Between Anarchy and Hierarchy

To my parents

Between Anarchy and Hierarchy

A Theory of International Politics and Foreign Policy

Robert H. Lieshout
Department of Political Science
University of Nijmegen, The Netherlands

Edward Elgar
Aldershot, UK · Brookfield, US

© Robert H. Lieshout 1995

All rights reserved. No part of this publication may be reproduced, stored in a retrieval system or transmitted in any form or by any means, electronic, mechanical or photocopying, recording, or otherwise without the prior permission of the publisher.

Published by
Edward Elgar Publishing Limited
Gower House
Croft Road
Aldershot
Hants GU11 3HR
UK

Edward Elgar Publishing Company
Old Post Road
Brookfield
Vermont 05036
US

British Library Cataloguing in Publication Data
Lieshout, Robert H.
  Between Anarchy and Hierarchy: Theory of
  International Politics and Foreign
  Policy
  I. Title
  327.101

Library of Congress Cataloguing in Publication Data

Lieshout, R. H.
   Between anarchy and hierarchy : a theory of international politics
and foreign policy / Robert H. Lieshout
   Includes index.
   1. International relations—Philosophy. 2. International
relations—Social aspects. 3. International relations—Decision
making. I. Title.
JX1395.L485 1996   95–30786
327'.1'01—dc20   CIP

ISBN 1 85898 196 4

Printed and bound in Great Britain by
Hartnolls Limited, Bodmin, Cornwall

Contents

List of Figures and Diagrams

Preface

Between Anarchy and Hierarchy is, in the first place, an attempt to demonstrate that a general empirical behavioural theory purporting to explain social and political phenomena can indeed help us to gain a sound understanding of international issues, and thus of the issues that figure prominently in contemporary international politics, such as those of peace and security, of underdevelopment and of European integration. In the second place, this book is an endeavour to integrate into the more classic, 'realist' theories of international relations the theories in the field of bureaucratic decision making (including the making of foreign policy) that have been developed in the course of the last twenty years or so.

In the third place, this book is intended to pay back, at least in part, the intellectual debt I have built up with many people over the years. Among these creditors, Johan K. De Vree occupies a very prominent place. His books and articles, *and* the fascinating manner in which he conveyed his ideas during many lengthy conversations, induced me to succumb no longer to the temptations of a sceptical attitude towards the possibility of understanding social reality, and to search for an answer to the question, why, in international politics, things are as they are. My second creditor was never aware of the fact that I am deeply in his debt. This is Sir Karl Popper. His epistemological dissertations showed that difficult problems can often be explained much more simply than we would deem possible at first sight. Moreover, they made clear that it ought also to be the scientist's ambition to aim for the greatest possible simplicity in his search for truth. A third creditor is Jan W. van Deth. When in 1981 I was confronted for the first time by the products of what is sometimes called the science of comparative politics, it was his appreciation of my bewilderment that made me decide to take up the study of the epistemological foundations of the social sciences.

Other of my creditors are Dick W.P. Ruiter, Frans A. van Vught and Don F. Westerheijden. Their comments on previous versions of the manuscript gave me the hope that perhaps I had something worthwhile to say, and thus the motivation to try and do it better next time. I am also indebted to Kees Aarts, Hans Blommestein, Bas Denters, Auke van Dijk,

Mark Frederiks, Martin van Hees, Wil Hout, Henk van der Kolk, Anton Weenink, Wouter Werner and, again, Don F. Westerheijden, for their precise and inspiring comments on the penultimate version of this text, or parts of it. Special mention should go to my editor, Jacqueline Stamper-Whiteside. Although she kept reassuring me that my English was very fine indeed for a Dutchman, this did not stop her 'improving' almost every sentence I wrote.

Finally, I owe a very considerable debt to the head of my former department at the University of Twente, Jacques Thomassen. But for his willingness to give me all the scope I needed to develop my scientific interests in a direction that was unfamiliar for him too, this book would never have been written. Moreover, by adopting the rather thankless role of devil's advocate when going through my manuscripts, he has saved me from many mistakes.

Without doubt my largest debt is to my parents – and not only from an intellectual point of view. I dedicate this book to them.

Robert H. Lieshout
Malden

NOTE

As will become clear in Chapter 2, in the epistemological approach I shall adopt in this book, literally everything can be an 'individual', including billiard balls, bureaucrats and states. For this reason, I shall be referring to the individual as 'it'. However, where I am concerned with analysing the behaviour of human individuals only (as for example in Chapter 8), I shall be using the masculine gender. This is deemed to apply to men and women, except when a contrary intention is evident from the context.

1. Introduction

In this book I shall be expounding a general empirical theory that seems to offer a fruitful explanation for the ways in which cooperation and conflict may develop in international politics. The core of the theory is the perception that states endeavour to maintain their own position in the international system, and that the likelihood of success for their endeavours depends, on the one hand, on the structure of the international system in which the states find themselves, and on the other, on the way in which the processes of (collective) decision making take place within those states. I have chosen this starting point because I am convinced that the evolution of cooperation and conflict in international politics cannot be explained in a satisfactory manner, without taking into account both the structure of the international system, and the ways in which decision making is organized within the states that are constitutive of the international system.

In Chapter 2, I begin by discussing the epistemological considerations that should make it clear that, if we wish to find an answer to the question 'why are international politics the way they are?', it is vital to construct a theory that is universal as well as falsifiable. Then, in Chapter 3, I formulate the theory's explanatory principle, the *primum mobile*, which makes it possible to provide a productive answer to precisely that question. Subsequently, in Chapter 4, I introduce the variables that, together with the explanatory principle, are crucial to a proper understanding of cooperation and conflict in international politics. Taken together, Chapters 3 and 4 should provide 'some first principles in the most important of sciences, the knowledge of the human community, and its operations'.[1]

Next, in Chapter 5, I apply these first principles to some of the understanding that has been developed in the context of analysing the three non-cooperative games employed most frequently by students of international relations: the Prisoner's Dilemma, the Stag Hunt and the Game of Chicken.

In Chapter 6, I then argue that what distinguishes an anarchical from a hierarchical system is that the latter has at its disposal an agency capable

1

of forcing the actors in the system to fulfil their promises to one another. In this chapter I also make an initial assessment of how the presence or absence of such an agency influences the ways these systems react to the changes continually taking place in their environment, such as climatological changes, demographic developments, and technological revolutions.

In the international system just as in national systems, force is the *ultima ratio* of power. However, in the case of a conflict between states in the anarchical international system, force stands more to the fore as the potential arbiter of that conflict, than it does in a situation of conflict between human individuals in hierarchical national systems. From this it follows that there are characteristic differences between anarchical and hierarchical systems with respect to the ways in which the members of such systems are able to solve their common problems, and their ability to manage crises in their mutual relationships. I analyse these differences in Chapters 7 and 8.

In the final chapter, I discuss the feedback relationships that govern the evolution of the international system. The central point in my argument is that states will differ in respect of their ability to adapt themselves to changes in their environment, and that those differences are the consequence of the diverse ways in which (collective) decision making is organized within these states; and that, moreover, these differences in adaptability will influence the behaviour of the states in the international system, and thus may result in changes in the structure of the international system.

The theory I set out in *Between Anarchy and Hierarchy* is derived by deduction, while one of the central topics in the theory concerns the problem of collective goods provision. This indicates that I am trying to apply an 'economic' approach to the study of political phenomena. 'Political economists' differ among themselves as to what precisely this politico-economic approach is about. Nevertheless, they seem to be agreed that it does in any case include the following four elements (I shall deal with all four as I develop my argument):

. political economy concerns the attempt to formulate explanations for social and political phenomena that can be derived from an axiomaticized, consistent system of statements;
. moreover, political economy involves the ambition to explain *all* social and political phenomena in terms of the behaviour of actors (be they states or human individuals) who try to maximize their utility;

accordingly, also the behaviour of students of international relations can be viewed as utility-maximizing behaviour;

. political economy is in particular concerned with the problem of collective goods, that is to say, goods where there is no clear one-to-one relationship between those who contribute to the production of the good and those who profit from the production of that good (cf. De Jasay 1989 and Margolis 1982, pp. 8–9);

. finally, political economy has to do with the problem how the political institutions of a community should be organized for the furtherance of the welfare of the citizens of that community. To put it another way: working on the assumption that government ought to promote the welfare of citizens, political economy is about the attempt to formulate an answer to the question of which tasks government ought to undertake, and which it ought not. This interpretation is in line with Adam Smith's classic description of the subject matter of political economy in his *Wealth of Nations*:

> Political economy, considered as a branch of the science of a statesman or legislator, proposes two distinct objects; first, to provide a plentiful revenue or subsistence for the people, or more properly to enable them to provide such a revenue or subsistence for themselves; and secondly, to supply the state or commonwealth with a revenue sufficient for the publick services. (Smith 1979ed.b, I, p. 428)

NOTE

1. See: 'A Letter from Governor Pownall to Adam Smith, L.L.D., F.R.S., being an examination of Several Points of Doctrine, laid down in his "Inquiry in to the Nature and Causes of the Wealth of Nations"' (Mossner and Ross (eds) 1987ed., p. 337).

2. Epistemology

I CAUSAL EXPLANATIONS AND THEORETICAL OBSERVATIONS

Whenever we try to explain a certain kind of behaviour '(e)' – be it the behaviour of states in the international system or that of civil servants in a department of foreign affairs – we usually look for another kind of behaviour '(c)', which must have brought '(e)' about. To put it another way: most of the time we assume that a certain cause '(c)' will be necessary and sufficient to explain the occurrence of the effect '(e)'. We tacitly assume that – to use an expression of David Hume's – a *necessary connexion* exists between cause and effect. Accordingly, we conceive a causal explanation to exist of only two elements, which are related to one another in the following way: '(c) → (e)'.

However, David Hume showed two centuries ago that this simple causal model cannot be correct as far as the explanation of empirical phenomena is concerned. In his famous *A Treatise of Human Nature*, Hume argues that such an inference can only be valid in sciences like algebra and arithmetic, which are concerned with *demonstrative* knowledge, i.e. the *comparison of ideas*, but not in the empirical sciences, which try to explain observable behaviour and can therefore only produce *probable* knowledge. For, when we try to detect the nature of this 'necessary connexion' between empirical phenomena, and cast our eyes on 'the *known qualities* of objects', we shall immediately discover that 'the relation of cause and effect depends not in the least on *them*' (Hume 1981ed., p. 77, emphasis in original). Clearly, it is impossible to explain an effect by a cause (or causes) alone, for 'there is no object, which implies the existence of any other if we consider these objects in themselves' (Hume 1981ed., p. 86). In this way, Hume discovered that in the empirical domain necessity and inevitability do not exist.

Hume's argument may be illustrated using Julius Caesar's decision to cross the Rubicon. This decision cannot have been the necessary effect, the inevitable consequence, of Caesar's receiving the news that the supporters of his rival, Pompey, had gained the upper hand in the Roman

4

Senate, *because* Caesar might have done an infinite number of things in reaction to the news. For instance, he could have returned to Transalpine Gaul, played a game of dice, etc., etc. Caesar's behaviour '(e)' cannot be explained by one or several causes '(c)', since it is possible to derive any kind of effect whatsoever from some cause. In the words of David Hume, 'the mind can always *conceive* any effect to follow from any cause, and indeed any event to follow upon another' (Hume 1981ed., p. 650, emphasis in original).

It appears, then, that if we want to explain a certain kind of behaviour – be it the behaviour of human beings, billiard balls, or states – such an explanation must contain a third element at least. An element that enables us to reduce the number of possible effects from a certain cause. Without this third element all effects are equally likely. This third element of a causal explanation I shall call a 'theory' or a 'point of view'. A theory, a 'connecting principle, as Adam Smith termed it (Smith 1980ed., p. 45) – explains why '(c)' and '(e)' belong together. To be a little more precise: we can deduce from a theory the 'hypotheses' – the 'laws' – that describe the conjunction of '(c)' and '(e)'. Consequently, the model of a causal explanation has to have the form as shown in Figure 2.1.

Figure 2.1: The model of causal explanation

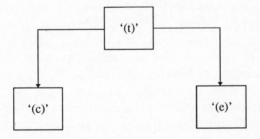

Following Wittgenstein, Karl Popper summarizes Hume's discovery that nothing is inevitable in the empirical domain, in a similar fashion:

A necessity for one thing to happen because another has happened does not exist. There is only logical necessity ... the necessary link between *a* and *b* is neither found in *a* nor in *b*, but in the fact that the corresponding ordinary conditional (or 'material implication', $a \twoheadrightarrow b$) ... follows *with logical necessity* from a law of nature – that it is necessary, relative to a law of nature. (Popper 1980ed., p. 438, see also Popper 1971ed., II, p. 363, emphasis in original)

We can conclude from Hume's discovery that cause and effect do not exist independently of ourselves. Cause and effect are, to paraphrase the historian R.G. Collingwood, no mere objects, something outside the mind which knows them, but the result of an activity of thought (cf. Collingwood 1946, 1957ed., p. 218). It is the individual who decides, from his own point of view, by means of a theory, which of the infinite number of possible observable phenomena will be causes and effects and which not. Whether the individual is conscious of this thought process is an entirely different matter.[1]

For the sake of clarity, I should emphasize that it is also the case that, where we have no other ambition than to observe certain facts with no desire to explain them (we do not want to theorize about the relationships between those facts), we shall nevertheless – unconsciously – be using a theory, simply because we shall have to make a choice about which facts actually to observe. Every observation excludes other possible observations, and as such implies a point of view on which observable facts to take into account and which not. Theory necessarily precedes observation. It is in this sense that all observations are theoretical observations. As the methodologist William Whewell remarked in this connection, 'there is a mask of theory over the whole face of nature' (quoted in Medawar 1984ed., p. 130).[2] This implies that the scientist who aspires to do no more than merely to observe and to describe his observations, engages in the same theoretical activity as his more ambitious colleague who wants to explain observable phenomena.[3]

In the context of this argument we need not pay much attention to the question of where we get our theories from, and the debate on *inductivism*, the doctrine that reality impresses itself upon us one way or another. (See, for a brief summary, Lieshout 1984, pp. 3–5.) It is interesting to note that, in this respect, Hume showed himself to be an inductivist. In the *Treatise*, he defended the position that we derive our theories from our experience of the 'constant conjunction' of certain phenomena (Hume 1981ed., pp. 98–106). This so-called 'doctrine of the primacy of repetitions' is, however, untenable in the light of the following argument that Popper developed:

> All the repetitions which we experience are *approximate repetitions*; and by saying that a repetition is approximate I mean that repetition *B* of an event *A* is not identical with *A*, or indistinguishable from *A*, but only *more or less similar* to *A*. But if repetition is thus based upon mere similarity, it must share one of the main characteristics of similarity; that is, its relativity. Two things which are similar are always similar *in certain respects*. ...

Generally, similarity, and with it repetition, always presuppose the adoption of *a point of view*: some similarities or repetitions will strike us if we are interested in one problem, and others if we are interested in another problem. But if similarity and repetition presuppose the adoption of a point of view, or an interest, or an expectation, it is logically necessary that points of view, or interests, or expectations, are logically prior, as well as temporally (or causally or psychologically) prior, to repetition. (Popper 1980ed., pp. 420–22, emphasis in original)

Immanuel Kant may be regarded as the first philosopher who, having been awakened from his self-confessed 'dogmatic slumber' by the study of Hume's work, explicitly refutes the intuitively plausible idea on which inductivism is based. The idea, that is, that we can know reality independently of our theories about that reality. In his *Prolegomena* Kant formulates the (in his own words) 'apparently daring proposition', that 'the understanding does not draw its laws ... from nature, but prescribes them to nature' (Kant 1783, 1953ed., p. 82).[4] The normative character that Kant attributes to empirical laws – nature ought to behave in accordance with the laws prescribed by the intellect – is of particular interest. I shall return to this subject in the next section.

There is a second aspect to the 'inductivistic illusion' that I should deal with briefly. It concerns the fallacy that a research method can be found, a calculus can be constructed, which, provided it is applied in the proper manner, would generate theories. The invention of a theory is, however, always a creative act, and, as such, can never be the result of the application of the proper research method (whatever that may mean). It was not without good reason that Karl Popper used to begin his lectures on Scientific Method by explaining to his students that no method for discovering scientific theories exists (Popper 1983, pp. 5–6). When we are looking for new theories, it might be helpful to make observations, to analyse empirical findings with the help of statistics, but it might be just as profitable to go for a walk in the woods or to drink a good glass of wine.

II THE 'SEARCHLIGHT THEORY OF KNOWLEDGE'

To make it clear what a theory (a point of view) actually 'does', I shall in this section discuss the 'searchlight theory of knowledge', which Sir Karl Popper put forward (Popper 1968ed., pp. 127–8 and Popper 1971ed., II, pp. 260–61). In this connection, it is of the utmost importance fully to realize that at any given moment an infinite number of phenomena might be observed. From this it follows that, with each observation, we make a selection from the infinitely large set of possible observations. This also implies that, if we try to explain why things happen the way they happen, we select in just the same way a certain number of phenomena from this universe of possibly observable phenomena – the 'boundless region of individual facts', as the philosopher Adam Ferguson has called it (Ferguson 1792, I, p. 276) – and then divide these phenomena into causes and effects. It is we who determine what is, and what is not, relevant to the explanation of certain phenomena. (Whether we are aware of doing so, is of course quite another matter.)

This is also true of Caesar's decision to cross the river Rubicon. What the great general had eaten for breakfast that day is tacitly assumed to be irrelevant to his decision to march against Rome. The same goes for an infinite number of other things, such as the clothes he wore, the colour of the leaves on the trees on the banks of the Rubicon, etc., as opposed to his receipt of the news that the supporters of his rival Pompey had gained the upper hand in the Roman Senate.

Now, let us think of our brain as a lamp. A lamp that starts burning the moment we are born.[5] This lamp illuminates the universe of possibly observable phenomena. Were we to find ourselves in the position of having no device that would enable us to aim the light from the lamp (i.e. if we had no notion of what might or might not be relevant), then the infinite universe of possibly observable phenomena would be illuminated only weakly. In other words, in that situation the number of possible causes and effects would be equal to the universe of possible observations. David Hume describes this perplexing situation as follows: 'and indeed there is nothing existent, either externally or internally, which is not to be consider'd either as a cause or an effect' (Hume 1981ed., p. 75). We would not be able to distinguish essentials from inessentials. Caesar's breakfast would appear to us to be just as important to his decision to cross the Rubicon, as the news about the developments in the Roman Senate. Our position then would be comparable to that of the philosopher who has come to the understanding that everything is connected with everything else, but also – and this sounds altogether rather less exalted – to that of Buridan's ass. This hungry ass was unable to decide which of two stacks of hay was the more appetizing to start its meal with and, as a result, eventually died of hunger in the midst of plenty.[6]

Buridan's ass is not capable of making a choice because it lacks, as it were, the instrument that would enable it to determine which things are more and which things are less relevant. The statement that 'everything is connected with everything else' is as profound as it is silly. Even if it were true, what good would this 'knowledge' do us? The only thing that would have happened is that the universe of all possibly observable phenomena would have been renamed the universe of all possible causes and effects. In short, we still know nothing at all. It will be obvious that this relates to a purely hypothetical situation. In reality we shall not find ourselves in this position (and this also goes for the philosopher who has discovered that everything is connected with everything else). From birth we are able to make choices. From the very beginning we dispose of information that enables us to distinguish between important and unimportant matters (although this does not preclude the possibility that this information may turn out to be incorrect). Thanks to the innate and acquired theories that we have at our disposal, we are capable of aiming the lamp, and of turning the lamp into a searchlight.

With the help of a point of view, a theory, we determine what will be cause and effect and what not. To return to the example of Caesar's march on Rome: the 'cause' is the news of the victory of Pompey's supporters in the Roman Senate; the 'effect', Caesar's decision to cross the Rubicon. Were someone subsequently to ask us whether the clothes Caesar was wearing that day might not also have influenced his decision, then our answer would have to be that, according to our theory, the way Caesar was dressed is irrelevant. (Remember the direction of the arrows in the model of causal explanation in Figure 2.1.)

We can word this perception somewhat differently. Our theory excludes the possibility of Caesar's breakfast or the way he was dressed contributing anything to explaining the fact that he crossed the Rubicon on 11 January, 49 BC. The empirical content of a theory, in the words of A.F. Hayek, 'consists in what it forbids'. It will be clear that this is in line with the normative character of Kant's dictum that the understanding does not draw its laws from nature, but prescribes them to it. According to Hayek, a theory 'describes merely a range of possibilities. In doing this it excludes other conceivable courses of events' (Hayek 1967, p. 32). The emphasis should be on the adjective 'conceivable'. We can imagine that events might take a different course. This is also the core of Hume's argument (see the previous section): 'The mind can always *conceive* any effect to follow from any cause, and indeed any event to follow upon another' (emphasis in original).

To sum up: the answer to the question of what a theory actually does, boils down to the notion that a theory, a point of view, enables the individual to ignore certain things as being irrelevant. By stating that certain, conceivable, courses of events are impossible, a theory gives the individual a certain grip on the environment. It is this idea that has led the biologist Garrett Hardin to interpret science as 'the search for the definition of the impossibilities of this world' (Hardin 1960, p. 306).

Figure 2.2: The searchlight theory of knowledge

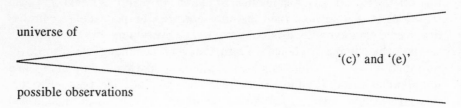

universe of

'(c)' and '(e)'

possible observations

Theories provide us with prescriptions, as it were, on how to act successfully in certain circumstances. This realization makes it clear that the rules − the laws − that can be deduced from theories cannot be divided into two mutually exclusive categories: on the one hand the empirical rules, and on the other the normative rules. Both kinds of rules tell us something about reality and both have a normative component. De Vree has expressed this as follows: 'Every rule, of whatever kind in whatever field, can indeed be looked upon as a standard of conduct to which actual conduct should or may conform to a certain (variable) degree' (De Vree 1982, p. 277).

The analogy of the searchlight − to which, incidentally, we should not attach too much weight, and which we should certainly not take too literally − shows that a point of view has to be of good quality, as otherwise we would not be able to focus the lamp. If it is of poor quality, a very real danger arises that the light will disperse in all directions, with the result that we shall again find ourselves in the situation of everything appearing to be connected to everything else, and that, in consequence, we are unable to make a choice between what is and what is not relevant.

In the next section, I shall discuss what requirements have to be met if the point of view (the theory) is to be of good quality. This discussion will take place using the rules applicable to those wishing to play the game of empirical science. The criteria I shall develop in the course of my argument are aimed in particular at making it possible to determine what, formally speaking, is the best point of view. What sort of point of view gives us the firmest grasp of our environment? On the basis of these formal requirements, it then becomes possible to compare various points of view, and to determine the kind of points of view that serve us best. To avoid any possible misunderstanding, I should add that, in the next section, I shall concern myself only with *formal* criteria. I shall not go into questions like these: What is the *material* content of the various points of view (what kind of explanation do they offer as to why things are as they are)? How well have these viewpoints stood up to being tested? How severe were those tests?

III THE RULES OF THE EMPIRICAL SCIENCE GAME

A. Why Things Are as They Are

As the fate of Buridan's ass makes abundantly clear, confusion will do us no good at all. Empirical science concerns the endeavour to reduce confusion as much as possible, and empirical scientists are pre-eminently involved in devising the means by which this reduction can be brought about. This they do first of all by inventing and articulating the 'principles' which help make it possible to order reality. So the first rule of the empirical science game runs as follows:

Rule 1:
Empirical scientists shall formulate the principles with the help of which it becomes possible to explain why things are as they are.

I am quite prepared to admit that this rule is worded in such a way that some elucidation may be in order. The following considerations will help, I hope, to make it clear what is intended by this first rule of empirical science.

We increase our hold on reality by inventing the regularities that govern the world and *why* they do so. Just like all other information processing systems, we impose a structure, a regularity, upon reality. If nothing is familiar, if we are unable to make any prediction as to what is going to happen (however unreliable this prediction may turn out to be afterwards!), if, in short, every possible course of events appears equally probable, we cannot survive. Indeed, 'nothing is so practical as a good theory'.[7] The perception that the better we are able to order reality, the higher our chances of adapting ourselves successfully to our environment, has been articulated by Adam Ferguson as follows:

Multiciplicity without order distracts and perplexes the mind; and the highest species of suffering, perhaps, that could be devised for a being merely intelligent, would be for him to look round on a world of numberless individuals, of which no two had any resemblance or connection together. ... The knowing is distinguished from the

ignorant, no doubt by the great number of particulars it has perceived or observed;
but still more by his proficiency in comprehending the many under the few denomi-
nations, in which they are or may be stated. (Ferguson 1792, I, p. 273)

I should point out that empirical theories are not the only systems of
thought that have the property of making the world more predictable.
Religions and ideologies may possess precisely the same property.

Empirical scientists must never be content with recording the
bewildering variety of observable phenomena. As Imre Lakatos has
observed: 'science, after all, must be demarcated from a curiosity shop
where funny local – or cosmic – oddities are collected and displayed'
(Lakatos and Musgrave (eds) 1970, 1974ed., p. 102). Rule 1 should not,
however, be interpreted to mean that empirical scientists have continually
to invent 'new' principles. Not even the most gifted of empirical
scientists is expected to do so. Nor should we forget, as I have explained
in Section I, that the invention of these principles is a creative act, and, as
such, impervious to rules. What empirical scientists, in their endeavours
to explain why things are as they, are required to do, is to make the
principle they are employing explicit, and to think through its
implications. A touch of genius, however desirable, is not a requirement
for being an empirical scientist, but a large amount of perseverance is.

From my discussion of rule 1 it will be clear that little importance
should be attached to the objections that many an author has raised
against a science that is nothing more than a reduction of reality. We
shall have to make a reduction, because otherwise we shall not be able to
survive. It is with this in mind that, in *The Open Universe*, Sir Karl
Popper reaches the conclusion that 'science may be described as the art of
systematic over-simplification – the art of discerning what we may with
advantage omit' (Popper 1982a, p. 44).[8] Empirical scientists attempt –
just like 'ordinary' people – to get a grip on a perplexing reality, and
they do so in precisely the same way. With the assistance of a point of
view as to why things are as they are, they are able to put certain things
on one side as being irrelevant. Although in certain (fashionable)
intellectual circles, admitting to be a reductionist more or less comes
down to, as Richard Dawkins aptly puts it, 'admitting to eating babies',
reductionism is really nothing more than 'just another name for an honest
desire to understand how things work' (Dawkins 1986, 1988ed., p. 13). It
is a very defensible proposition that the 'only thing' that distinguishes
empirical scientists from 'ordinary' people, is that the former pay more
attention to the quality of their point of view. The quality requirements
concerned have been set out in the rules of the game that I shall deal with
in the next two sub-sections.

The understanding that we get a grasp on reality by means of a reduction of that reality, which enables us better to systematize that same reality, implies that we do not get a grip on reality by formulating definitions. To be sure, since Aristotle it has become the tradition to think that definitions generate knowledge, but nothing is further from the truth. Witness the fruitless discussions that may ensue about the question of what precisely the essence of 'a puppy' would be, or the question whether the black-and-white spotted animal with horns and an udder ought to be called a cow or a horse.[9] Properly considered, a definition has no other function either in common parlance or in empirical science, than that of a convenient shorthand. Using a definition, a single word can replace a lengthy description. As it happens, which particular single word is chosen is quite arbitrary. (Although, naturally, it is also convenient to choose a word that follows common usage.) It is completely irrelevant what the black-and-white spotted animal with horns and an udder will be called, in actual fact. The only thing that matters is that, once we have decided to call such an animal a cow, we continue to do so. Otherwise chaos still reigns.[10]

B. Consistency

Not every point of view can be communicated intersubjectively, that is to say, can be subjected to a critical discussion, sometimes simply because we are not aware of the fact that we have a point of view. By the way, this is a phenomenon more common in the social sciences than one would wish – witness all those social 'scientists' who proclaim that their ambitions go no further than observing empirical phenomena (finding out about 'what goes with what') and recording these observations, and who, 'in all modesty', admit that they have not yet reached the stage where they would also be able to explain these phenomena (having any idea 'why what goes with what').[11] But where a point of view has to be communicated intersubjectively, it is not enough to be aware of the fact that we have a particular point of view. For this purpose, the point of view must also be internally consistent. Only if this is in fact the case, can the viewpoint then be the subject of a rational discussion, and as such become part of what has been called the *context of justification*.

In the previous section, I hope to have demonstrated conclusively that the most important property of theories is that they *exclude* other, conceivable, courses of events. When we try to articulate a certain viewpoint, for example because we want to convince others that this particular point of view gives us the firmest hold on reality, then it becomes apparent that this crucial property can only be maintained if the system of statements in which we have set out our point of view is internally consistent. That is to say, that we can deduce no statements from that system that contradict one another. For, if this were to be the case, then every possible statement can be deduced from that system and, accordingly, no statement whatsoever can be excluded from that system.[12] Karl Popper makes the following observation in this connection:

> But the importance of the requirement of consistency will be appreciated if one realizes that a self-contradictory system is uninformative. It is so because any conclusion we please can be derived from it. Thus no statement is singled out, either as incompatible or as derivable, since all are derivable. A consistent system, on the other hand, divides the set of all possible statements into two: those which it contradicts and those with which it is compatible. (Among the latter are the conclusions which can be derived from it.) This is why consistency is the most general requirement for a system, whether empirical or non-empirical, if it is to be of any use at all. (Popper 1980ed., p. 92)

If this requirement for points of view to be internally consistent were to be abandoned, then every rational discussion would become impossible. Given that in that situation everybody could then parry any point of criticism – which, in the final analysis, comes down to demonstrating that a certain point of view contains inconsistencies – with a simple 'what of it?', or a devout 'my heart tells me I'm right'.[13]

In the light of the above, the second rule of the empirical science game runs as follows:

> *Rule 2*:
> In their endeavours to explain why things are as they are, empirical scientists shall deem a possible statement about observable phenomena to be part of the context of justification if, and only if, the axiomatic (theoretical) system from which the statement has been deduced is internally consistent, that is to say, it is not possible to deduce from this system both the statement '(a)' and its negation '~(a)' (cf. Lieshout 1984, pp. 8 and 9).

The second rule of empirical science can also be worded like this: an empirical scientist shall never reconcile himself to inconsistencies in his theory; he shall endeavour to eliminate them. This implies that the second rule entails the rejection of *instrumentalism*, the doctrine that holds that, in the end, scientific theories are nothing but instruments that enable us to act successfully. After all, an instrument (a piece of equipment) will be judged on its usability, but a theory with which we try to explain why things are as they are, must ultimately be judged on its internal consistency. If an exceedingly useful theory turns out to be inconsistent, and it proves to be impossible to eliminate these inconsistencies, then this theory does not fit into the *context of justification*, and in consequence, empirical scientists will have to deem this theory to have been refuted. For if they were to accept the fact that a particular theory is inconsistent, and were to elevate usefulness to be *the* criterion on which theories would be judged, then the search for better theories would come to a halt. As Alfred Tarski puts it: 'it is inimical to the progress of science to measure the importance of any research exclusively or chiefly in terms of its usefulness and its applicability' (Feigl and Sellers (eds) 1949, p. 77).[14]

C. Empirical Content

As I have said before, the property that distinguishes theories is that they enable us to exclude certain, conceivable, courses of events. From this, the conclusion can be drawn that, the more a theory excludes (the higher its empirical content, as this is usually called), the more it tells us about reality (the greater its *informativity*, to use Swanborn's term) (Swanborn 1981, 1987ed., pp. 37–40). This conclusion can be expressed in the third rule of the empirical science game.

Rule 3:
In their endeavours to explain why things are as they are, empirical scientists shall strive to formulate consistent axiomatic systems with an increasing empirical content; that is to say, that the set of potential falsifiers of those systems becomes larger and larger.

The concept of 'empirical content' often leads to misunderstandings, and is frequently confused with the concept of 'logical content'. I would like therefore to point out that the *logical content* of a theory concerns the class of statements about observable phenomena that are permitted by the theory (that are in agreement with the theory), whereas the *empirical content* of a theory consists of the class of statements about observable phenomena that are excluded by the theory (see Figure 2.3).

Figure 2.3: Empirical and logical content

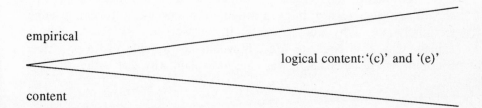

empirical

logical content: '(c)' and '(e)'

content

An empirical theory may be deemed to have been falsified where a phenomenon is observed that, according to the theory, cannot occur. To be more precise, from the *explanatory principle* (as set down in the *axioms* of the theory) statements can be derived (the *theorems*) from which, by using *existential assumptions* (see Chapter 3, Section I), new statements can be deduced (the *hypotheses),* which forbid certain conceivable events to occur. A hypothesis states that it is *impossible* that a certain course of events will take place. If this course of events is nonetheless observed, then this observation is recorded in a *potentially falsifying statement*, after which it is up to the researcher – or his colleagues – to decide what the implications of this statement are for the validity of the explanatory principle.[15]

The fourth rule of the empirical science game also follows from the endeavour to formulate theories with an ever higher empirical content.

Rule 4:
In their endeavours to explain why things are as they are, empirical scientists shall formulate statements about observable phenomena that can be deduced from empirical theories and that are stated in strictly universal terms; that is to say, these statements cannot be replaced by a finite number of singular statements.

Empirical scientists attempt to formulate *strictly universal hypotheses*. They prefer such statements, because in the case of a strictly universal statement the class of potentially falsifying statements is infinitely larger than in the case of a singular statement. A strictly universal hypothesis tells us infinitely more about reality than a singular hypothesis.

I should like to emphasize that rule 4 is about strictly universal hypotheses that can be derived from a consistent theory, and not about hypotheses that are formulated in strictly universal terms. The reason is that an *ad hoc* hypothesis, even if worded in strictly universal terms, does not provide us with information. Such a hypothesis does not tell us anything about the ways in which reality is organized. The following example illustrates rather nicely that, ultimately, we are not interested in *ad hoc* statements at all, but in systems of statements that explain why things are as they are. Let us suppose there is this really smart monkey, which, when it is put in front of a typewriter, types the formula, $E = MC^2$. Admittedly, this would be quite an impressive performance, but should we also regard it as a triumph in our quest for knowledge? Definitely not. Why not? Because, if we were to ask the monkey to explain why E is equal to MC^2, it would not be able to do so. Albert Einstein, on the other hand, was able to explain why that is the case, and that is why he is considered to be one of the greatest empirical scientists of all time.

Ad hoc hypotheses are of no interest, because they do not exclude anything. Since they are not embedded in a consistent system of statements, they are compatible with all other possible statements (this applies to every single statement). De Vree has articulated this as follows:

> Our knowledge is systemic in character too. That is to say, the content, meaning and significance of every single notion or concept, of every single statement or observation, is a function of *other* notions, concepts, etc. Our knowledge, the systems of concepts that we have developed, these contain information only as far as they display order and organization, as they do in fact have a certain structure, within which it is clear precisely how its separate elements – i.e. notions and statements, including observational statements – connect with one another, and what their meaning, implications and consequences are. And single statements and researches only contain information in so far as they increase the information content of those systems of concepts. (De Vree 1986, p. 354, emphasis in original)[16]

D. A Normative Theory

To summarize, my remarks in Section III boil down to the assertion that empirical theories are a superior form of theory. Since they are formulated as axiomatic, consistent systems of strictly universal statements, empirical theories provide us with the firmest possible hold on reality, and this hold becomes firmer as the empirical content of those systems of statements increases. However, it cannot be denied that in daily life – and also in scientific life – we are happy to use theories that clearly violate the four rules that I have formulated above. How can we explain this paradox? The answer to the paradox entails the realization that the development of empirical theories usually demands considerable effort, and that we are therefore ready to settle for less. Information cannot be acquired without cost. One might say that the rules of the empirical science game are part of a *normative* theory about how we ought to search for truth. The theory exhorts empirical scientists to ignore the costs that are bound up with the search for better and better theories. As Bertrand Russell has stated: 'The scientific attitude of mind involves a sweeping away of all other desires in the interest of the desire to know' (Russell 1918, 1957ed., p. 47). It is with this in mind that we can formulate a fifth rule of the empirical science game. This rule is as follows:

Rule 5:
In their endeavours to explain why things are as they are, empirical scientists shall be ready to play for high stakes: they shall be prepared to invest heavily in their research, in terms of energy, time and intellectual capacity, and they shall be willing, time and again, to put their investments at risk.[17]

Not, for that matter, that we for one moment cherish the illusion that empirical scientists can live up to this rule all of the time. When we consider the behaviour of human individuals – such as that of empirical scientists – then it will be obvious that the 'desire to know' is susceptible to considerations of costs and benefits too. (I shall go into this question more extensively in Chapter 3, Section III.)

Empirical scientists are sometimes confronted with the fact that, from the theory they espouse, statements can be deduced that conflict with one another, or with statements about observed phenomena. If this happens, then their first duty, according to the rules of the empirical science game, is to eliminate such inconsistencies. After all, they are not allowed to put up with inconsistencies. Moreover, there can be no question of the costs attached to eliminating these inconsistencies, in terms of energy, time and intellectual capacities, being taken into consideration. (See also my previous observations on the relationship between consistency and instrumentalism.) In everyday life, however, what it will cost to eliminate these inconsistencies and whether eliminating the inconsistencies will be more productive than restoring consistency, are factors that play a decisive role in our thinking. We tolerate inconsistencies if the benefits of eliminating the inconsistencies do not outweigh the costs of doing so. It is not my intention to create the impression that in everyday life information and energy are opposed to one another, for that is definitely not the case. The only thing I wish to point out is that, in our daily lives, information and energy are interwoven to such an extent that it is impossible to consider the one apart from the other.

IV CONSPIRACY THEORIES AND EMPIRICAL THEORIES

A. Methodological Individualism and Methodological Collectivism

In Chapters 3 and 4, I shall formulate the basic principles and central ideas of a general behavioural theory to explain social and political phenomena. In Chapter 7, I shall elaborate this theory with regard to decision making and the management of conflict in the international state system. In this connection I shall assume that, in the international system, states are the only units that can exhibit 'behaviour'. This means that I assign the explanatory principle to states, and that, accordingly, states are the only elements in the international system that are able to make choices. Subsequently, in Chapter 8, on the basis of the same general behavioural theory, I shall formulate a theory about decision making and the management of conflict in bureaucracies. In that chapter, I shall start from the assumption that individual human beings are the only units in the system that are capable of 'behaviour'. This is usually called *methodological individualism*. James Buchanan describes this principle as follows: 'individualism as an analytical method suggests simply that all theorizing, all analysis, is resolved finally into considerations faced by the individual person as decision-maker' (Buchanan and Tullock 1962, 1965ed., p. 315). Finally, in Chapter 9, I shall argue that the integration of both theories is essential for a proper understanding of the evolution of the international system, and that such an integration is indeed feasible.

In all honesty, I have to acknowledge that my intention of developing a theory that includes both the field of the traditional theory of international relations and that of the more recent theory of bureaucratic decision making (including foreign policy decision making) is a little unusual.[18] It is generally assumed that a theory intended to explain the behaviour of states cannot explain the behaviour of human individuals as well, and vice versa. The most important argument advanced in support of this assumption is that states are merely theoretical constructs, whereas human beings really exist. Many an author, following Popper, even combines this argument with 'the demand that social phenomena, including collectives, should be analysed in terms of individuals and their actions and relations' (Popper 1968ed., p. 341).[19] However, this demand is untenable in the light of the following two epistemological considerations.

The first argument is (see also Section I) that the empirical scientist is not obliged to formulate an explanation of the behaviour of states in the international system, nor of individual human beings in the context of (government) organizations, in terms of the behaviour of the human individuals concerned. The decision to reduce this behaviour to 'considerations faced by the individual person as decision-maker', can only be the result of a choice on the basis of methodological considerations (the emphasis in methodological individualism should be on *methodological*, and not on individualism). As such it does not imply a naïve individualism (the idea that social and political processes can only be explained in terms of the behaviour of the individual humans involved, since only the latter really exist). The scientist not only decides for himself which theory he wishes to use (bearing in mind the rules of the empirical science game), but also to which element in which system he will assign the explanatory principle. Which element he chooses depends on the problem the scientist is interested in, the results he expects to get from the choice he has made, and a host of other practical matters, such as the accessibility of data and the amount of time available. From the epistemological standpoint, there are no objections to a *methodological* collectivism. Obviously, such objections do exist with respect to a naïve collectivism – the idea that, in the context of explaining social and political phenomena, the behaviour of individual human beings can only be the manifestation of processes of interaction between certain social entities or collectivities (such as classes, peoples, states or civilizations). There is nothing against a 'state-as-sole-actor' approach to international political phenomena, just as long as the 'assumption of comprehensive rationality' (see Chapter 3, Section I) is not introduced as well (cf. Allison 1971, pp. 26 and 31–5).

The second argument is that it may seem quite natural to explain social and political phenomena in terms of the behaviour of the individuals concerned, since the latter, unlike collectivities, can be observed,[20] but that we should nevertheless not lose sight of the fact that individuals, too, can only be observed in the light of theories. The implication of this is that, from an epistemological point of view, 'the human individual' is just as much a theoretical construct as is 'the state'.

To sum up, the position I have adopted comes down to the assertion that, methodologically speaking, 'the state' can be an 'individual' too. Whenever we want to explain something, we shall have to formulate an explanatory principle, and subsequently to assign this explanatory principle to one or more elements in the system in question (see also Chapter 3, Section I). These are the elements that are assigned the designation 'individual', and it is up to the researcher to decide which element, or elements, are the most likely candidates for this designation.

There is also a material argument in defence of the decision in Chapter 7 to assign the explanatory principle to 'the state'. The purport of this argument is that it can be shown that a state adapts itself to its environment in the same manner as an individual human being. A state is also subject to what I shall call the 'dictate of reality'. The behaviour of a state is likewise at any given moment the result of an evolutionary process, in which information that existed to begin with is discarded, modified, retained or developed, in so far as the state judges this information to contribute to a successful adaptation to the environment (see also Chapter 3, Section I). Although it does have to be said that, in general, a state is less sensitive to changes in its environment, at least in comparison with a single individual, as a result of the state's greater power (and that, because of this greater power, it can allow itself to remain less sensitive to changes more easily and for longer), and in consequence will adapt itself more slowly and with greater difficulty to changes in its environment.

B. Hidden or Invisible Hands?

The theory that I shall develop in the rest of this book explains the dynamics of the social and political processes between individuals, in terms of the goals the individuals try to attain, and the unintended consequences of this goal-oriented behaviour on the quality of the system in question. This implies that I conceive the order that can be observed in the interaction between individuals to be the result of their actions, but not the result of their design.[21] To put it somewhat differently, and following the philosopher Robert Nozick, I shall try in this book to formulate an 'invisible-hand explanation' of the dynamics of international relations and bureaucratic decision making, rather than a 'hidden-hand explanation'.[22]

The overriding objection to hidden-hand explanations is that they cannot be empirical theories. They cannot be falsified, and therefore belong to the category of conspiracy theories. However intricate the alleged conspirators' intrigues, the principle on which conspiracy theories are based is very simple. Anything that exists *must* have been contrived by someone or something (be it God, the gods, the Jews, the plutocrats or the imperialists, to name but a few popular conspirators) in order to reach a certain goal (world domination, the realization of the spirit of the nation). And no doubt this, in a certain sense commendable, simplicity, is one of the major reasons for the enduring popularity of conspiracy theories.[23]

In order to avoid possible misunderstandings, I should immediately add that the above does not imply that I am of the opinion that it never happens that people conspire in order to achieve certain ends. The only thing I am trying to do, is to point out the insurmountable problem we confront if we assume that *everything* is the result of a conspiracy (in other words, that everything in existence is no more than a 'move' by someone or something in some 'game' for the attainment of some end). The problem, that is, that it is logically impossible to derive statements that could conflict with other possible statements about observable phenomena, from such a theory.

The theories of imperialism as developed by Magdoff and Galtung, for instance, and the theory of the state as formulated by Miliband, are typical examples of conspiracy theories (Magdoff 1969, Galtung 1971 and Miliband 1969, 1973ed.). Whatever behaviour 'the state' exhibits, it is nothing more than a move by the 'executive committee of the ruling class' to strengthen the position of that ruling class.[24] Also, when the state takes measures that at first sight seem to go against the interests of the ruling class, such as the introduction of a 40-hour working week, then this is no more than the outcome of a subtle game the better to disguise the oppression and exploitation that is actually happening. Or when, in contradiction to what the theories of imperialism predict, we can find in the archives of the ministries of foreign affairs no trace of secret transactions between civil servants on the one hand, and shipping tycoons and oil barons on the other hand, then this can only mean that the conspirators were able to erase all traces of their illegal practices, or that the harmony of interests between government officials and plutocrats was so complete that it was unnecessary for them to communicate with one another. More than that, when evidence is indeed found for the opposite contention – government officials do in fact often appear to have opposed capitalists – then this evidence is nothing more than an indication that the conspirators were able to cover up their machinations by leaving false trails.

In the light of my discussion of what constitutes the distinctive quality of a theory in Sections II and III, it should be clear how fundamental my objection to conspiracy theories is. It can in any case be illustrated quite easily with the help of the meteorological 'theory', which confidently predicts that tomorrow it will rain or not. This meteorological theory is likewise true at all times and in all places. But with this 'theory', nobody needs to explain to us that it is completely worthless. For what good will it do us to know that tomorrow it will rain or not? Absolutely nothing! Such a 'theory' – and this applies equally to every conspiracy theory – does not tell us anything at all about reality, because it is always true. Since this kind of theory, in the words of the historian Patrick Gardiner 'can never be proved wrong ... nobody is left any the wiser for that' (Gardiner 1952, p. 110). The bio-physicist John R. Platt reaches the same conclusion:

> a 'theory' of this sort is not a theory at all, because it does not exclude anything. It predicts everything, and therefore does not predict anything ... This is not science, but faith; not theory, but theology ... a theory is not a theory unless it can be disproved. That is, unless it can be falsified by some possible experimental outcome. (Platt 1964, p. 350)

Karl Popper, in his turn, tries to elucidate the idea that a theory only tells us something about reality if it is falsifiable, by paraphrasing a statement of Albert Einstein's: 'in so far as a scientific statement speaks about reality, it must be falsifiable: and in so far as it is not falsifiable, it does not speak about reality' (Popper 1980ed., p. 314).[25]

Since empirical science is ultimately not about the certainty of always being right but about the possibility of being proved wrong, an empirical scientist wishing to explain the behaviour of states in the international system, or that of human individuals in the context of (government) organizations, ought to prefer an invisible-hand explanation to a hidden-hand explanation.

NOTES

1. Adam Smith suggests that we are possibly only aware of this activity of thought when something quite unexpected happens to us (Smith 1980ed., pp. 41–2).

2. Cf. D.S. Kothari: 'The simple fact is that no measurement, no experiment or observation is possible without a relevant theoretical framework' (quoted in Prigogine and Stengers 1984, p. 293). That this fact has to be emphasized time and again is an indication that things are not as simple as Kothari would have us believe.

3. Margaret and Harold Sprout quote 'a famous economist', who supposedly has said that 'the most vicious theorists are those who claim to let the facts speak for themselves' (Sprout and Sprout 1965, 1979ed., p. 45).

4. 'Der Verstand schöpft seine Gesetze ... nicht aus der Natur, sondern schreibt sie dieser vor' (Kant 1783, 1922ed., p. 72).

5. This is a typical example of a so-called 'as if' explanation. See for an exposition of the notion of an 'as if' explanation: Friedman 1966, pp. 19–23 and Lieshout 1984, pp. 10–11 and 31–2.

6. See Boulding (1962, 1963ed., pp. 81–7) for a thorough discussion of the situation in which Buridan's ass finds itself.

7. The psychologist Kurt Lewin is the author of this much-cited assertion. See, for instance, Janis and Mann 1977, p. xv.

8. Cf. the historian E.H. Kossmann: 'All of us ought to be so keenly aware of the inextricable complexity of history that we should not criticize a historian for simplifying matters. Of course he does. If he did not he would not be able to say anything meaningful' (Kossmann 1987, p. 232).

9. The examples are taken respectively from Popper and Von der Dunk (Popper 1971ed., II, pp. 13–14 and Von der Dunk 1975, p. 37). Speaking of this kind of discussion, Vilfredo Pareto observes that 'from the rigorously scientific view all these terminological questions do not have the slightest importance' (quoted in Margolis 1982, p. 14).

10. This also entails definitions having to be read from right to left (at any rate as far as formal languages are concerned, as used in mathematics, and the Indo-European languages with the exception of Farsi). As Karl Popper has said '*a definition ... must be read back to front, or from right to left*; for it starts with the defining formula, and asks for a short label to it' (Popper 1971 ed., II, p. 14, emphasis in original).

11.   The expressions 'what goes with what' and 'why what goes with what' are taken from
       the chapter by Converse in *Ideology and Discontent* (Apter (ed.) 1964).

12.   See for a formal derivation of this proposition, for example, Popper 1968ed., pp. 317
       and 319–21 and Nagel and Newman 1959, 1971ed., pp. 50–51.

13.   For the sake of clarity, I should emphasize that the requirement that no contradictory
       statements should be deduced from an axiomatic system, obtains – and in Popper's
       quotation this is actually said in so many words – for *all* axiomatic systems, be they
       normative theories, mathematical theories, or empirical theories. All axiomatic systems
       must be internally consistent if they are to have any informative content at all. In
       addition, empirical theories must satisfy the requirement of also being externally
       consistent. The latter means that statements about observable phenomena that can be
       derived from such axiomatic systems, should not conflict with statements about
       observed phenomena.

14.   Cf. Popper: 'In testing theories, we must attempt to falsify them. In trying out
       instruments, we only have to know the limits of their applicability. If we falsify a
       theory, we always look for a better one. But an instrument is not rejected because there
       are limits to its applicability: we expect to find such limits' (Popper 1983, p. 114).

15.   An observation of this kind does not 'automatically' lead to a refutation of the theory.
       In the first place, because the refutation of a theory requires a decision, and,
       accordingly, can never be an automatism. In the second place, because there may be
       good, theoretical, reasons for questioning the value of the observation.

16.   Cf. Adam Smith: 'it gives us a pleasure to see the phenomena which we reckoned the
       most unaccountable, all deduced from some principle ... and all united in one chain far
       superior to what we feel from the unconnected method, where everything is accounted
       for by itself, without any reference to the others' (Smith 1980ed., p. 244).

17.   In *The Theory of Moral Sentiments*, Adam Smith remarks that 'the resolute firmness of
       the person who acts in this manner, and in order to obtain a great though remote
       advantage, not only gives up all present pleasures, but endures the greatest labour both
       of mind and body, necessarily commands our approbation ... There is the most perfect
       correspondence between his sentiments and our own, and at the same time, from our
       experience of the common weakness of human nature, it is a correspondence which we
       could not reasonably have expected. We not only approve, therefore, but in some
       measure admire his conduct and think it worthy of a considerable degree of applause'
       (Smith 1979ed.a, p. 190).

18.   Although Graham Allison, one of the most important advocates of a foreign policy
       approach to explaining the behaviour of states, does not rule out the possibility of such
       a 'grand model' in advance (Allison 1971, p. 255).

19.   In the same vein, Peter Ordeshook argues that 'any adequate understanding of group
       choice or action ultimately must be reducible to an understanding of the choices that
       individual human beings make in the context of institutions for the purpose of attaining
       individual objectives' (Ordeshook 1986, p. xii).

20.   Cf. Hans Morgenthau: 'It is always the individual who acts, either with reference to his
       own ends alone or with reference to the ends of others. The action of society, of the
       nation, or of any other collectivity, political or otherwise, as such has no empirical
       existence at all' (Morgenthau 1946, 1965ed., p. 187).

21.   Cf. Adam Ferguson: 'Every step and every movement of the multitude, even in what
       are termed enlightened ages, are made with equal blindness to the future; and nations
       stumble upon establishments, which are indeed the result of human action, but not the
       execution of any human design' (Ferguson 1773ed., p. 205).

22.   The expression 'invisible-hand explanation' is clearly inspired by Adam Smith's
       famous metaphor (see also Chapter 8, Section III). According to Nozick 'an invisible-
       hand explanation explains what looks to be the product of someone's intentional

design, as not being brought about by anyone's intentions. A hidden-hand explanation explains what looks to be merely a disconnected set of facts that (certainly) is not the product of intentional design, as the product of an individual's or group's intentional design(s)' (Nozick 1974, p. 19).

23. The human tendency to interpret the world anthropomorphically appears to be another important reason for the enduring popularity of conspiracy theories. In this connection it is worth mentioning Fred Wilson's proposition, that the inclination to think anthropomorphically constitutes the major obstacle to scientific progress, but that, by learning to adopt a critical attitude, which 'is, or ought to be, part of the training of any competent scientist', this inclination can be suppressed (Wilson 1985, pp. 341–2).

24. Cf. Karl Marx and Friedrich Engels: 'The executive of the modern State is but a committee for managing the common affairs of the whole bourgeoisie' (Marx and Engels 1848, 1968ed., p. 5).

25. Popper also cites Einstein's original remark: 'in so far as the statements of mathematics speak about reality, they are not certain, and in so far as they are certain, they do not speak about reality' (Popper 1980ed., p. 314).

3. The Explanatory Principle

I THE EXPLANATORY PRINCIPLE

A. Introduction

After all these detours, it is high time to make a start on the exposition of the theory. But first, for good measure, I shall indicate briefly and informally what terms like 'axiom', 'assumption', 'theorem' and 'definition', mean in the context of my argument, since I shall be employing them frequently in the remainder of the book.

Strictly speaking, an *axiom* is a theorem in a theory that cannot be deduced from the other theorems that are part of that theory. In this book I shall reserve the term for the assumptions that constitute the explanatory principle. The latter sets the theoretical system in motion, so to speak, and determines the relationships between the other elements of the theory. In the present theory there is only one such assumption, and therefore it has only one axiom.

The (existential) *assumptions* can be divided into two classes: assumptions of place and assumptions of time. Following John Stuart Mill's usage, I shall speak of assumptions of 'coexistence' and assumptions of 'succession': 'every phenomenon is related ... to some phenomena that coexist with it, and to some that have preceded and will follow' (Mill 1843, 1981ed., p. 323). On the one hand, there are assumptions relating to the environment in which the explanatory principle, the 'mechanism', finds itself at time t. On the other hand, there are assumptions regarding the development, the evolution, that the system (mechanism *and* environment) in question has gone through in the past, and will go through in the future. The assumptions of 'succession' concern the dynamics of the theory. Formally speaking, existential assumptions are also axioms – they cannot be derived from the theory, and, after all, the existence of someone or something has to be presumed too – but since the assumptions of succession and coexistence have a function in the theory different to that fulfilled by the assumptions that make up the explanatory principle, I have given them another name.

The statements that can be deduced from axioms and assumptions, I shall call *theorems*. Naturally, these deductions have to be valid ones. In the following chapters I shall formulate various theorems. With a view to the readability of the text, I shall keep these deductions informal. Undoubtedly, some readers will be of the opinion that it would have been better if I had avoided the word 'theorem', in view of the informal character of these deductions. However, this would surely be attaching too much importance to a word. Which brings me to the role *definitions* play in an argument. As I have already explained in Chapter 2, Section III, definitions can be no more than a convenient shorthand. A definition enables us to substitute a single word for a description of a complex of phenomena (or, properties). The only thing that matters here is that, once we have introduced a certain definition, we adhere to it (Popper 1971ed., II, p. 14). For the sake of completeness, I conclude this terminological exercise with the observation that, in the course of my argument, I shall pay no attention to the operationalization of the theorems that will be deduced. That is to say, I shall not go into the way in which these theorems can be translated into hypotheses that contain falsifiable statements about reality.

B. Utilities and Probabilities

In order to make the workings of the explanatory principle as clear as possible, I shall for the moment assume a system in which only one individual is present. (This may be a human individual, like Robinson Crusoe on his island, but also a state.) I shall, by the way, in the course of my exposition of the explanatory principle, tacitly replace this assumption from time to time with the assumption that in the system under consideration two or more individuals are present.

Definition 1:
A *system* consists of a set of elements that are somehow interrelated, that is to say, the conduct or state of any one of the elements is influenced by the conduct or state of the other elements.

Definition 2:
An *individual* is the only element within a system that is capable of behaviour governed by the mechanism formulated in the axiom.

Definition 3:
The *environment* of an individual consists of all the other elements in the system (individuals or otherwise) of which the individual is a part.

Assumption 1:
Only one of the elements in the system under consideration is capable of behaviour
that is governed by the mechanism formulated in the axiom.

Figure 3.1 depicts the relation between system, individual and
environment, on the assumption that there is only one individual present
in the system.

Figure 3.1: System, individual and environment

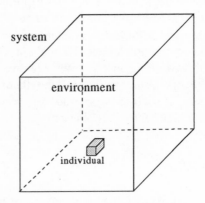

Source: From: *The Second Law* by Atkins. Copyright © 1984 by Scientific American Library.
Used with permission of W.H. Freeman and Company.

Definition 4:
Information concerns everything that reduces the degree of entropy in a system
(everything that reduces disorder and uncertainty in a system).

A system contains information if, and to the extent that, it displays a
certain degree of order or organization; if, formally speaking, the manner
in which the elements are arranged is not the most probable one. Where
the latter situation does however obtain, which means it is impossible to
detect whether any rearrangement of the elements has occurred, then the
entropy in the system has reached its maximum value (Atkins 1984, p.
73).

This also applies to systems of statements, such as (empirical) theories.
Such systems contain more information – that is to say, display a greater
degree of order and organization – the less ambiguous the connections
are between the various elements in the systems, the fewer inconsistencies
the systems contain, and the fewer undecidable questions they produce.

(Remember, once again, the fate of Buridan's ass; this poor ass was unable to choose, because each behavioural alternative looked equally attractive to it.)

We can conceive of empirical science as the conscious attempts by individual human beings to make explicit and to structure their knowledge of the world. Earlier I adduced arguments for why, ultimately, we have no interest in singular statements (see Chapter 2, Section III). Owing to their axiomatic structure, empirical theories are pre-eminently suited to establishing relationships between (statements about) observable phenomena, and it is by means of *deduction* that we are able to establish these connections. This implies, by the way, that the method of deduction should not be regarded as the counterpart for the method of induction. The method of deduction is about the ways in which statements can be deduced in a valid way from other statements, and, accordingly, is not about the production of 'new' knowledge, whereas this last is expressly (but mistakenly) the case with respect to the method of induction.

At the heart of the concept of information used here, is the degree of order in a system. That degree of order is relatively high in an empirical theory, because of its axiomatic structure. The axioms determine the mutual relationships between the elements of the theory, and make it possible to remove everything that is superfluous.[1]

Axiom:
Individual behaviour comprises overt behaviour, a change in the relationship between the individual and its environment, as well as covert behaviour, which behaviour entails changes in the nature and the quality of the information the individual has at its disposal. It follows from the individual's choosing of a certain behavioural option from a subjectively available set of such options; where the probability that the individual will choose a certain behavioural option is a function of the marginal utility of the outcome (the payoff) associated with this particular option, in the sense that, the greater the expected marginal utility of the outcome associated with a certain option, the higher the probability that the individual will choose that option. (Cf. De Vree 1983, pp. 235–7.)

Definition 5:
The *expected marginal utility* of the outcome (o) of a certain behavioural option consists of the sum of the marginal utility of (o) at time t, and the marginal utilities of all the other outcomes to which the individual expects (o) to lead at times $t+1$, $t+2$, ..., $t+n$, multiplied by the subjectively estimated probability that these outcomes will be realized, that is to say:

$$Eu(o) = \sum_{i=0}^{n} u(o^{t+i})\, p(o^{t+i}) \qquad (3.1)$$

In other words: axiom and definition state that the probability that an individual will choose a certain behavioural option, is proportional to the balance of expected costs and benefits that the individual assigns to this behavioural option, and the balance of expected costs and benefits assigned to the other behavioural options subjectively available to it, *and* the subjectively estimated probability that these costs and benefits will materialize.

The proposition that the individual is able to choose a behavioural option from a subjectively available set of such options, presupposes that the individual is able to order this set of behavioural options on the basis of the outcomes associated with the various subjectively available behavioural options. It is assumed that the individual, where it may choose between two behavioural options which it expects to lead to outcomes o_1 and o_2 respectively, is able to determine which of these outcomes it prefers, and that it acts accordingly. More specifically, this means that the individual either strictly prefers o_1 to o_2, or o_2 to o_1, but not o_1 to o_2 *and* o_2 to o_1 (the *assumption of asymmetry*). At the same time it is assumed that, if the individual knows its preference with respect to o_1 and o_2, it is also able to place the outcome associated with a third behavioural option o_3 somewhere on the ordinal scale set by o_1 and o_2. Supposing that the individual strictly prefers o_1 to o_2, then either o_3 is strictly preferred to o_2, or o_1 is strictly preferred to o_3, or both relationships hold (the *assumption of negative transitivity*) (Kreps 1990, pp. 18–22).

These assumptions include both random behaviour and rational behaviour. I shall speak of rational behaviour, where the individual's scale of preference for the outcomes of the behavioural options available to it exhibits a certain degree of consistency over time. The latter does *not* imply that the individual cannot change its mind – it initially preferred o_1 to o_2, now it prefers o_2 to o_1 – but it *does* imply that the individual does not change its mind constantly.[2] This is called the 'minimal', or 'thin', definition of rationality.

The probability concept introduced in the axiom concerns *relative*, or *conditional,* probability: the probability p that an event a will occur, given b, is equal to r:

$$p\,(a,b) = r \qquad (0 \le r \le 1)$$

I shall apply this concept of probability to everything that satisfies the axioms of the theory of probability.

This is not of course the place to go into the age-old controversy about the proper interpretation of probability as, on the one hand, *subjective* probability (the fact that we speak of the probability of the occurrence of a certain event *a* is a reflection of our incomplete knowledge; if our knowledge of the world were complete, then we would be able to predict the occurrence of *a* with certainty), or, on the other hand, as *objective* probability (given a certain condition *b*, the probability that event *a* will occur will either increase or decrease). I shall confine myself to the observation that empirical scientists, in their endeavours to understand why things are as they are, ought to employ the objective interpretation of probability.[3] In the theory being considered, I shall assume, by the way, that the individual, either consciously or unconsciously, will use the subjective interpretation of probability. The more often its expectation – that given *b* event *a* will occur – has proved in the past to be correct, the more confident the individual will become that it disposes of certain knowledge in this area. In other words, the individual's estimated probability of event *a* is not constant, and is based on the individual's past experience.[4]

In the light of what was discussed in Chapter 2, the general meaning of axiom and definitions should be clear. Behaviour is only possible if the individual has information, i.e. if it is capable of choosing a certain behavioural option from a set of such options. The latter can only be done if the outcomes attaching to the behavioural options the individual has at its disposal are not equally attractive.

Utilities are *postulated entities*, which the researcher – the one wishing to understand the ways in which social and political processes develop – uses in attempting to gain this understanding. As such, utilities are indeed 'empty of empirical content'.[5] Witness also Jeremy Bentham's defence of 'the principle of utility': 'is it susceptible of any direct proof? it should seem not: for that which is used to prove everything else, cannot itself be proved: a chain of proofs must have their commencement somewhere. To give such proof is as impossible as it is needless' (Bentham 1982ed., pp. 12–13; cf. Mill 1910ed., p. 32). Also, this 'empirical emptiness' implies that the idea that the individual tries to maximize its utility should not be equated with a negative image of human nature. At this stage of the argument it is left entirely open which things the individual will attach the greatest utility to, be it weapons, wealth, prestige, or, in the words of Robert Gilpin, 'beauty, truth and goodness' (Keohane (ed.) 1986, p. 305).

The axiom also applies to non-voluntary behaviour. The fact that people are often forced to act in a certain way, because someone holds out the prospect of significant costs if they do not act like this (for example, they pay taxes or protection money under the threat of violence), does not signify that these people 'have no choice', as the saying goes. They do have a choice, although, admittedly, it is a choice they would rather avoid, since it is one between two behavioural options that are both valued negatively – the one more negatively (becoming the victim of violence), and the other less (paying taxes or protection money).

Moreover, the axiom implies that the rationality of the individual must be 'bounded', as the economist Herbert Simon has called it (Simon 1947, 1961ed.), and for this reason it involves the rejection of the assumption of 'objective' or 'comprehensive' rationality. That this must be so, follows from the consideration that the theory in which it is postulated – (i) that the individual is able to choose a behavioural option from a set of such options, and, at the same time, (ii) that this individual is objectively rational – must be inconsistent. For the 'assumption of omniscience' (Simon 1957, pp. 202–3) implies that the individual would make its choice on the basis of a complete knowledge of all outcomes associated with each of the behavioural options subjectively available to it. But the class of 'outcomes associated with a behavioural option' is, as a matter of fact, infinitely large. This means that an individual wishing to act in a comprehensively rational manner, would never be able to choose, tied up as it would be for the rest of its short life discovering all the outcomes attaching to all the subjectively available behavioural options. The individual would suffer the same fate that befell Buridan's ass.[6] Indeed, the decision to act in an objectively rational manner from then on, would have to be taken on arbitrary grounds! In this way it also becomes clear that irrationalism necessarily precedes rationalism (cf. Popper 1971ed., II, pp. 228–31).

Contrary to what the protagonists of 'bounded rationality' seem to think, the assumption of comprehensive rationality cannot be rejected because it is inconsistent with the facts. A rejection on the basis of that argument only leads to an infinite regress.[7] The assumption should be rejected – and this *is* a valid argument – because, in conjunction with the axiom that states that individuals are able to make choices, it leads to an inconsistent system of statements.[8]

C. Dynamic Opportunism

With the help of a second and third assumption, we introduce dynamics into the theory. The individual's choice at time *t* is influenced by what happened in the past, and by what appears to be going to happen in the future. The second assumption concerns Gossen's famous First Law. This law is to the effect that, to paraphrase Joseph Schumpeter, as the individual goes on acquiring successive increments of a good, the intensity of its desire for one additional unit declines monotonically until it reaches – and then conceivably falls below – zero (Schumpeter 1954, 1982ed., p. 910).

> *Assumption 2*:
> The marginal utility that the individual expects at time t from the future realization of an outcome (o) associated with a certain behavioural option will decline monotonically and fall below zero, in proportion as the total utility of that outcome realized in the past is greater.

A discussion of some of the implications of this assumption will have to wait until Section III and later chapters.[9]

The third assumption, largely as a result of Axelrod's *The Evolution of Cooperation* (Axelrod 1984), has nowadays gained the status of 'unproblematical background knowledge' in the study of international relations. It is the 'reasonable' one, that the present value to the individual of a certain outcome is less, the more distant in time the realization of the outcome (Taylor 1987, p. 61). This means that in the situation that two outcomes o_1 and o_2 have the same expected marginal utility, but that o_1 can be realized at time t, whereas o_2 can be realized not earlier than time $t+1$, the individual will prefer o_1 to o_2.

> *Assumption 3*:
> The marginal utility that the individual expects at time t from the future realization of an outcome (o) associated with a certain behavioural option will become smaller, the longer the period of time the individual expects it to be before this outcome is realized.[10]

This assumption also implies that the individual will attach less value to the loss of an investment intended to bring about the outcome of a certain behavioural option, where, however, this outcome has not yet been realized, the further back in the past that investment was made.

It can be deduced from assumption 3, that in a system with more than two individuals and in which no agency capable of enforcing the rules of the system exists, there is an increased likelihood that the individuals will subordinate the 'abstract' idea of the importance of maintaining these rules to their 'concretely felt' self-interests. David Hume was also of course familiar with the one-sided battle between an abstraction like 'the rule of law' and the demands of a 'passionate minority'. He realized that individuals are all too easily prepared to ignore strictly universal legal rules, which serve an abstract goal – such as, for instance, the rule that individuals ought to be treated on an equal basis with no regard for birth, language, race or sex – whenever this suits them. Precisely because the advantages of breaking such a legal rule lie in the present, and the disadvantages (the eventual collapse of the legal order) lie in the future. Hume observes:

> All men are sensible of the necessity of justice to maintain peace and order; and all men are sensible of the necessity of peace and order for the maintenance of society. Yet, notwithstanding this strong and obvious necessity, such is the frailty or perverseness of our nature! it is impossible to keep men, faithfully and unerringly, in the paths of justice. Some extraordinary circumstances may happen, in which a man finds his interests to be more promoted by fraud or rapine, than hurt by the breach which his injustice makes in the social union. But more frequently, he is seduced from his great and important, but distant interests, by the allurement of present, though often very frivolous temptations. This great weakness is incurable in human nature. (Hume 1985ed., p. 38; cf. Hume 1985ed., p. 474, and Hume 1981ed., pp. 477–501)

Joseph Schumpeter is also of the opinion that the individual is inclined to opportunism. Witness the argument he develops to support his proposition that people rarely allow themselves to be persuaded by the irrefutable arguments in favour of capitalism. This follows from the fact that:

> any pro-capitalist argument must rest on long-run considerations. In the short run, it is profits and inefficiencies that dominate the picture. In order to accept his lot, the leveler or the chartist of old would have had to comfort himself with hopes for his great-grandchildren. In order to identify himself with the capitalist system, the unemployed of today would have completely to forget his personal fate and the politician of today his personal ambition. The long-run interests of society are so entirely lodged with the upper strata of bourgeois society that it is perfectly natural for people to look upon them as the interests of that class only. For the masses, it is the short-run view that counts. Like Louis XV, they feel *après nous le déluge*, and from the standpoint of individualist utilitarianism they are of course being perfectly rational if they feel like that. (Schumpeter 1942, 1976ed., pp. 144–5)[11]

The individual prefers consumption to investment. In the rest of the book I shall frequently return to the theme that it depends on the environment in which the individual finds itself whether, and to what extent, the individual will be able to suppress this inclination. For the moment, I shall restrict myself to the observation that, the more stable and, therefore, the more predictable the individual's environment, the more weight the individual will attach to its long-term interests.

D. The Dictate of Reality

When I now turn to a discussion of the relationship between the individual and its environment, it will be clear that the individual can only survive in its environment if it has 'good' or 'correct' information about that environment at its disposal. The individual can only hope to maximize its utility, whatever that may entail, if it is able to adapt itself to its environment – and the 'laws' that govern that environment – and not the other way around. If the individual wants to survive, it will have to conform to the *dictate of reality* (cf. De Vree 1990, II, pp. 359–70). Discovering how the environment is constructed is of course a question of learning. The individual will more or less deliberately 'test' the information it has subjectively available on its usefulness for maximizing the individual's utility. This learning process will go on by means of trial and error. The individual will behave more 'rationally', that is to say, will be better able to make choices, to the extent that this process of 'error elimination', as Popper calls it (Popper 1982ed.b, pp. 44–53), leads to more transparent and realistic information about the individual's environment.

It will also be clear that, the more 'favourable' the environment is to the individual, in the sense that the individual will have to expend less effort in order to be able to survive, the greater the likelihood that the individual will (continue to) exhibit 'random' behaviour. To put it another way, the more the individual is protected from the consequences of its mistakes – which result from incorrect expectations about the way the environment functions – the higher the probability that the individual will persist in unsuccessful behaviour. In a hypothetical 'perfect' environment – an environment in which the individual would be able to survive without ever having to exert itself – the individual would not be able to learn anything at all. Moreover, in such a perfect environment all behavioural options would look equally attractive, and, consequently, it would be impossible for the individual to order its set of behavioural options. It appears, then, that a 'perfect' environment is inconsistent with the axiom that the individual is able to choose, in precisely the same way as 'perfect' knowledge is. On this subject, Adam Ferguson has observed that man:

is destined to learn, and his lot must have the severities of a school, not the pampering of sensuality and sloth. ... If we attempt to conceive such a scene as the atheist contends would be required to evince the wisdom and goodness of God; a scene in which every desire were at once gratified without delay, difficulty or trouble; it is evident, that on such supposition the end of every active pursuit would be anticipated, exertion would be prevented, every faculty remain unemployed, and mind itself no more than a consciousness of languor, under an oppression of weariness, such as satiety and continued inoccupation are known to produce. (Ferguson 1792, I, pp. 177 and 178)

Likewise it will be obvious that the individual will continue to behave more randomly, the less able it is to discover the consequences of its actions. In their well-known article 'Rational choice and the framing of decisions', Tversky and Kahneman rightly pointed out that 'accurate and immediate feedback' is a prerequisite for effective learning (Hogarth and Reder (eds) 1987, p. 90). Such feedback is, however, lacking where it takes some time before the consequences of the individual's actions become visible, and/or can be shifted on to others, and when changes in the environment cause the consequences of the individual's actions to remain hidden from the individual. The idea that the lack of accurate and immediate feedback increases the likelihood of random behaviour, has been expressed rather neatly by Joseph Schumpeter, when he tries to explain why 'normally, the great political questions take their place in the psychic economy of the typical citizen with those leisure-hour interests that have not attained the rank of hobbies, and with the subjects of irresponsible conversation'. This is so, according to Schumpeter, because the citizen is a member of:

an unworkable committee, the committee of the whole nation, and that is why he expends less disciplined effort on mastering a political problem than he expends on a game of bridge. ... It will help to clarify the point if we ask ourselves why so much more intelligence and clear-headedness show up at a bridge table than in, say, political discussion among non-politicians. At the bridge table we have a definite task; we have rules that discipline us; success and failure are clearly defined; and we are prevented from behaving irresponsibly because every mistake we make will not only immediately tell but also be immediately allocated to us. These conditions, by their failure to be fulfilled for the political behavior of the ordinary citizen, show why it is that in politics he lacks all the alertness and the judgment he may display in his profession. (Schumpeter 1942, 1976ed., p. 261)

The behaviour of the individual is at any given moment the result of an evolutionary process. It is an inherently dynamic affair, in which information that existed originally is discarded, modified, or retained, in the measure that the individual believes this information to contribute to a successful adaptation to the environment. It will be clear that the more stable – and, consequently, the more predictable – the environment in which the individual finds itself, the greater the likelihood that the individual will be able to adapt successfully. But – and this cannot be emphasized enough – there is absolutely no guarantee that a successful adaptation will indeed take place.

It is by no means certain that the process of adaptation by trial and error will lead to unambiguous and realistic understanding. Where this does not happen, the individual will begin to exhibit pathological behaviour. The individual will also begin to behave pathologically when, owing to the unpredictability of the environment, all the individual's attempts to impose a structure on reality fail, *and* when the individual is confronted with a 'new' environment in which its 'old' understanding, for whatever reason, is no longer successful. In the latter situation the individual will cling to its 'old' perceptions the more stubbornly, the more successful that understanding has been in the 'old' environment. The individual realizes full well that it is losing its grip on the environment, but it will deny that this has anything to do with its understanding. The lack of success is blamed on 'bad luck' or 'mere coincidence' and, in any case, considered to be something that will pass. Whereas, when after a while the bad luck turns out nevertheless to be structural, the individual will not be able to gain new insights.

In this context I should also mention that, the more successful a given perception has been, the greater the individual's inclination to suppose that it has gained a sound understanding of how the environment functions (cf. my discussion of the subjective interpretation of reality). The result is that the individual will be more prepared to postpone consumption and to invest with an eye to the future, and of course, the more the individual has invested as a result, the less it will be prepared to modify this understanding.

II A NATURAL SYSTEM

We are the children of chaos, and the deep structure of change is decay. At root, there is only corruption, and the unstemmable tide of chaos ... This is the bleakness we have to accept as we peer deeply and dispassionately into the heart of the Universe. (Atkins 1984, p. 200)

A. The First and Second Law

The mechanism postulated in the previous section is no more than a formalism, which enables us to connect utilities to (behavioural) probabilities. As such it is 'true in all possible worlds'. In order to give the theory some empirical content, I introduce a fourth assumption, which states that the system of which the individual is a part is a natural system.

Assumption 4:
The system of which the individual is a part is governed by the laws of thermodynamics.

Viewed from the perspective of thermodynamics, every natural system – and thus man, too – represents a certain amount of energy that is, to a greater or lesser extent, organized. Witness Einstein's famous assertion that $E = MC^2$: matter and energy are equivalent. Matter is energy in a compressed form (this also explains the existence of 'black holes' in the universe). Different forms and kinds of matter 'merely' represent different ways in which, or differ in the proportion that, energy is organized.

Of the four basic laws of thermodynamics, the First and Second Law are of particular importance for a sound understanding of the ways in which social and political processes develop. The First Law states that the total amount of energy in the universe remains constant. *Energy is neither produced nor destroyed, but is transformed.* The economist Thomas Sowell observes in this connection that, 'although we speak loosely of "production", man neither creates nor destroys matter, but only transforms it – and the knowledge of how to make these transformations is a key economic factor' (Sowell 1980, p. 47). A natural system is only capable of performing work by means of the transformation of energy, and this transformation is only possible by destroying the organization of other natural systems (such as food and fuel). This entails that, the better a natural system is organized, the more energy it contains and the better it is able to extract energy from other natural systems.

The Second Law of thermodynamics says that *the transformation of energy is always accompanied by an increase in entropy*. The efficiency of these energy transformations is always less than 1 (in other words, a *perpetuum mobile* is impossible). The most important implication of both laws together is that a natural system can only maintain itself by destroying the organization of other natural systems,[12] and that this process must eventually lead to the destruction of the organization of the natural system itself.[13] To be sure, this is certainly not a recent observation. Thomas Hobbes, too, is familiar with it, although that great philosopher uses different words to describe it:

> I put for a general inclination of all mankind, a perpetual and restless desire of power after power, that ceaseth only in death. And the cause of this, is not always that a man hopes for a more intensive delight, than he has already attained to; or that he cannot be content with a moderate power: but because he cannot assure the power and means to live well, which he hath present, without the acquisition of more. (Hobbes 1947ed., p. 64)[14]

Whatever kind of behaviour the individual exhibits, be it overt behaviour or covert behaviour (such as the processing of information), it requires the individual to do some work. (This even applies to sleeping!)

Definition 6:
Energy refers to everything that makes it possible to bring about a change in the state of a system.

From now on, however, I shall make no further use of the word 'energy'. Although it has the merit of being neutral, it also sounds rather artificial in the context of the study of social and political phenomena. So, instead, I shall in future speak of 'power', a word more familiar to political scientists and students of international relations.

B. The Pursuit of Power

In the light of my discussion of the *dictate of reality*, the following theorem can be deduced from the axiom that the individual tries to maximize its utility, and the assumption that the world in which the individual lives is governed by the laws of thermodynamics:

Theorem 1:
The individual will choose, from the set of behavioural options subjectively available to it, the behavioural option with which is associated the outcome with the highest expected marginal utility in terms of power.

The individual has power (in other words, 'exists') if it is able to bring about a change in the state of a system.

The tenor of the argument developed thus far shows a great resemblance to the approach to social and political phenomena that Thomas Hobbes set out in his *Leviathan*. Witness also his definition of power. According to Hobbes 'THE POWER of *a man*, to take it universally, is his present means, to obtain some future apparent good' (Hobbes 1947ed., p. 56, emphasis in original). In his dissertations on power, however, Hobbes does not take sufficiently into account that the power of the individual not only depends on the amount of material resources at its disposal (fossil fuels, physical strength, food, weapons, et cetera), but also on the efficiency with which the individual is able to use these 'objectively' available material resources. The power of the individual does not only depend on the amount of material resources it has, but also on its ideas (theories) of how to use these material resources. In short, the individual's power consists of two elements: information and material resources.

This leaves the problem that material resources can only *be* material resources by virtue of the information they contain. A way out of this problem would be to reserve the term 'material resources' for information stored in the individual's environment. But then there is the complication that the theories and ideas the individual disposes of also belong, strictly speaking, to the individual's environment (since the individual is no more than a mechanism that is able to make choices). I think the best thing to do is simply to cut this Gordian knot, and to speak in future of the material resources of the individual when it concerns matters and processes in the individual's environment that can be observed, that is to say, that take place in the individual's 'operational environment', as Harold and Margaret Sprout have called it. And from now on I shall use the term 'information' with respect to all things and developments that concern the theories and the ideas of the individual and that cannot be observed, that have to do with its 'psychological environment' (Rosenau (ed.) 1969, pp. 48–9).

Definition 7:
Material resources refers to everything in the 'operational environment' of the individual that makes it possible for the individual to bring about a change in the state of the system of which it is a part.

This solution means, by the way, that from now on I shall write information between single quotation marks ('information'), whenever I speak of information in the formal sense, that is in the sense of definition 4.

III POWER AND INFORMATION

Who wants mere understanding, when power is offered instead? (Hardin 1960, p. 197)

A. The Value of Consistent Information

In this section I shall discuss several other implications of the explanatory principle postulated in Section I. These are of the utmost importance for a sound understanding of social and political processes.

Theorem 2:
The individual is only able to acquire new information, if it is able to relate this information to the information already at its disposal.

This theorem corresponds with what I have analysed at length in Chapter 2, namely, the proposition that all observations are 'theoretical' observations. According to the axiom, this must be so, because, if the individual cannot somehow make a connection between what is already familiar to it and what is new, then there is no way in which the individual would be able to assess the marginal utility of this new information (and, consequently, would ignore it).

Theorem 3:
The individual will value information in proportion to the contribution the individual expects this information to make to the maximization of its power.

Theorem 4:
If the individual detects that recently observed phenomena or newly acquired understanding are inconsistent with the information already at its disposal, it will either try to ignore the inconsistency (deny that an inconsistency exists), or try to remove it. Which behavioural option the individual will choose (and to what extent) is dependent on the marginal utility, in terms of power, the individual attaches to ignoring or resolving this external or internal inconsistency.

These theorems have also been discussed extensively in Chapter 2, and in particular in the course of my discussion of the second rule of the empirical science game and my rejection of the doctrine of instrumentalism. The information the individual has at its disposal is valued by the individual in proportion to its contribution to a successful adaptation to the environment. 'Successful', that is, in terms of the amount of power the individual has.

Since internal and external inconsistencies decrease the likelihood of successful behaviour, the individual will try to avoid them as much as possible. As far as internal inconsistencies are concerned – the individual realizes that it holds certain ideas that are mutually inconsistent – these can be removed in two ways. On the one hand, the individual can make a choice in favour of one of the inconsistent ideas and reject the other; on the other, the individual can search for fresh understanding in which the inconsistent notions are merged in a synthesis. As far as external inconsistencies are concerned – the individual discovers that its expectations about reality do not agree with the observed facts – there are four behavioural options available (see also Figure 3.2).

The individual can, in the first place, ignore the inconsistency. In the second place, the individual can attempt to 'immunize' its existing information, that is to say, it can try to save its existing information by devising 'conventionalist stratagems' that reduce the empirical content of that information. In the third place, it can attempt to improve its existing information by adopting conventionalist stratagems that increase the empirical content of that information.[15] And, finally, in the fourth place, the individual can try to replace its existing information with 'better' information.

Figure 3.2: Possible reactions to a detected external inconsistency

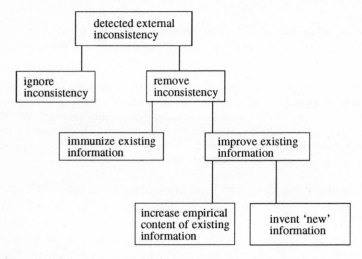

B. Five Factors

The answer to the question whether the individual will ignore or try to remove a detected inconsistency, appears to depend on the following five factors:

1.   *The relevance of the inconsistency.* Does the inconsistency relate to matters of vital importance, matters that are immediately relevant to the individual's day-to-day functioning? Or does it involve a question that is far removed from the individual's everyday worries, as is the case with abstract knowledge? The less threatening to its power the individual expects the inconsistency that has been detected to be, the higher the probability that the individual will ignore the inconsistency; and, conversely, the more the individual believes its power to be in danger as a result of the inconsistency, the greater the likelihood that it will try to remove the inconsistency. This proposition also implies that – in the case of an external inconsistency – the more the individual believes its

power to be at stake, the higher the probability that the individual will try to remove this inconsistency by immunizing the existing information. Another implication is that, as far as the individual is concerned, its 'everyday theories', so to speak, must fit with reality, but that when it comes to abstract theories or information about things that seem to have no immediate relevance to its own life or experience, it is quite prepared to put up with the greatest nonsense.

2. *The expected (alternative) costs involved.* The higher the anticipated costs (in terms of power, time and intellectual capacity) of trying to remove an inconsistency that has been detected, as compared to the expected costs of ignoring the inconsistency, the higher the probability that the individual will ignore the inconsistency. Conversely, the lower the expected costs of trying to remove an identified inconsistency, as compared to the anticipated costs of ignoring the inconsistency, the more likely it is that the individual will try to remove the inconsistency. Whereby it is assumed – in the case of an external inconsistency – that the individual expects the costs of immunizing the existing information to be lower than the costs of improving the existing information.

3. *The amount of power and information already at the individual's disposal.* The less power and information the individual has, the fewer (cognitive) means it has at its disposal for removing the inconsistency identified. The smaller the amount of power and information the individual has, the more improbable it becomes that the individual will expect it to be worth its while to find out how the inconsistency can be removed and to be able to do so.

4. *The amount of non-reusable power the individual has invested in the information that has turned out to be inconsistent (in relation to the amount of power the individual has).* The more an individual has invested in a certain point of view, and the less possible it is to turn this investment to other purposes, the lower the probability that the individual will be prepared to give up that viewpoint if it is confronted with an inconsistency. This probability will decrease further, the less power the individual has. The empirical scientist whose theory, after many years of strenuous effort and hardship, is refuted the first time it is put to a severe test, will very probably take refuge in conventionalist stratagems in order to save the theory, or ignore the results of the test, and simply adhere to the theory without making any modifications.[16]

It will be clear that the individual will also take into account how long ago it made this non-reusable investment. The longer ago the investment was made, the less value the individual will attach to the loss of the investment (cf. my discussion of assumption 3).

5.   *The extent to which the information that has turned out to be inconsistent has contributed to the individual's power (in relation to the amount of power the individual has).* The less the inconsistent information has contributed to the individual's power, the more prepared the individual will be to remove the inconsistency (provided, of course, that the information does not relate to matters of little or no importance to the individual); whereas, conversely, the more that information has contributed to the individual's power, the more probable it becomes that the individual will ignore the inconsistency.[17] The more successful a career the empirical scientist I introduced just now has made in the academic world, during (and by virtue of) the long years of hard work in which he developed his theory, the greater the probability that, when the theory turns out to be inconsistent, he will simply ignore the inconsistency.

At the same time, Gossen's First Law should apply here too. This means that, as the scientist becomes more and more successful as a result of the theory he has developed, the marginal utility of another increment of success becomes smaller and smaller, up to a point at which the scientist will be prepared to reconsider his theory.

Naturally, these factors can neutralize or reinforce one another. I must admit that at this moment I can give no indication of how much weight should be attached to each of the five factors in their mutual interaction. Although it seems a matter of course to suppose that of the first three (static) factors, the third is the most important, and of the last two (dynamic) factors, the first.

An example of the five factors being able to reinforce one another, concerns the (fictional?) social sciences graduate who finds out, in practice, that he has been taught quite a lot of nonsense during his studies. This graduate will be inclined to ignore this new information, and this inclination will become stronger and stronger, the more he expects it to cost him to reconcile this new information with the information acquired during his studies, the more dependent his present position is on his academic degree, the greater the amount of non-reusable power, time and intellectual capacity invested in his academic education, and the more successful his career up to now has been, thanks to his academic background. To put it somewhat more formally:

Theorem 5:
The marginal utility of the outcome attached to the behavioural option of ignoring an inconsistency (denying that it exists) will increase, the less threatening to its power the individual expects this inconsistency to be, the higher the (alternative) costs of removing this inconsistency are (compared to those of ignoring the inconsistency), and the less power and information the individual has; *and* the greater the amount of non-reusable power invested in the information that has turned out to be inconsistent the individual believes there to be, and the more it believes this investment to have contributed to its power up to now.

Whereas, conversely, the marginal utility of the outcome associated with the behavioural option of trying to remove an inconsistency will increase, the more threatening the individual expects this inconsistency to be to its power, the lower the (alternative) costs of removing this inconsistency are (compared to those of ignoring the inconsistency), and the more power and information the individual has; *and* the smaller the amount of non-reusable power invested in the information that has turned out to be inconsistent the individual believes there to be, and the less it believes this investment to have contributed to its power up to now.

In the light of my discussion of the five factors that influence the individual's decision either to ignore or to remove an inconsistency, it should at least have become clear why only a few will attach great importance to an activity that has as little to do with day-to-day reality, and that, moreover, is also very costly (in terms of power, time and intellectual capacity), as the endeavour to explain why things are as they are (cf. also my discussion of the fifth rule of the empirical science game). Why, in the words of David Hume, 'the empire of philosophy extends over a few; and with regard to these too, her authority is very weak and limited' (Hume 1985ed., p. 169).[18]

In this connection I should not omit to mention that, in the eyes of the individual, it is never a question of an unambiguous choice between either information or power. It is always a choice between more of the one and less of the other. A powerful individual can afford to acquire 'correct' information about its environment, but, at the same time, because it is so powerful, it has less need to do so: it can allow itself the luxury of arbitrary behaviour. Whereas, conversely, a powerless individual cannot bear the costs of acquiring 'correct' information about its environment, while at the same time, because it is so powerless, having a greater need to do so: it cannot afford the luxury of arbitrary behaviour. This implies, moreover (if I do not take the two 'historic' factors 4 and 5 into account), that the probability increases that an individual will persist in unsuccessful behaviour, in proportion as the individual is less powerful.

C. How 'New' Insights Emerge

At the end of this section on power and the processing of information, and once again in anticipation of my discussion of the implications for the interaction between two or more individuals of the explanatory principle I have postulated, I wish to go into the question how – assuming an isolated group of individuals (for instance, the inhabitants of an island) – new theories about how reality is structured can develop.

In a group of individuals, the process of *error elimination* that every individual goes through separately is influenced by the understanding and behaviour of the other individuals in the group. The individual learning process is made easier by the fact that the individual can imitate the example of other individuals in the group. Generally speaking, the individual will try to imitate the ideas and behaviour of those members of the group who, in the eyes of the individual, have adapted themselves most successfully (in terms of power) to the dictate of reality. This implies that, where the environment is stable, the perceptions and behaviour of the 'adult' individuals in the group will tend to become more or less identical in matters that are vital to their survival. This tendency will become stronger, the more successful (in the opinion of the individuals) this understanding and behaviour have proved to be in the struggle for survival (cf. Alchian 1950, p. 219). Deviant opinions and deviant behaviour usually have to do with matters deemed by the adult members of the group to be relatively unimportant.

The foregoing also implies that the probability that an individual will develop deviant theories about how the world is structured increases, the longer the period in which the individual, for whatever reason (a protracted illness, geographical separation), has little or no contact with the other members of the group. The longer this period of isolation, the more probable it becomes that the individual will form its own ideas about how its environment works. The individual will run into problems when this period of separation comes to an end, and, subsequently, the deviant nature of its ideas becomes clear to all. The individual (and not the other individuals in the group!) now faces the choice between adjusting its deviant theories to those that are dominant in the group, or sticking to its own theories. Which behavioural option the individual will choose depends first of all on the length of the period of separation. This must have been long enough for the individual to discover that its theories fit with reality, that is to say, that they enable the individual to adapt successfully to the environment. If this condition is not fulfilled, then the likelihood increases that the individual will abandon its own theories. Where this condition is in fact met, it becomes more probable that the individual will refuse to give up its deviant theories. In that case, an (intellectual) entrepreneur has been born, someone who thinks (whether rightly or wrongly, that will remain to be seen) that things can be combined more effectively than the way they are at present (cf. Schumpeter 1961ed., pp. 66–7 and 74–5) – whereby the probability that the individual will actually choose this option increases, in proportion to the length of the period of separation, and to the contribution the deviant theories have made to the individual's power during this period.

IV ALTRUISM

The explanatory principle I have been expounding in the previous sections corresponds more or less to the rational actor model that is employed in most of the social sciences, including international relations. Time and again this model has the objection raised against it that it would not be able to explain altruistic behaviour. That is to say, behaviour by which the individual puts a part of its power, or, in the extreme case, its entire power, at the disposal of another individual, or group of individuals, without apparently getting something in return (Hardin 1977, pp. 13–14). My decision to elucidate the implications of the explanatory principle by assuming a system in which only one individual is present, does not really help to refute this objection. But the objection still does not hold. It is my contention that the implications of the explanatory principle can be reconciled very happily with altruistic behaviour. I shall devote this section to the arguments in support of this contention, and I shall do so on the basis of a brief examination of the argument developed by Howard Margolis in his *Selfishness, Altruism and Rationality*. By virtue of this book, Margolis is currently regarded by many as one of the most important exponents of the above objection.

It is regrettable, by the way, that the critics of the rational actor model also attempt to justify their position by interpreting the model in a particular way, and to elevate it to *the* interpretation of the model. Theorem 1 states that the individual tries to maximize its power. Nothing is said in the theorem about the ways in which the individual can best achieve this goal. In this regard, literally everything is still possible. But the critics of the rational actor model cannot live with this indeterminacy.

They claim that the model implies that the individual is able to survive in one way only, which is by pursuing its own self-interest, or, a little more insinuatingly, its 'narrow' self-interest. (In their view there is apparently no difference between individualism, the idea that any element in a system can be analysed on its own, and egoism, the endeavour to strengthen one's position at the expense of the community.) After which they demonstrate, to their own satisfaction, that the natural and social world is full of behaviour that contradicts *this* explanatory principle, and conclude that another explanation, one that leaves more room for altruistic behaviour, is in order.

Margolis also applies this technique. He, too, maintains that the rational actor model implies that 'all human behaviour can be explained in terms of narrow self-interest', and shows subsequently that this explanation quite often fails to account for actual behaviour (Margolis 1982, p. 7). Significant in this respect is his interpretation of, what he calls, 'the Darwinian argument'. According to Margolis, it is an 'immediate consequence' of this argument that 'self-interested creatures, other things being equal, will be able to leave more descendants carrying their genes than would non-self-interested creatures. Hence natural selection will favor self-interest' (Margolis 1982, p. 26). But this conclusion is wholly unwarranted. As a matter of fact the 'Darwinian argument' does not say anything at all about the relationship between the extent to which the individual pursues its self-interest and its chances of being successful in evolution. This would also conflict with the 'blind' (or should I say 'contingent'?) nature of the evolutionary process. The 'Darwinian argument' hinges on the perception – see also my discussion of the relationship between the explanatory principle and the dictate of reality – that as the individual is better adapted to its environment, so the probability increases that the individual will be able to reproduce itself and to pass its genetic information on to the next generation.[19] Why one individual is better adapted than another is a matter of chance – in the shape of genetic variation and variation in the environment – and of the cumulative effect of the selection mechanism over the generations (cf. Hardin 1960, Dawkins 1986, 1988ed. and Gould 1989).

Still, the question remains whether the explanatory principle allows for altruistic behaviour. Margolis thinks that this is not the case. In his opinion, such behaviour can only be explained if, instead of the rational actor model, we postulate a decision rule, which Margolis calls the 'Fair Share principle', on the basis of which the individual, consciously or unconsciously, determines how it will allocate a certain amount of its resources: for its own benefit (private values), or for the benefit of the group of which it is a member (social values). This decision rule takes two things into consideration – how large a share of its own resources the individual has previously devoted to group-interest, and the situation of the group as a whole (for example the level of collective goods provision within the group) – and is as follows:

> The larger the share of my resources I have spent unselfishly, the more weight I give to my selfish interests in allocating marginal resources. On the other hand, the larger the benefit I can confer on the group compared with the benefit from spending marginal resources on myself, the more I will tend to act unselfishly. (Margolis 1982, p. 36)

The question now is whether this decision rule, in contrast to what Margolis claims, can also be deduced from the explanatory principle. In order to be able to answer this question affirmatively, I shall first have to introduce the notion of a lexicographical, or – to follow John Rawls, who thinks this term too cumbersome – lexical, order (Rawls 1971, pp. 42–3).

In this connection, a lexicographical order means that the individual, assuming there to be a set of subjectively available behavioural options $\{b_1, b_2, b_3..., b_k\}$, will (up to a certain limit) give absolute priority to the realization of the outcome associated with, say, b_1. This implies that the individual, up to the moment when the total utility derived from the realization of the outcome attaching to b_1 reaches a certain level, is unable to make a tradeoff between, on the one hand, the expected marginal utility of an extra unit of the outcome associated with b_1, and, on the other, the expected marginal utility of a unit of the outcomes attached to the other behavioural options. My proposition is that the individual's set of subjectively available behavioural options is partly ordered lexicographically. The individual gives absolute priority to the realization of certain outcomes, which, for the sake of convenience I shall call the basic necessities of life, until a certain level has been reached. (Until the moment this level has been attained, it is irrelevant whether this is the result of the individual's own exertions or those of the other members of the group.) From the moment the individual believes that level has been reached – which, generally speaking, comes down to the fact that the individual believes it is sufficiently powerful to maintain itself successfully against other individuals – the individual will exhibit behaviour that accords with the regularities postulated in the 'FS principle': that is, the larger the marginal utility of group-interest behaviour compared to that of self-interest behaviour (to follow Margolis's terminology), the higher the probability that the individual will choose group-interest behaviour; and, the more the individual has shown group-interest behaviour in the past, the greater the likelihood that the individual will choose self-interest behaviour. But the moment the individual believes that it has dropped below that key level, the individual will no longer use this decision rule. The kinds of behaviour that, according to Margolis, would be in direct contradiction to the rational actor model, can in this interpretation be seen as manifestations of the level of prosperity attained in certain parts of the world.

To sum up, altruistic behaviour is not prohibited by the explanatory principle. This goes for accidental altruistic behaviour – by mistake the individual puts part of its power, or perhaps even all of its power, at the disposal of another individual or group of individuals – as well as for what may be called consistent altruistic behaviour, for instance on the basis of the 'FS principle'. And here the probability that an individual will exhibit the latter kind of altruistic behaviour increases, the better able to maintain itself among the other individuals in the system the individual believes itself to be.

All that remains for me to do at the end of this section is to point out that altruistic behaviour can also be a form of successful behaviour (in terms of power), in the sense that altruistic behaviour can also be regarded as a kind of investment. The individuals I have assisted in the past will maybe feel obliged to assist me, if I get into trouble myself. It will be obvious that, the more powerful an individual, the more easily it can allow itself to make more of these risky investments. The risk consists in the fact that, if the individual is itself in trouble, it will not be in a position to enforce these favours in return. We need only recall the sad truths rehearsed in the well-known blues: 'Nobody knows you when you're down and out'. The risky nature of the investment is another reason why altruistic behaviour is less common among (very) poor people than among people who are well-off.

NOTES

1. The importance of order also explains why many empirical scientists feel that a solution to a given problem has to be elegant. Paul Dirac, a physicist, has expressed this feeling as follows: 'it is more important to have beauty in one's equations than to have them fit experiment. It seems that if one is working from the point of view of getting beauty in one's equation, and if one has really a sound insight, one is on a sure line of progress' (quoted in Medawar 1984ed., p. 262). The relation between 'beauty' and 'truth' is also a recurrent theme in the work of Adam Smith. In his essay 'Of the nature of that imitation which takes place in what are called the imitative arts', he observes that, when we listen to a well-composed concerto, 'the mind in reality enjoys not only a very great sensual, but a very high intellectual, pleasure, not unlike that

which it derives from the contemplation of a great system in any other science' (Smith 1980ed., p. 205). While to give another example, in the *Wealth of Nations* he speaks of: 'the beauty of a systematical arrangement of different observations connected by a few common principles' (Smith 1979ed.b, II, pp. 768–9). A theory's elegance certainly belongs to the good, theoretical, reasons on the basis of which we may decide to ignore a potentially falsifying statement (see Chapter 2, Section III).

2. Bearing in mind that, as Riker and Ordeshook have pointed out, it may at times be perfectly rational to act in a perfectly random manner (Riker and Ordeshook 1973, p. 14). See, for an extensive analysis of the assumptions that underlie this so-called rational actor model, Elster 1983, pp. 6–9 and Elster 1979, 1984ed., pp. 68–71.

3. See Popper 1980ed., pp. 332–3, for the axioms of the theory of probability. See Popper 1983, pp. 281–300, for a discussion of the subjective and objective interpretations of probability.

4. This is what L.J. Savage calls the *personalistic* point of view: 'probability measures the confidence that a particular individual has in the truth of a particular proposition' (Savage 1954, p. 3).

5. As A. Rosenberg finds out to his amazement (Rosenberg 1976, p. 148).

6. If we were to assume that the system is 'closed', and will forever remain closed, then we could say that the number of consequences of the various behavioural options involved is indeed finite. But whatever this assumption might mean – would the system not have to be very 'limited' indeed, if the individual were ever to be able to calculate all the consequences of all the behavioural options involved? and, moreover, would the individual who knows for certain that all its endeavours will be in vain (and especially in that very short term), ever bother to choose a behavioural option? – the fact remains that this extra assumption needs to be introduced in order to make the theory consistent again, and, with Occam's razor in hand, we ought to prefer the theory that postulates subjective rationality.

7. For if we demand that an assumption must accord with reality (a kind of empirical test in advance), then we run into the problem of how to test that this is indeed the case. This can only be done by means of a theory from which the assumption in question can be deduced in the shape of a hypothesis. If it subsequently turns out that, for the time being, that hypothesis cannot be refuted, then we are at liberty to introduce the assumption into the theory. However, the test theory from which the assumption has been derived as a hypothesis naturally rests on assumptions too, which, in their turn, need to be tested for their verisimilitude using other test theories, and so on *ad infinitum*.

On the same basis, the demand formulated by Milton Friedman should also be rejected. According to Friedman, assumptions should be 'descriptively false' (the famous 'F-twist'). But how could we establish that an assumption meets this demand? Only, by formulating a test theory, etc. etc. (Friedman 1966, p. 14).

8. Cf. also Riker and Ordeshook's criticism of the argument developed by Herbert Simon, that there is a difference between, on the one hand, the unrealistic 'maximizing' principle, and, on the other hand, the realistic 'satisficing' principle: 'unless we ask decision makers to play God, maximizing and satisficing are the same thing' (Riker and Ordeshook 1973, p. 23).

9. Iain Hampsher-Monk has pointed out that Gossen's Law was anticipated by Jeremy Bentham in his 'Measurement of subjective states': 'the quantity of happiness produced by a particle of wealth (each particle being of the same magnitude) will be less and less at every particle; the second will produce less than the first, the third than the second, and so on' (quoted in Hampsher-Monk 1992, p. 324).

10.   Conventionally, it is assumed that the individual employs an exponentially increasing discount parameter *w*, which remains constant through time, to assess the present value of future outcomes, that is to say:

$$Eu(o) = \sum_{i=0}^{n} w^i \, [u(o^{t+i}) \, p(o^{t+i})] \qquad (3.2)$$

where $0 < w < 1$ (Taylor 1987, p. 61). It should be noted, however, that the added assumption that the value of *w* remains constant through time, does pose a problem. In Chapter 5, Section II, I shall explain why this assumption cannot be maintained.

11.   The reason for Auguste Comte's rejection of the science of political economy may be cited in support of Schumpeter's proposition. In Comte's view, political economy tends 'to answer to all complaints that in the long run all classes, and especially the one most injured on the existing occasion, will enjoy a real and permanent satisfaction; a reply which will be regarded as derisive, as long as man's life is incapable of being indefinitely lengthened' (cited in Hayek 1952, 1979ed., p. 351).

12.   According to Atkins it would be more correct to refer to the *energy principle* and the *entropy principle* respectively, but that nevertheless one usually speaks of the First and Second Law of thermodynamics (Atkins 1984, p. 32).

13.   Cf. in this connection the following quotations taken from *Order out of Chaos* by Prigogine and Stengers:
>   The cultural implications were far-reaching, and they included a conception of society and men as energy-transforming engines. But energy conversion cannot be the whole story. It represents the aspects of nature that are peaceful and controllable, but below there must be another, more 'active' level ... The world is described as an engine in which heat is converted into motion only at the price of some irreversible waste and useless dissipation. Effect-producing differences in nature progressively diminish. The world uses up its differences as it goes from one conversion to another and tends toward a final state of thermal equilibrium, 'heat death'. In accordance with Fourier's law, in the end there will no longer be any difference of temperature to produce a mechanical effect. (Prigogine and Stengers 1984, pp. 111 and 115–16)

14.   Shakespeare makes Richard II sigh, after the latter has resigned his crown to Henry Bolingbroke:
>   Nor I, nor any man that but man is,
>   With nothing shall be pleased till he be eased
>   With being nothing.
>   (*The Tragedy of King Richard the Second*, Act 5 Scene 5)

15.   Hans Albert has coined the expression 'immunization'. See, for a discussion of the concept of 'conventionalist stratagems', Popper 1980ed., p. 82, Lakatos and Musgrave (eds) 1970, 1974ed., pp. 100–101 and Lieshout 1984, pp. 13–15.

16.   Karl Marx provides us with a very nice example of a scientist who ignores facts that contradict his theory, in respect of his doctrine of the impoverishment of the proletariat, if not absolutely, then at least relatively. According to Leszek Kolakowski it is obvious that Marx:
>   was determined to find in capitalism a relentless tendency to degrade the worker, and that he resisted facts which indicated that the worker was getting better off. Bertram Wolfe has pointed out that in the first edition of *Capital* various statistics are brought down to 1865 or 1866, but those for the movement of wages stop at 1850; in the second edition (1873) the statistics are brought up to date, again with

the exception of those on wages, which had failed to bear out the impoverishment theory. This is a rare but important case of disingenuousness in Marx's treatment of factual data. (Kolakowski 1978, 1981ed., I, p. 290)

17.   Tolstoy has expressed this idea in the following way:

I know that most men – not only those considered clever, but even those who are very clever and capable of understanding most difficult scientific, mathematical, or philosophic, problems – can seldom discern even the simplest and most obvious truth if it be such as obliges them to admit the falsity of conclusions they have formed, perhaps with much difficulty – conclusions of which they are proud, which they have taught to others, and on which they have built their lives. (Tolstoy 1898, 1938ed., p. 218)

18.   To avoid possible misunderstanding, in Hume's time 'the empire of philosophy' was still equated with 'the empire of science'.

19.   Margolis's interpretation of the Darwinian argument is unconvincing for another reason also. According to Margolis, the argument implies that groups in which individuals have a propensity to act in the interest of the group stand a better chance of being successful in the struggle for survival between groups, than groups consisting entirely of self-interested individuals (Margolis 1982, pp. 26–35). The most significant objection that can be raised against this interpretation is that Margolis completely ignores the possibility that the desired objective, 'the survival of the group', may be the unexpected, unintended by-product of the attempts by the members of the group to adapt themselves successfully, in terms of their *own* power, to their environment. A group can be successful in the struggle for survival, without any of its members, in the words of Roland McKean, arising in the morning and asking themselves, 'what can I do today for Pareto optimality?' (McKean 1965, p. 498). It is interesting to note in this connection, that Darwin was inspired particularly by the work of Malthus and Adam Smith, who did have an eye for the unintended social repercussions of purposeful individual behaviour.

4. Interaction

I POWER AND DISTANCE

In this chapter, I shall be discussing some of the implications that follow if the assumption that there is only one individual present in the system were to be replaced by the assumption that there are two individuals present in the system. At the same time, I shall be introducing certain concepts, such as demand behaviour, credibility, dependence, harmony of interests and conflict of interests, which I shall be using frequently in the following chapters.

Assumption 1*:
Only two of the elements in the system under consideration, i and j, are capable of behaviour that is governed by the mechanism formulated in the axiom.

The other assumptions introduced in the previous chapter still apply. Both individuals may differ from one another in an infinite number of ways, for instance, as far as human individuals are concerned, with respect to their gender, intelligence, colour of skin and physical strength, or, in the case of states, as regards their gross national product, form of government, number of inhabitants, and geographic location, but they are alike in the manner in which they connect utilities and behavioural probabilities. What they also have in common is that they are situated in a system that is governed by the laws of thermodynamics, that Gossen's First Law applies to them, and that both value less an outcome associated with a certain behavioural option, the longer the time they expect it to take before this outcome will be realized. Moreover, for the sake of elucidating the mechanisms of interaction, I shall once again from time to time tacitly substitute the assumption that there are more than two individuals in the system for the assumption that there are only two individuals in the system.

It is the essence of interaction that individuals influence one another by their behaviour. That is to say: i's behaviour increases or decreases the attractiveness to j of a certain behavioural option from the set of such options subjectively available to it, and vice versa. Behaviour that has this effect I shall call, following De Vree, demand behaviour.

Definition 8:
Demand behaviour is any kind of behaviour by an individual *i* that has the effect that it induces a change in the attractiveness of the behavioural options subjectively available to another individual *j*.

This definition will speak for itself. The inclination of *i* and *j* to interact with one another, I shall call the *affinity* between *i* and *j* (cf. chemistry, where affinity stands for the attraction between elements that causes them to combine with one another).

Whether the individuals will interact − will engage in demand behaviour towards one another − and the extent to which this will be the case, depends on the power they have at their disposal and the distance between them. The more powerful individual *i* is, the greater the probability that *i*'s attempts to maximize its own power will lead to a change in the marginal utilities that *j* attaches to the various behavioural options subjectively available to it. At the same time it will be clear that, the greater the distance between the individuals (from a social, intellectual, political or geographical point of view), the more of their power they will have to expend in order to 'reach' the other individual. This understanding led Kenneth Boulding to the formulation of his *law of diminishing strength*. (Boulding formulated this law in the context of his analysis of the behaviour of states, but it also applies to the behaviour of human individuals.) This law states: '*the further, the weaker*'; that is, the further from home any nation has to operate, the longer will be its lines of communications, and the less strength it can put in the field' (Boulding 1962, 1963ed., p. 231, emphasis in original).[1]

I have worded my observations in the foregoing paragraph in such a way that it may be clear that two individuals can interact with one another without being aware of the fact that they do so. In that regard, it is easy to see that, in a system with two individuals that differ in power, the probability that the more powerful individual will not be aware of the fact that it engages in demand behaviour towards the other individual, will be greater than the probability that the less powerful will be unaware of doing so − whereby the probability that the more powerful individual will not be aware of the fact that it engages in demand behaviour towards the other individual, increases to the extent that the difference in power between the two individuals will be greater. In a situation in which *i* and *j* do in fact realize that they are able to influence one another, each of them will only do so if it is of the opinion that this will contribute to the maximization of its power. This implies that, the more i and j have to offer to one another (i.e. the greater their respective power), the more they will want to interact with one another, and, at the same time, the more of their power they will have to expend in order to be able to do so. This also means that an attempt to influence the other individual is not without risk. It will only pay i to interact with j where the latter disposes of a certain amount of power, and, accordingly, also poses something of a threat to i. For, as Stephen Walt observed with respect to states, 'the greater a state's total resources (i.e., population, industrial and military capability, technological prowess, etc.), the greater a potential threat it can pose to others' (Walt 1985, p. 9).[2]

The individual will prefer to interact with those individuals that are powerful enough to strengthen its own power and just not powerful enough actually to threaten its own power. (This is not to say that the individual's behaviour is at any one moment guided by this rule. This is typically a rule the individual will have to learn and re-learn in the course of time. It is, by the way, very doubtful whether the individual in a continually changing world will ever reach this optimum, and subsequently will manage to stay there over a prolonged period of time.) The greater the difference in power between the two individuals, the less the more powerful individual will be interested in influencing the behaviour of the other individual, whereas, conversely, the more interested the less powerful individual will be in influencing the other's behaviour. Another implication of the foregoing is that, in a system with several more or less powerful individuals, most of the demand behaviour will be focused on the most powerful individuals in the system.

If I now return to my discussion of the concept of 'distance', in Stephen Walt's view distance (in his terminology 'proximity') constitutes *the* most important factor in the explanation of the pattern of alliances so characteristic of the bipolar system that was established after the Second World War:

> the effects of proximity help explain why the alliance choices of ... important states make the Soviet situation even worse. Because the Soviet Union is the largest power on the Eurasian land mass, it poses a significant threat to the many states on or near its borders. As a result, Soviet relations with neighboring countries are generally imperial or hostile: those countries are either under *de facto* Soviet control or allied with the U.S. Although geographic proximity may in some cases make it easier for the Soviet Union to use military power against its neighbors, this situation also provides the independent states of Eurasia with a powerful incentive to seek allies elsewhere to deter such an attempt or to defeat it should it occur. ...
>
> For the medium powers of Western Europe and Asia, the U.S. is the perfect ally. It is sufficiently powerful to contribute substantially to their defense, it is driven by

its own concerns to oppose Soviet expansion, and yet it is sufficiently distant from those allies so that it does not itself pose a significant threat ... More than any other factor, geography explains why so many of the world's significant powers have chosen to ally with the U.S. (Walt 1985, p. 36)

It cannot be denied that distance constitutes an important element in explaining the manner in which states *and* human individuals behave towards one another. The smaller the distance between individuals, the greater the likelihood that they will interact, whereas, conversely, the greater the distance between individuals, the lower the probability that they will interact and, accordingly, will be able to threaten one another.[3] Nevertheless, Walt is assuming too much when he concludes that geographical distance, more than any other factor, explains why the United States, until the collapse of the Soviet empire after the fall of the Berlin Wall in 1989, was the natural ally of the states on the Eurasiatic continent that tried to maintain their independence in the face of the Soviet threat. It is not possible to consider the effects of distance without taking the effects of power into account as well. If Walt were to persist in his claim that distance is the decisive factor in international politics, then he would have a hard time explaining why all those states on or near the borders of the Soviet Union decided to ally themselves with the United States, and not with, to take another country far away, Brazil. My point is that, if the United States had not also been a superpower, capable of launching an attack on the Soviet Union with nuclear weapons (which is altogether in a different league from 'contributing substantially' to the defence of these countries), then it would have made little sense for the countries on the fringe of the Soviet empire to enter into an alliance with the United States. For, if the United States had been unable to strike at the Soviet Union and to inflict unacceptable damage, then such an alliance would have lacked a credible deterrent against the Soviet Union. In that case, those countries would not have tried to counterbalance the Soviet threat by means of an alliance with the United States. In other words, they would not have exhibited *balancing* behaviour. Instead they would have attempted to reach a settlement with the Soviet Union: that is to say, they would have exhibited *bandwagoning* behaviour (see also Chapter 6, Section III).

Perhaps this is unnecessary, but for the sake of clarity I conclude this section by summarizing in the following theorem the most important implication that can be drawn from the argument developed so far:

Theorem 6:
The smaller the distance between i and j, and the greater their respective power, the greater the likelihood that they will engage in demand behaviour towards one another.[4]

II CREDIBILITY

A. Definition

In a crucial passage in his *Politics among Nations*, Hans Morgenthau defines political power as 'a psychological relation between those who exercise it and those over whom it is exercised. It gives the former control over certain actions of the latter through the impact which the former exert on the latter's minds' (Morgenthau 1978ed., p. 30). Although this definition has the drawback that it may erroneously create the impression that in politics there exists no such thing as the dictate of reality, at the same time it has the merit that it makes clear that the extent to which individuals will be able to engage in demand behaviour towards one another is not merely a function of the 'objective' circumstances in which they find themselves. This is so, because the probability that individual j will alter its behaviour in consequence of i's behaviour also depends on the credibility of i's behaviour in the eyes of j. The likelihood that i's behaviour will lead to a change in the marginal utilities that j attaches to the behavioural options subjectively available to it (the probability that i is able to influence j) is also a function of j's perception of the rewards and sacrifices that seem to be involved in i's behaviour, as well as of j's belief that i will be willing to realize these rewards and sacrifices.

Definition 9:
The *credibility* of i refers to j's expectation that i is able and willing to execute the threats and to fulfil the promises that, according to j, seem to be involved in i's behaviour.[5]

An increase in an individual's credibility, say i, will, generally speaking, enable the individuals in the system to use their power more efficiently. This applies to j as well as to i. For, the greater i's credibility, the less uncertain j will be as to the implications of i's behaviour. This implies that j will dispose of more 'information', and, in consequence, will be able to use its power more efficiently. While, as far as i is concerned, the greater its reputation to execute its threats and to fulfil its promises (and, naturally, the more powerful i is, the more easily it will be able to do so), the less of its power i will have to employ to induce a change in the marginal utilities j assigns to the various behavioural options subjectively available to it – whereby the credibility of i increases in proportion to j's belief that i is more powerful than j and that the distance between them is shorter.[6]

The credibility of i is based on j's knowledge of i's power, and is therefore based to a certain extent on j's experiences with i. It will be clear that, the shorter the distance between i and j, the greater the probability that both individuals will interact, and will gain this experience.

An individual's credibility constitutes a very important component of its power in its relations with other individuals. Especially when the individual interacts very frequently with those other individuals (e.g. where the individual participates in an organization, such as in government), and when the pace of the interaction processes in which the individual takes part – i.e. the frequency with which the individuals involved are confronted with deadlines – is such that it does not permit the individual (provided it would like to do so) to find out whether the individuals that try to engage in demand behaviour towards it, actually are capable of fulfilling the promises and executing the threats that seem to be involved in their behaviour.

At the same time, however, things are such that, the higher the frequency with which i and j interact, the greater the probability that their credibility towards each other will be damaged. Moreover, the faster the pace of the interaction process in which i and j take part, the greater the probability that this indeed will be the case. This somewhat abstruse proposition may quite easily be illustrated using the following two examples. In a crisis – such as the autumn 1962 confrontation between the United States and the Soviet Union following the Soviet decision to deploy missiles in Cuba – all that the decision makers involved can go on is one another's reputation. The last thing they will have time for is to start a thorough investigation into whether these reputations are justified or not (leaving aside that this may be a very risky undertaking indeed). Besides, in a crisis, the decision makers will not have time to fulfil the promises they have made, nor to execute the threats they have uttered, or they will, as a result of the time pressure and the multiplicity of events, simply forget all about them (cf. Allison 1971, pp. 185–244). My second example of the above proposition is much more commonplace, and therefore perhaps more striking. In the relationship between parent and child, from the point of view of efficiency it is the parent's credibility that is of the utmost importance. Accordingly, a parent will go to great lengths to protect his or her credibility, if not to enhance it. But the parent who has forbidden the child to act in a certain way under threat of punishment, will inevitably lose some of that credibility in the event that the child, despite the threat, acts in the forbidden way, while at the same time the milk threatens to boil over, the telephone rings, and there is someone at the door.

B. To Make Promises and to Keep Them

It also follows from the foregoing argument with respect to the importance of credibility for the power of the individual, that the individual, in order to protect its credibility, will not be eager to commit itself to another individual for a certain period of time (for example, in the case of human individuals, by entering into a forward contract, or, in the case of states, by concluding a treaty of mutual assistance). It will be clear too that, the more powerful the individual, the more easily it will be prepared to commit itself to another individual. Another implication of my argument is that, the more of the individual's power that may be at stake if it commits itself to another individual, the shorter the time for which the individual will be prepared to do so. This also means that, the less predictable the future is (the less stable the system of which the individuals are a part), the less the likelihood that the individuals will be prepared to commit themselves for a given length of time – whereby this probability decreases even further, in proportion as the individuals have less reliable information about one another (which again depends on the degree of stability of the system). On the other hand, however, the individual may, by committing itself to another individual, strengthen its own power and thereby increase its chances of survival in an uncertain world. It is impossible to say in advance which course of action the individual should follow. The individual will have to learn, by means of trial and error, the proper balance between commitment and non-commitment in a changing world.

The more importance an individual attaches to its credibility, the greater the probability that that individual, in the event that it had entered into some forward contract or concluded some treaty of mutual assistance and has subsequently come to regret that it did so, will nevertheless perform more or less as promised. *Even* if the system lacks an authority capable of enforcing the fulfilment of this promise (and this condition applies to all anarchical systems, such as the international system). How much weight the individual will attach to its credibility depends not only on the stability of the system of which the individual is a part, but also on the number of potential contracting parties in the system. The smaller the number of potential contracting parties, the more the individual will value its credibility (cf. Williamson 1975, pp. 26–30). The more important their credibility to the individuals in an anarchical system, the greater the probability that this system will develop into, what Hedley Bull has called, an *anarchical society*.[7]

The argument developed in this section also implies that, conversely, the less the individual expects its credibility to be at stake were it to break its promise – for example, because it expects that its non-performance will go unnoticed, or that in the future it will have nothing to do with the individual it made the agreement with (which expectation again depends on the number of potential contracting parties) – and the more costly it expects performance to be, the greater the likelihood that the individual will not keep its promise.

In a system with two individuals, the more powerful individual, call it i, will be more ready to enter into an agreement than the less powerful individual, in this case, j. The more powerful individual will also be better able to bear the costs of performance *and* non-performance (whether by the less powerful individual or by itself). In the case of a forward contract to realize some common objective that is equally profitable to both individuals, i will attach less weight to j's possible non-performance than j will to i's possible non-performance – whereby the probability that i will tolerate j's non-performance will increase the more powerful i is, and the greater the difference in power between i and j. This also implies that j is more likely than i to exhibit so-called free rider behaviour (see Chapter 5, Section V). At the same time the less powerful individual is also the one that can least afford the destruction of 'information' that non-performance entails. Here again we encounter the ambiguous relationship that exists between power and information (see also Chapter 2, Section III). This is also the case if we look at the behaviour of the more powerful individual with respect to the protection of its credibility. Although this individual can more easily afford to subordinate its credibility to opportunistic considerations, there is a limit to the extent that it can do so – which limit, of course, will be further away the more powerful the individual is. This understanding that even the most powerful cannot disregard their credibility with impunity, has been expressed by Adam Ferguson in his *An Essay on the History of Civil Society* as follows:

Where the citizen is supposed to have rights of property and of station, and is protected in the exercise of them, he is said to be free; and the very restraints by which he is hindered from the commission of crimes, are part of his liberty. No person is free, where any person is suffered to do wrong with impunity. Even the despotic prince on his throne, is not an exception to this general rule. He himself is a slave, the moment he pretends that force should decide any contest. The disregard he throws on the rights of his people recoils on himself; and in the general uncertainty of all conditions, there is no tenure more precarious than his own. (Ferguson 1773ed., pp. 260–61)

Another implication of my argument, is that the more powerful individual i will be more prepared than the less powerful individual j to tolerate deviant behaviour from the other individual, i.e. behaviour that reduces the degree of predictability in the system.

To conclude this section, I should like to point out the following. The more powerful an individual is *vis-à-vis* the other individuals in the system, and the more aware it is of this difference in power (the individual has learned from experience that it is much more powerful than the other individuals), the smaller it expects the costs to be of putting its credibility (or part of it) at stake, and the greater the probability that the individual will in fact do so. Lawrence Freedman is certainly right when he observes that it is only prudent '*not* to allow one's credibility to be put to the test over matters where few interests were at stake' (Freedman 1981, 1989ed., p. 223, emphasis in original).[8] However – and that is just the way it is – it is *precisely* in matters that appear to be relatively unimportant that the individual will be inclined to be careless with its credibility. So we see that the weight that an individual assigns to a certain matter depends on the perceived difference in power between the individuals involved. The more powerful an individual believes itself to be in comparison with the other individual, the less importance it will attach to that matter, and the more careless it will be. In this way, the very powerful will get themselves involved time and again in adventures that in the end will damage their credibility. We have only to think of the United States and the Soviet Union and the various interventions they became entangled in over the past few decades (Vietnam, Afghanistan, the Lebanon, Somalia, to name but a few). Not to mention all those people holding power – ministers, high officials, managers, chairmen of the board and the like – who were eventually brought down, after they had tried to settle an apparently unimportant issue quickly (in their own favour) by a demonstration of their power that ought to have convinced the other party that it would not be worth its while to pursue the matter any further. (Many a successful detective story is based on this idea.)

III DEPENDENCE

A. Definition

From my discussion of credibility it may have become clear that credibility is a rather elusive source of power. Although an individual's credibility will be related to certain 'objective' elements – the resources the individual disposes of, the individual's capacity to fulfil its promises, to execute its threats and to speak the truth – still, in the end, everything depends on what *other* individuals believe the individual to be capable of. An individual's credibility only exists in the light of the expectations other individuals have formed about its behaviour. (Which is not to deny that the individual, in its turn, will form expectations about the other individuals' expectations about its preparedness to fulfil its promises and to execute its threats.) We might say that credibility as a component of the individual's power has more to do with 'information' than with resources. When it comes to dependence, the reverse is true.

A very nice characterization of a relationship of dependence was given by the former Canadian Prime Minister Pierre Trudeau, when he described the relationship between Canada and the United States as 'in some ways like sleeping with an elephant. No matter how friendly or even-tempered the beast ... one is affected by every twitch and grunt' (quoted in Waltz 1979, p. 192). Accordingly I define dependence as follows:

Definition 10:
Individual j is *dependent* on individual i in some form or other where the latter disposes of sufficient power to strengthen or weaken the power of j.

Theorem 7:
The more power i has at its disposal, and the shorter the distance between i and j, the more j is dependent on i.

Individuals i and j are dependent on one another where they are able to help *and* to hurt one another, and they are better able to do so to the degree that both individuals are more powerful and the distance between them is smaller. At the same time the proposition holds (and this has already been said in the previous section in so many words), that the more dependent i and j are on one another, the more weight they will attach to their credibility.

Even though a relationship of dependence relates more to the 'objective' aspects of the relationship between individuals i and j, it will be obvious that they will have to learn that such a relationship exists, and this learning process will inevitably take some time. This learning process will take longer in proportion as the individuals attach less weight to the relationship, and the stability of the system of which the individuals are a part is smaller.

B. Dependence as a Source of Conflict and Prosperity

Every relationship of dependence has a positive and a negative side (as my definition of dependence has, I hope, made clear). As Adam Smith has shown in his famous example 'from a very trifling manufacture ... the trade of the pin-maker', it pays the individual to give up a position of autarchy. The division of labour leads to 'universal opulence' (Smith 1979ed.b, I, pp. 14 and 22).[9] This applies to human individuals as well as to states. A policy of isolating a country from foreign influences will in the long run be detrimental to the welfare and well-being of the citizens of that country, however great the advantages of such a policy in the short run may appear to be. This theme figures prominently in the work of the economist P.T. Bauer. In his view, the underdevelopment of many African and Asiatic countries must not be regarded as the evil legacy of Western colonialism. According to him, it is precisely the other way around. 'The poorest and most backward countries have until recently had no external economic contacts and often have never been Western colonies. ... The level of material achievement usually diminishes as one moves away from the foci of Western impact' (Bauer 1981, 1982ed., pp. 67 and 70; see also Bauer 1984, pp. 21 and 157).[10]

At the same time, it cannot be denied that participating in the division of labour (including at an international level) means that the individual will have to run certain risks. A relationship of dependence, after all, may also be a source of possible conflict with other individuals. It is illustrative in this connection, that one of the two exceptions to a system of free trade that Adam Smith was prepared to admit, applied to industries that are necessary for the defence of the country (Smith 1979ed.b, I, p. 463). The more dependent individuals are on one another, the greater the probability that they will trade *and* that they will fight. Kenneth Waltz has observed in this connection that:

> the myth of interdependence [the myth that an increase in relations of interdependence between states promotes the likelihood of world peace; RHL] both obscures the realities of international politics and asserts a false belief about the conditions that promote peace, as World War I conclusively showed. 'The statistics of the economic interdependence of Germany and her neighbors,' John Maynard

Keynes remarked, 'are overwhelming.' Germany was the best customer of six European states, including Russia and Italy; the second best customer of three, including Britain; and the third best customer of France. She was the largest source of supply for ten European states, including Russia, Austria-Hungary, and Italy; and the second largest source of supply for three, including Britain and France (Keynes 1920, p. 17). And trade then was proportionally much higher than now. The governments were more involved internationally than they were in their national economies. Now governments are more involved in their national economies than they are internationally. This is fortunate. (Waltz 1979, pp. 158–9)[11]

John Gaddis, who quotes Waltz approvingly, adds in his *The Long Peace*, 'nor did the fact that the United States was Japan's largest trading partner deter that country from attacking Pearl Harbour in 1941. Since 1945, there have been more civil wars than interstate wars; that fact alone should be sufficient to call into question the proposition that interdependence necessarily breeds peace' (Gaddis 1987, p. 224).

It appears then that no civilization is possible without violence (or the threat of it). This implies that the increase in global relationships of dependence will not in itself usher in an era of world peace. The unprecedented levels of trade, cooperation and welfare that have been reached in the course of this century, and the massacres of the First and Second World War: these are the two sides of the same coin. (See also Section IV.)

Theorem 8:
The extent to which i and j are dependent on one another increases in proportion as both individuals are more powerful, the distance between them is smaller, and their credibility greater; and, conversely, the extent to which both individuals are dependent on one another decreases in proportion as i and j are less powerful, the distance between them is greater, and their credibility less.

Two things remain to be discussed in this section. The first concerns the implication that can be drawn from my argument that, the more j believes itself to be dependent on i, the greater the probability that j will attempt to influence i. The behaviour of the nine member states of the European Communities after the Arab–Israeli War of 1973 constitutes a good illustration of this in the field of international relations. Once the European dependence on Arab oil had become all too apparent, European initiatives 'spontaneously' sprang up to promote a European–Arabian rapprochement and an independent role of the European Communities in the Middle East peace process. Simply heart-warming was the West European solicitude for the fate of the Palestinians. Now, more than twenty years later, West European dependence on Arab oil has decreased considerably, partly due to a sharp increase in the use of nuclear energy in the member states of the European Communities (with the exception of the Netherlands), and the exploitation of the oil fields in the North Sea (which exploitation, by the way, only became profitable after the price of oil as a result of the crisis of 1973–74 had reached record levels), and we do not hear much any more of a European-Arab dialogue, a European peace initiative, let alone of the West European concern for the fate of the Palestinian people.

The other matter concerns Kenneth Waltz's panegyric, in his *Theory of International Politics*, on the virtues of the bipolar world that came into existence after the Second World War (Waltz 1979, pp. 132–83). According to Waltz, this bipolar world – the remnants of which survive to the day on which I write – is a safer world than the multipolar world that existed from 1850 to 1945. One of the reasons he advances to explain why this is so, is that the two superpowers that buttressed this bipolar world, the United States and the Soviet Union, were far less dependent on one another, from an economic as well as a military point of view, than were the great powers in the previous period.[12] However, Waltz overlooks the fact that, as far as one, rather important, aspect is concerned, the degree of dependence between the United States and the Soviet Union was far higher than was ever the case between Great Britain, France, Germany, Russia, Austria-Hungary, Japan and the United States, in the previous hundred years. Both superpowers were able (and the United States and the Russian Federation are still able, notwithstanding the considerable arms reductions they have agreed upon) to inflict damage on one another on a scale and with a swiftness that was believed to be impossible until the end of the 1940s. Because of the expansion of the nuclear weapons arsenals of both superpowers, and the fact that they came to have missiles (ICBMs and SLBMs) that could transport these nuclear weapons almost unhindered to their targets (the military bases and the industrial and population centres of the enemy), the United States and the Soviet Union were, from the end of the fifties, more dependent on one another than two other great powers ever had been in world history. We need not be surprised, therefore, to find that each of the superpowers, in spite of all the advantages that in Waltz's view go with bipolarity, tried to free itself time and time again from the other's hold (with the so-called *Strategic Defense Initiative* (*SDI*) at the beginning of the eighties as the last attempt in the series). This also suggests that the fact that the United States and the Soviet Union managed to keep their conflicts at a level of low intensity, or else fought them by proxy, has less to do with *Mutual Assured Destruction* (*MAD*) than is often assumed fairly uncritically. It was at least as important that, in the years after the Second World War, both superpowers were able – as always this was a matter of chance and ability – to gain experience of one another, and on the basis of this experience to develop rules for their mutual relationships (cf. Mearsheimer 1990, pp. 16–17 and 26–7).[13] The long series of conflicts about Berlin and the Cuban missile crisis in particular, appear to have provided them with the opportunity to make clear to their opponent what kinds of behaviour one was prepared to accept and what kinds not, and to develop a sound understanding of the opponent's potential.

IV HARMONY OF INTERESTS AND CONFLICT OF INTERESTS

In this section, I shall be considering two further conclusions that can be drawn from the argument I have developed in this chapter. I have already discussed them more or less explicitly in the foregoing sections, but since they conflict quite sharply with the common-sense view as to how the world ought to be organized, they merit separate treatment. Common sense has it that the probability that individuals will get into conflict (including violent conflict) with one another decreases as the power differential between them becomes smaller. It is also a common assumption that an individual is better off in proportion as it is less dependent on other individuals – for example a state that manages to disengage itself more and more from the global division of labour. In the light of the approach that I have been expounding in Chapters 3 and 4, however, the first assumption is completely mistaken, and the second only partly correct.

My first unorthodox conclusion is that, in the situation where two individuals i and j are powerful enough to make a contribution to the realization of a certain behavioural option – be it by active assistance or by passive acquiescence – the degree of harmony of interests between i and j with respect to the realization of this behavioural option increases in proportion as the difference in power between them becomes greater; whereas, conversely, the degree of conflict of interests between i and j increases in proportion as the difference in power between them gets smaller – where harmony of interests and conflict of interests are defined respectively in the following way:

Definition 11:

In a situation in which it is not possible for individual *i* to realize the outcome of a certain behavioural option without the active assistance or passive acquiescence of individual *j*, then there exists a complete *harmony of interests* between individuals *i* and *j* with respect to the realization of this outcome if *j* behaves itself in accordance with *i*'s wishes without *i* having to expend any amount of its power, however small, to bring *j*'s behaviour about; whereas, conversely, there exists a complete *conflict of interests* between individuals *i* and *j* with respect to the realization of this outcome if *i* is unable to persuade *j* to behave itself in accordance with (or more in accordance with) *i*'s wishes, even if *i* would expend all of its power to bring about this change in *j*'s behaviour.

If I subsequently make a distinction based on the nature of the outcome that *i* is trying to realize with *j*'s active assistance or passive acquiescence – does the outcome concern a private good or collective good? (see Chapter 5, Section I for the definition of a collective good) – and I also assume that *i* is more powerful than *j*, then the following proposition holds. As far as *i* is concerned, a harmony of interests with *j* will come about more easily with respect to the realization of a private good, and a conflict of interests with regard to the realization of a collective good; whereas, conversely, as far as *j* is concerned, a harmony of interests will come into existence more readily with respect to the realization of a collective good, and a conflict of interests with regard to the realization of a private good.

A division of labour between *i* and *j* leads to an increase in the power of both individuals, and, in that sense, there exists a harmony of interests between them. At the same time, however, this division of labour, and the specialization it involves, implies that *i* and *j* become something of a threat to each other's power (if it so happens that one of them, for whatever reason, does not perform). The consequences of this dependence vary with the initial positions of *i* and *j*. In a situation where *i* is far more powerful than *j*, and where the distance between them is small, then *j* will be very reluctant to act in a manner that may get it into conflict with *i*, while *i*, for its part, will feel less threatened if *j* acts in a way that will increase *j*'s power. With the result that the probability increases that a harmony of interests between both individuals will come about in respect of the realization of a certain outcome – where the probability that this will indeed be the case increases, the more stable the system is of which they are a part. This may also be formulated as follows. Where *i* or *j* faces the decision to assist actively or to acquiesce passively in an attempt by the other individual to increase its power, then, the greater their difference in power, and the greater the distance between them, the lower is their *sensitivity to gaps in payoffs*, the expression introduced by

Joseph Grieco (Grieco 1988, pp. 500–501). However, if the power differential between i and j is small, and the distance between them likewise, then j will be very reluctant to act in accordance with i's wishes, because any increase in i's power, however small, may threaten its own power. Consequently, the likelihood increases that there will be a conflict of interests between both individuals – where the likelihood that this indeed will happen increases in proportion as the system of which they are a part is less stable. And, accordingly, the smaller the power differential between i and j, and the smaller the distance between them, the greater their sensitivity to gaps in payoffs.

In view of these considerations, I shall from now on assume that the expected marginal utility to individual i of the outcome (o_k) associated with a certain behavioural option in the set of behavioural options subjectively available to i – which behavioural option is to the effect that i actively assists with or passively acquiesces in an attempt by individual j to increase its own, i.e. j's, power – is a convex combination of i's own outcome, o_s, associated with this behavioural option, and the difference between i's and j's outcome, o_d. The expected marginal utility of (o_k) is not only a function of the 'absolute' outcome o_s that i expects to receive, multiplied by the probability with which i expects o_s to realize itself – as in equation (3.1) – but also of the 'relative' outcome o_d associated with this behavioural option, that is to say, the difference between its own outcome o_s and the outcome o_o it expects j to receive: $o_d = o_s - o_o$, again multiplied by the probability that o_d will be realized. Accordingly, we get the following expression (cf. Taylor 1987, p. 123):

$$Eu(o_k) = \sum_{i=0}^{n} u(\lambda o_s^{t+i} + (1-\lambda)o_d^{t+i})\, p(\lambda o_s^{t+i} + (1-\lambda)o_d^{t+i}) \qquad (4.1)$$

Where $0 \le \lambda \le 1$, and the weight that i attaches to o_d, as compared to o_s, increases (the value of the sensitivity coefficient λ approaches 0) in proportion as the power differential between i and j becomes smaller and the distance between them diminishes; whereas, conversely, the weight that i attaches to o_s as compared to o_d increases (the value of λ approaches 1) in proportion as the power differential between i and j becomes greater and the distance between them increases.[14]

Individuals are more envious of one another in proportion as the difference in power between them decreases and the distance between them diminishes.[15] More than two hundred years ago, David Hume put this understanding in the following words:

'Tis worthy of observation concerning that envy, which arises from a superiority in others, that 'tis not the great disproportion betwixt ourself and another, which produces it; but on the contrary, our proximity. A common soldier bears no such envy to his general as to his sergeant or corporal. (Hume 1981 ed., p. 377)[16]

Kenneth Organski, who in his work has criticized this common misconception again and again, observes in his *World Politics*, 'The relationship between peace and the balance of power appears to be exactly the opposite of what has often been claimed. The periods of balance, real or imagined, are periods of warfare, while the periods of known preponderance are periods of peace' (Organski 1958, 1968ed., p. 294).[17]

A world of equals, whatever its merits, is a dangerous world. In my view, it is no coincidence that Thomas Hobbes started his characterization of the state of nature, the situation where 'every man is enemy to every man', with the claim that:

NATURE hath made men so equal, in the faculties of the body, and mind; as that though there be found one man sometimes manifestly stronger in body, or of quicker mind than another; yet when all is reckoned together, the difference between man, and man, is not so considerable, as that one man can thereupon claim to himself any benefit, to which another may not pretend, as well as he. For as to the strength of body, the weakest has strength enough to kill the strongest, either by secret machination, or by confederacy with others, that are in the same danger with himself. (Hobbes 1947ed., p. 80)[18]

The second unorthodox conclusion that can be drawn from the argument I developed in the previous sections is that, if i were able to make itself completely independent of j, both individuals would eventually be worse off. It makes sense in this connection to stay with the distinction that Kenneth Waltz, following many others, draws between *interdependence as sensitivity* and *interdependence as mutual vulnerability* (Waltz 1979, pp. 139–46). The first kind of interdependence means that the two individuals i and j are able to adapt themselves quite easily to changes in their environment and to changes in their demand behaviour towards one another. Interdependence as sensitivity points to their capacity to learn quickly. The second kind of interdependence, in contrast, refers to the fact that i and j are unable, or able only with the greatest difficulty, to adapt themselves to changes in their environment and to changes in their demand behaviour towards one another. The crucial point is that, in a world that is continually undergoing changes, prudence requires that i and j try to avoid interdependence as mutual vulnerability as much as possible (although a certain degree of this kind of interdependence will be the inevitable by-product of every, in itself profitable, specialization), but, at the same time, to promote their interdependence as sensitivity as much as possible (although this does not imply that they must give up all specialization in the context of long-term projects). Such a policy will be the more prudent as the world in which *i* and *j* find themselves is more susceptible to change (see also Chapter 5, Section III). Naturally, such a process of continual adaptation involves costs at any given moment, but in the long run it leads to a more successful adaptation of *i* and *j* (in terms of their power) to one another and to their environment.[19]

NOTES

1. The relationship between power and distance is analogous to the relationship between 'income' and 'price' in economics, in the sense that power refers to the (disposable) income of an individual that considers buying a certain good, and distance to the price of that good.
2. Cf. also Adam Smith: 'The wealth of a neighbouring nation ... though dangerous in war and politicks, is certainly advantageous in trade' (Smith 1979ed.b, I, p. 494).
3. Witness David Hume's explanation of why the Greek city-states were almost continually at war with one another. This was the 'natural effect of their martial spirit, their love of liberty, their mutual emulation, and that hatred which generally prevails among nations that live in close neighbourhood' (Hume 1985ed., p. 404).
4. Theorem 6 captures what may be called the 'mechanics of interaction'. If we ignore the probabilistic nature of all things empirical, we may express the relationship between power, distance and interaction (and its intensity) in the form of the following equation:

$$I_{ij} = \frac{C_o P_i P_j}{D^\delta_{ij}} , \; i \neq j \in \{i, j\} \tag{4.2}$$

Equation (4.2) is, as a matter of fact, equivalent to Newton's gravity law. It states that the intensity of the interaction between two individuals *i* and *j* (their gravitational attraction), I_{ij}, changes in proportion with changes in the power of *i*, P_i, or of *j*, P_j (in their respective mass), and with changes in the distance between them – whereby C_o is a constant and δ a positive integer, indicating (in the case of geographical distance) the difficulty of the terrain that *i* and *j* have to traverse before they may actually interact with one another: the more difficult the terrain, the higher the value of δ (in Newton's formulation: $\delta = 2$) (cf. Lieshout 1992, p. 414). As we shall see in Section II of this chapter, however, an understanding of mechanics is not enough if we wish to understand international relations and foreign policy.
5. The individual's reliability, in the sense of its reputation for speaking the truth, should also be considered to be a part of the individual's credibility.
6. Kenneth Organski gives expression to the same concept when he observes that 'a reputation for power confers power, whether or not it is justified' (Organski 1958, 1968ed., p. 109).

7.   According to Bull, the states in an anarchical society (he erroneously confines himself
      to states; such societies may also be established among human individuals) 'regard
      themselves as bound by certain rules in their dealings with one another, such as that
      they should respect one another's claims to independence, that they should honour
      agreements into which they enter, and that they should be subject to certain limitations
      in exercising force against one another. At the same time they co-operate in the
      working of institutions such as the forms of procedures of international law, the
      machinery of diplomacy and general international organization, and the customs and
      conventions of war' (Bull 1977, pp. 13 and 26–7).

8.   Freedman makes this remark in response to the following observation by Thomas
      Schelling:

> If the question is raised whether this kind of 'face' is worth fighting over, the
> answer is that this kind of face is one of the few things worth fighting over. Few
> parts of the world are intrinsically worth the risk of serious war by themselves,
> especially when taken slice by slice, but defending them or running risks to protect
> them may preserve one's commitments to action in other parts of the world and at
> later times. 'Face' is merely the interdependence of a country's commitments; it is
> a country's reputation for action, the expectation other countries have about its
> behavior. (Schelling 1966, p. 124)

9.   The growth of the global division of labour in recent centuries (the rise of the 'modern
      world-system', to use Immanuel Wallerstein's expression) has led to an unprecedented
      prosperity. How much prosperity has increased may be illustrated rather nicely by the
      following quotation taken from Bernard Mandeville's *Fable of the Bees* about the
      enormous advances that, according to him, had already been made at the beginning of
      the eighteenth century:

> If we trace the most flourishing Nations in their Origin, we shall find that in the
> remote Beginnings of every Society, the richest and most considerable Men among
> them were a great while destitute of great many Comforts of Life that are now
> enjoy'd by the meanest and most humble Wretches: So that many things which
> were once look'd upon as the Invention of Luxury, are now allow'd even to those
> that are so miserably poor as to become the Objects of publick Charity, nay
> counted so necessary, that we think no Human Creature ought to want them.
> (Mandeville 1924ed., I, p. 169)

10.   In his essay 'The underdevelopment of development literature: the case of dependency
      theory', Tony Smith refers to empirical research from which it appears that, 'as a
      general rule ... the countries most integrated into the world economy have tended to
      grow more quickly over a longer period than those that are not' (Smith 1979, p. 250).

11.   Waltz refers to Keynes's *The Economic Consequences of the Peace*. It should be noted
      that Waltz's summary of Keynes's findings is incorrect, in so far as, according to
      Keynes, Germany was the best customer of seven, and not six, European states:
      Russia, Norway, Holland, Belgium, Switzerland, Italy and Austria-Hungary (Keynes
      1919, 1971ed., p. 10).

12.   As far as military dependence is concerned, Waltz manages to do so only by claiming
      that a state's military dependence varies to the extent to which that state must rely on
      other states for its security (Waltz 1979, p. 168). I thank Marc van Ooijen for making
      this clear to me.

13.   To be sure, Waltz does not deny the importance of such a learning process (Waltz
      1979, p. 173).

14.   As Duncan Snidal notes in his 'Relative gains and the pattern of international
      cooperation', 'A plausible curvilinear specification is that relative gains concerns peak
      when states are roughly equal and drop off when one state is either far behind, or far
      ahead of, the other' (Snidal 1991, p. 725). In his article Snidal, however, confines

himself to the discussion of a less complicated monotonic relationship, which is to the effect that, 'for any pair of states, the smaller state will be more concerned with the relative gains consequences of their interaction ... The larger state may overcome the smaller state's greater reluctance to cooperate by offering it more than an equal share of the benefits' (Snidal 1991, p. 720).

15. According to Robert Nozick, an individual is (strongly) envious of another individual, if it prefers the situation in which both individuals do not have a certain kind of object or attribute, to that in which the other has this kind of object or attribute while the individual itself does not have this kind of object or attribute (Nozick 1974, p. 239; cf. Schoeck 1969, 1987ed., p. 8). In the strategy of *Mutual Assured Destruction*, which implies that each of the superpowers is at all times able and willing to respond to an attack by the other superpower by launching a counter-attack that will cause unacceptable damage to the attacker, it is (tacitly?) assumed that the superpowers will behave as envious individuals. For, according to the strategy, the power that has become the victim of a nuclear attack will prefer the situation where both powers are destroyed to that in which it resigns itself to the other power's victory.

16. Mandeville employs, very much in style, a somewhat more frivolous analogy: 'Envy then is a Compound of Grief and Anger; the Degrees of this Passion depend chiefly on the Nearness or Remoteness of the Objects as to Circumstances. If one, who is forced to walk on Foot envies a great Man for keeping a Coach and Six, it will never be with that Violence, or give him that Disturbance which it may to a Man, who keeps a Coach himself, but can only afford to drive with four Horses' (Mandeville 1924ed., I, pp. 135–6).

17. Dougherty and Pfaltzgraff quote Charles P. Schleicher, who observes that 'peace is most in jeopardy when power is evenly balanced and war less likely when there is a preponderant power' (Dougherty and Pfaltzgraff 1981ed., p. 27).

18. Cf. also the statement made in 1776 by the Parliament of Paris, cited by E.H. Kossmann, 'Chaos ... is the inevitable consequence of perfect equality, and it will cause the collapse of society' (Kossmann 1987, p. 18). I should add that the probability that the weakest will indeed be able to confederate 'with others, that are in the same danger with himself' with a view to killing the strongest, decreases to the extent that the difference in strength between the strongest and the others becomes larger.

19. Robert Gilpin, too, reaches the conclusion that, 'in the long term, economic power is neither the possession of particular monopolies and/or technologies nor economic self-sufficiency, but rather the capacity of the economy to transform itself and to respond to changes in the global economic environment' (Gilpin 1987, p. 77).

5. Behavioural Theory and Game Theory

I INTRODUCTION

In Chapter 4, Section 1, I have argued that the individuals i and j are part of the same system if they are able to influence one another's behaviour. Or, to put it somewhat differently, if the decisions of the one individual have consequences for the decisions of the other individual. In my discussion, I have left open the possibility that these individuals are not aware of the fact that they are able to engage in demand behaviour towards one another. If I now assume that both individuals are in fact aware of this, then the analysis of their decisions fits into a special field of decision theory, i.e. game theory. For game theory analyses, in the words of Thomas Schelling (one of the founding fathers of this discipline), behavioural situations, 'in which each player's best choice of action depends on the action he expects the other to take, which he knows depends, in turn, on the other's expectation of his own' (Schelling 1958, p. 205). In this chapter I shall, by the way, only concern myself with a particular kind of games, namely the so-called *non-cooperative* games. This name does not signify that in such games the individuals are unable to cooperate with one another. What it does signify, is that the game is played in a world – as is assumed in assumption 1* as well – where no authority exists that is capable of enforcing the fulfilment of the promises the individuals may make to one another in the course of the game (cf. De Jasay 1989, pp. 26–30). In this chapter I shall be relating the conclusions I have formulated in the previous chapters to some important results of the analysis of non-cooperative games. In this way, I hope to provide a better understanding of the conditions on which individuals will decide to cooperate with one another, or, on the contrary, to refrain from cooperation.

Before I can make a start on my game-theoretic analysis of the possibilities and probabilities of cooperation (including international cooperation), I must first pay attention to the fact that the result of such cooperation (for example, a credible defence against a common enemy, an international trade agreement, or measures to protect the ozone layer), may be regarded as a *collective good*. That is to say, a good with the following properties: 1) it exhibits some degree of *jointness of supply*, which means that if one individual consumes the good, it does not become impossible for other individuals to consume that good too (cf. Blümel, Pethig and von dem Hagen 1986, p. 245); and 2) it is to some extent *non-excludable*, which implies that if one individual has provided the good, it is not feasible for that individual to exclude other individuals from consuming that good too (Olson 1965, 1971ed., p. 14). Moreover, as far as the consumers of the good are concerned, the good displays some degree of *non-rivalness*. A certain number of individuals may consume the good before congestion costs become noticeable and after that threshold has been reached the utility of the collective good to the consumers diminishes progressively in proportion as more and more individuals consume it (Head 1962, p. 202 and Taylor 1987, p. 7).

According to Russell Hardin, possible cooperation between individuals in order to reach a common objective becomes problematical, where each individual orders its preferences about the outcomes of its decision whether or not to cooperate in the provision of the collective good in such a way that each of them decides not to cooperate, regardless of what the others decide to do, even if each of them prefers the outcome that all of them decide to cooperate, over the outcome that none of them decides to cooperate. This means that Hardin equates the problem of collective action with the so-called *Prisoner's Dilemma* (Hardin 1982, p. 25). Michael Taylor has rightly taken exception to this 'strong definition' of a collective action problem. He proves that this definition does not take account of the fact that the provision of a collective good may also be a problem in situations in which the individuals order their preferences in the same manner as the players in what is commonly called the *Game of Chicken* (Taylor 1987, pp. 18–20). In this chapter I shall be arguing that cooperation can also pose a problem of collective action if the individuals involved order their preferences about the outcomes in the same way as the players in the so-called *Stag Hunt,* and above all wish to avoid the worst possible outcome.

II PRISONER'S DILEMMA

The Prisoner's Dilemma concerns the dilemma with which two prisoners, suspected of having committed a serious crime, are confronted by the prosecuting attorney who deals with their case. The latter knows there is not enough evidence to convict them of the crime, unless both of them confess. In order to get a conviction, the prisoners are interrogated separately, and each of them is told the following story. If both prisoners remain silent, then they can be charged only with a less serious crime, and a relatively light sentence of one year in prison for both of them would be requested. If both of them confess, then a sentence of five years in prison for both prisoners would be requested. However, were only one of them to confess and the other to remain silent, then a sentence of only three months for the prisoner who confesses would be requested, and the maximum sentence of ten years in prison for the prisoner who remains silent. The outcome of the game is that both prisoners confess to the prosecuting attorney.

The original Prisoner's Dilemma is a 2 x 2 game, which is played only once. There are two players. Each player has two alternative strategies at his disposal. In the present case, to cooperate with the other prisoner, i.e. to remain silent ('C'), or to defect, i.e. to confess ('D)'.[1] This game is unique among all 2 x 2 games, in that it has a single, very stable, but deficient (that is to say, Pareto-inferior) equilibrium (Rapoport and Guyer 1966, pp. 11, 15 and 18).[2] Rapoport and Guyer give a representation of the game and the utilities i and j attach to the four possible outcomes, in the same way as I have indicated in Diagram 5.1. (This is the so-called *strategic* or *normal* form.) The entries in the cells reflect the ordinal utilities that i and j attach to the various outcomes – where 4>3>2>1. The first entry in each cell represents the utility i attaches to that outcome, and the second the utility j attaches to it.[3]

Since it applies to i as well as to j that strategy C is *dominated* by strategy D, each of them chooses strategy D. D dominates C, because by choosing D each player will at least avoid the worst possible outcome, and may perhaps even end up with the best possible outcome. This is all very sensible as far as each player is concerned, but the result of their private considerations is the Pareto-inferior outcome that they both confess. Both players would be better off if both were to choose C rather than D. However, i as well as j faces the dilemma that, if he chooses C, this strategy may lead to the best possible outcome for them both, but that this outcome can only be reached if the other player also chooses C. Were the other not to do so, then choosing C will lead to the worst possible outcome from the individual player's point of view. Confronted with this dilemma, i and j see no other way out than to choose D.

Diagram 5.1: Prisoner's Dilemma

$$j$$

	C	D
C	3,3	1,4
D	4,1	2,2

i

The logic of the one-shot Prisoner's Dilemma leads to very pessimistic conclusions about the possibilities of cooperation between individuals. It implies that individuals may fail to cooperate, even if they are fully aware of the fact that it would be in their common interest to do so. Michael Taylor and, later, Robert Axelrod have shown that the prospects for cooperation look much less bleak if we allow for the fact that individuals will take into consideration that in the future they may have to deal with one another again (Taylor 1976 and Axelrod 1984). This more hopeful result of the repeated Prisoner's Dilemma is even obtained if it is assumed that, in any single game, each player attaches the same utilities to the four possible outcomes as do the players in a one-shot Prisoner's Dilemma.

To be sure, this hopeful result can only be obtained if it is assumed that the players are uncertain about the precise number of single games that constitute the repeated Prisoner's Dilemma. For, if the players were to know in advance how many constituent games there were in the repeated game, then they would again refrain from cooperating in each constituent game. That this must be so, follows from the following argument. Where the players know which game is to be the last in the repeated Prisoner's Dilemma, then this last game will turn into a one-shot Prisoner's Dilemma, and D will be their dominant strategy. This makes the penultimate game 'in strategic reality' the last game, and, accordingly, in this game also, D will be their dominant strategy. By reasoning backwards in this manner, they will decide to choose D in the first game of the repeated Prisoner's Dilemma as well (Luce and Raiffa 1957, pp. 98–9).

In a repeated Prisoner's Dilemma, a player can choose between more than two strategies. As a matter of fact the number of strategies available to a player is infinitely large. For example, he can choose the strategy 'all-C', which means that, in each constituent game of the repeated Prisoner's Dilemma, he chooses to cooperate, regardless of what the other player does. Or he can choose the strategy 'all-D', which means that in each constituent game he chooses to defect, whatever the other player does. A third possibility is the 'Tat-for-Tit' strategy, which prescribes that, in the first game, a player chooses D (just to be sure), and in each successive game chooses C, if and only if the other player chose C in the preceding game; if this is not the case, then the player again chooses D. A fourth possibility is the strategy 'Tit-for-Tat', which implies that in the first game a player chooses C, and in each successive game chooses C, if and only if the other player chose C in the preceding game; if this is not the case, then the player chooses D (cf. Taylor 1987, pp. 65–7).

Taylor and Axelrod subsequently argue that the players in a repeated Prisoner's Dilemma of indefinite length will eventually choose between either the unconditional strategy 'all-D', or a kind of conditional strategy, such as 'Tat-for-Tit' or 'Tit-for-Tat'. Each player makes his choice on the basis of a comparison of the expected outcome of the string of games if both players were to choose D in each and every game, with the expected outcome if both players were to choose C, conditionally, in every single game. But, as Axelrod observes: 'the future is less important than the present – for two reasons. The first is that players tend to value payoffs less as the time of their obtainment recedes into the future. The second is that there is always some chance that the players will not meet again' (Axelrod 1984, p. 12). The upshot of their argument is that if for both players *the shadow of the future*, as Axelrod has called this, is long enough – if, speaking more formally, the value of the discount parameter w (see Chapter 2, Section I) is sufficiently high – then both players will opt for a strategy of conditional cooperation, in this case 'Tit-for-Tat'.[4] With the result that the players will cooperate with one another in each constituent game of the repeated Prisoner's Dilemma, notwithstanding the fact that each of the players in every one of these games orders his preferences as to the outcomes in exactly the same way as do the players in a one-shot Prisoner's Dilemma.

No doubt Taylor and Axelrod have devised a very elegant solution for the problem of how players who are faced with the decision whether or not to contribute to a cooperative venture and who order their preferences as to the four possible outcomes in the same way as the players in the Prisoner's Dilemma, will choose to cooperate with one another. Nevertheless, their solution is unsatisfactory in several ways (see Pellikaan 1994, pp. 161–87 and 206–28, for an extensive discussion of the problems involved in their respective approaches). I shall confine myself to two points that are relevant in the context of my argument. My first point concerns one of the additional assumptions Axelrod introduces at the beginning of his discussion of the Prisoner's Dilemma. This assumption states that, 'there is no way to eliminate the other player or run away from the interaction. Therefore each player retains the ability to cooperate or defect on each move' (Axelrod 1984, p. 12). The effect of this assumption is that the environment is too nice to *nice strategies* (i.e. strategies that entail that the player will never be the first to defect). Too nice, in any case, compared with the environment in which states have to operate. In that case, this assumption ought to be replaced by one that stipulates that, after a player has vainly chosen C for a number of times in a repeated game against the same opponent, the player is eliminated from the game – where it will be impossible for the player to know in advance the number of games. (Besides, ought there not to be a small random chance that a single mistake of this kind will be fatal?) The introduction of an assumption of this kind results in the probability increasing that the players in a repeated Prisoner's Dilemma will play every constituent game as if it were a one-shot Prisoner's Dilemma, and, consequently, will refrain from cooperating with one another.

The hopeful result obtained by Taylor and Axelrod is also problematic in view of the assumption that the value of the discount parameter w remains constant. This assumption is necessary for their solution of the repeated Prisoner's Dilemma, but it has implications that cannot be reconciled with the behavioural theory I developed in the previous chapters. For instance, this assumption excludes the possibility that the players, thanks to the success of their cooperation, learn to see things more and more in a long-term perspective, with the result that the value of w increases in the course of time. At the same time, this assumption makes the reverse effect impossible, namely, that the players reach the conclusion that, because their cooperation has been so successful, they are now powerful enough to allow themselves to live from day to day, which means that at some point in time the value of w begins to decrease. Speaking more generally, this assumption does not provide the game with a dynamic setting. On the contrary, it ensures that the repeated Prisoner's Dilemma is entirely static in character. Michael Nicholson observes that the one-shot Prisoner's Dilemma 'represents a situation which almost never would be found in reality' (Nicholson 1989, 1990ed., p. 11). But, as a result of the assumption that the value of w is constant, this observation applies equally to the repeated Prisoner's Dilemma.

Nor is R. Harrison Wagner convinced. According to Wagner, the repeated Prisoner's Dilemma is not an accurate model of many of the situations to which it has been applied. In his view, it would be better to think in terms of a game in which the players get several chances to decide whether or not to cooperate with one another before they receive their payoffs. In this connection, he points out two additional conditions, neither of them very realistic in his eyes, that must be met before we can speak of a Prisoner's Dilemma. In the first place, that the game comes to an end immediately after each player has made his strategy known; and, in the second place, that each player chooses his strategy in ignorance of the other player's choice (Wagner 1983, p. 331). As far as this last condition is concerned, Wagner is certainly right in claiming that it is not very realistic. But, as Wagner himself observes, if this condition is replaced by the condition that the players choose sequentially and that the second player knows the strategy chosen by the first player, this still does not get the players out of a Prisoner's Dilemma. The introduction of this new condition *and* the corresponding representation of the game in the *extensive* form by means of a game tree (see Figure 5.1), however, do make clear that the first condition is indeed crucial for a Prisoner's Dilemma to exist. The dilemma exists because the Prisoner's Dilemma is a game of what I would like to call, the 'Red Queen type'. A game in which the players already know what Alice only finds out when she tries to correct herself after she has said that thunder is the cause of lightning, namely, that they will not get a second chance: "'It's too late to correct it," said the Red Queen: "when you've once said a thing, that fixes it, and you must take the consequences"' (Carroll 1871, 1954ed., p. 224).

Figure 5.1: Repeated choice in a one shot Prisoner's Dilemma

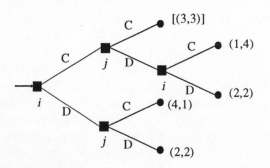

Source: Based on Wagner 1983.

As far as the story of the Prisoner's Dilemma is concerned, this means that the prisoner who initially remains silent, call him *i*, will be able to find out whether the other prisoner, *j* (who chooses his strategy after he has heard the choice *i* has made), has confessed or not, and that *i*, in the event that *j* has indeed confessed, subsequently gets the opportunity to confess too. In such a situation, *i* can safely try to reach the Pareto-optimal outcome by choosing the conditional strategy that stipulates 'choose C first; if it appears that the other chooses D, choose D as well'. With the result that, after *i* has chosen, *j* is faced with the choice between the outcomes (C,C) and (D,D), and then, naturally, will choose C. According to Wagner this result is generally valid: 'in any situation in which players choose one after the other, with full knowledge of each other's choices, conditional cooperation will be the optimal strategy as long as no one can count on having the last choice' (Wagner 1983, p. 333).

III STAG HUNT

In his *Discourse on the Origin of Inequality* (1755), Jean-Jacques Rousseau describes the attempts of a group of hunters to trap a stag, in the early state of nature. The task will take a day at least, and can only be completed successfully if none of the hunters shirks his obligations. Otherwise the stag will escape. Unfortunately, the hunters know from each other that they have 'no foresight', and that 'far from concerning themselves with a distant future, they hardly [think] of the next day' (Rousseau 1755, 1994ed., p. 57),[5] and that, consequently, they prefer the hare they can catch quickly to the stag they can only catch after a day's work, even though they find venison far tastier than hare. This knowledge means that each of the hunters will run off after a hare the moment he sees one, without troubling himself for one moment about the fate of his fellow hunters.

Thanks to the work of Kenneth Waltz and Robert Jervis, Rousseau's Stag Hunt is almost as well-known among students of international relations as the Prisoner's Dilemma. In his *Man, the State and War*, Waltz employs the Stag Hunt to demonstrate the relevance of a 'third image approach' to international politics (see Chapter 9, Section I). Jervis, in his turn, claims that states that have to decide whether or not to end an arms race, will be driven by the same considerations as Rousseau's hunters:

> If they cooperate to trap the stag, they will all eat well. But if one person defects to chase a rabbit – which he likes less than stag – none of the others will get anything. Thus, all actors have the same preference order, and there is a solution that gives each his first choice: (1) cooperate and trap the stag (the international analogue being cooperation and disarmament); (2) chase a rabbit while others remain at their

posts (maintain a high level of arms while others are disarmed); (3) all chase rabbits (arms competition and high risks of war); and (4) stay at the original position while another chases a rabbit (being disarmed while others are armed). (Jervis 1978, p. 167)[6]

The preferences of the players with regard to the four possible outcomes in the Stag Hunt can be represented in normal form as in Diagram 5.2.

Diagram 5.2: Stag Hunt

j

	C	D
C	4,4	1,3
D	3,1	2,2

i labels the rows (C, D).

The Stag Hunt belongs to the class of so-called coordination games. In this case it refers to a coordination game in which the players prefer the outcome that each of them chooses strategy C, to any other outcome. In the Stag Hunt, there is, however, the problem that there are two equilibrium outcomes (C,C) and (D,D), but as i and j prefer mutual cooperation to mutual defection, and as each knows that the other does so too, they will choose C, and accordingly will reach the Pareto-optimal outcome. This outcome is moreover a *coordination equilibrium*, which means that a player will not be better off, 'not only if he himself unilaterally changes strategy, but also if the *other* player changes strategy' (Taylor 1987, p. 71, emphasis in original).

The above conventional analysis of the outcome of the Stag Hunt appears to be intuitively satisfying, and, following Schelling and Rapoport and Guyer, we may call it the *natural outcome*. If a game with more than one equilibrium has only one Pareto-optimal equilibrium – that is to say, there is no other outcome in which both players are better off – then they will choose the strategy that contains this outcome (Rapoport and Guyer 1966, p. 15). But if this were to be the correct interpretation, then it becomes rather puzzling how Waltz reaches the conclusion that Rousseau's parable has precisely the same implications for the possibility of cooperation as the Prisoner's Dilemma, 'in cooperative action, even where all agree on the goal and have an equal interest in the project, one cannot rely on others' (Waltz 1954, 1959ed., p. 168). Besides, if things were as simple as the conventional analysis suggests, why does Jervis choose the Stag Hunt of all games to illustrate the proposition that 'although actors may know that they seek a common goal, they may not be able to reach it' (Jervis 1978, p. 168)? Are both authors simply mistaken, or is there perhaps something more, which is overlooked in the conventional analysis? It appears that the latter is indeed the case.

The conventional analysis of the Stag Hunt does not consider the possibility that each player in the Stag Hunt, above all else, will want to avoid the outcome that he alone chooses strategy C. However, it is exactly this that, according to Waltz, each player in the Stag Hunt worries about. Of course, it seems perfectly rational to choose C, but all depends on the rationality of the other player, 'to allow in my calculation for the irrational acts of others can lead to no determinate solutions, but to attempt to act on a rational calculation without making such an allowance may lead to my undoing' (Waltz 1954, 1959ed., p. 169). Waltz's argument boils down to the proposition that a player, who finds himself in a situation in which a wrong choice of strategy may lead to his ruin, will in the first instance order his available strategies lexicographically, on the basis of the possible outcomes they contain. The strategy the player chooses must meet the requirement that it does not contain the so-called *sucker-payoff*. He will only consider strategies that meet this requirement. If several of these strategies exist (in a one-shot game this is of course impossible, since in those games his choice is limited to either C or D), then the player would opt from this set of strategies for the one that also contains the natural outcome.

Such a lexicographical ordering of strategies follows first of all from the fact that, in the Prisoner's Dilemma as well as the Stag Hunt, neither of the players is capable of providing a certain amount of the collective good by himself. If, for instance, in the Prisoner's Dilemma i were to remain silent and j were to confess, then i would be providing a private good to j and not a collective good to them both. After all, i is himself excluded from the good, 'a prison sentence of three months'. The players choose strategy D, not because each of them hopes that the other will provide the desired collective good (at any rate a certain amount of it), but because each of them knows that he is unable to produce some of the collective good on his own. This is not all, however. It will not be every time a player faces the choice whether or not to contribute to the provision of a collective good, that the wrong choice will lead to his ruin. The more powerful a player is, and the lower the expected costs of the sucker-payoff are, the greater the probability that the player will be prepared to run the risk of incurring the sucker-payoff, and that he will choose C in order to be able to reach the Pareto-optimal outcome. The foregoing implies that, in order to determine the outcome of a coordination game such as the Stag Hunt, it will not be enough to know that the Pareto-optimal outcome is also the highest valued outcome. What is also needed is knowledge about the amount of power the players have at their disposal and the expected costs of the sucker-payoff. The less powerful the players, and the higher they expect the costs of the sucker-payoff to be (which may be expressed in a repeated coordination game by a low value of w), the greater the probability that they will choose D, although both players still prefer the outcome that each of them chooses C, to any other outcome.

IV GAME OF CHICKEN

In the Game of Chicken, two male adolescents are tempted to prove their manliness by participating in a game in which they drive their cars towards each other along the middle of the road at considerable speed. The player who swerves loses the game, and earns the reputation of being 'chicken'. The one who stays on course is the winner, and proves that he is the real man. The outcome of the game is that both players will swerve. Each of the players will prefer an outcome that exposes him as being chicken to the outcome of a head-on crash with possibly fatal results. The two players' order of preference for the four outcomes in the Game of Chicken can be represented in normal form as in Diagram 5.3.

Diagram 5.3: Game of Chicken

		j	
		C	D
i	C	3,3	2,4
	D	4,2	1,1

The players in the Game of Chicken constitute a so-called privileged group, that is to say, a group in which at least one of its members is able to provide a certain amount of the collective good – in this case 'survival' – alone, and who is also prepared to do so even if nobody else will do so (Taylor 1987, p. 36). But this sounds better than it is, for since the group is 'doubly privileged', problems arise immediately. Because i

as well as *j* can provide a certain amount of the collective good on his own, it becomes attractive to both players to try and become a free rider. For each of them there is an incentive: 'to attempt to bind himself irrevocably to non-cooperation (or at least to convince the [other] he is certain not to co-operate), an incentive deriving from his expectation that such a commitment will compel [the other player] to choose co-operation (on which he is able to free-ride)' (Taylor and Ward 1982, p. 355).[7] But in view of the fact that, according to the story, the temptations of a free ride do not outweigh the costs associated with the outcome that both players choose strategy D, each player still chooses C. This outcome of mutual cooperation is not, however, an equilibrium outcome: each player would improve his payoff if he alone were to choose D.

The danger that both players may fail to cooperate is anything but removed by assuming that they have a second chance, as Harrison Wagner did in his solution for the one-shot Prisoner's Dilemma. On the contrary, the last thing a player in the Game of Chicken needs, is that the other player knows that he (i.e. the former) will have a second chance. For, if *j* knew that *i* would have a chance to reconsider after *j* has made his choice, then *j* can safely choose D, since *i* will then choose C to avoid a catastrophe. This implies that Wagner's general conclusion that, whenever players choose one after the other in full knowledge of each other's choices, conditional cooperation is the optimal strategy as long as no player can count on having the last choice, does not hold in a Game of Chicken with repeated choice. In such a game both players will choose a strategy of conditional defection – a choice that may have disastrous consequences.

A repeated Game of Chicken is what Hugh Ward has called a 'game of ruin'. A game, that is, with the property that, after a certain number of rounds of play, in which both players choose strategy D, they reach 'the brink' (in a one-shot Game of Chicken the costs of mutual defection are such that the players immediately find themselves on the brink). If one of the players does not choose strategy C in the next constituent game, then the game will be over, since after that game each player will no longer be capable of providing some amount of the collective good alone – they may even have lost this capacity forever (Ward 1987, p. 28). This implies that, if *i* and *j* have the same idea about the moment they will find themselves on the brink, they will choose D in each constituent game of the repeated Game of Chicken until in their opinion this critical moment is reached, and then they will choose C as in the one-shot Game of Chicken. Subsequently, they will continue to choose C until they reach the conclusion that they find themselves no longer on the brink. If *i* and *j*, however, differ between themselves about the moment they will reach the brink, then the situation arises that the player who is the more worried of the two, say *i*, will choose C at a certain point, after which *j* can enjoy a free ride – profit from the collective good provided by *i* alone – until the moment that *i* judges that the players no longer find themselves on the brink, and again chooses D.

V THE PROBLEM OF THE FREE RIDER

In the foregoing sections I have used the tools of non-cooperative game theory to analyse the conditions on which players who find themselves in a system with no authority capable of enforcing the fulfilment of the promises they may have made to one another, will, or will not, cooperate with one another in order to reach some common objective. The most significant results of my analysis seem to me to be the two following. In the first place, that a player's decision to cooperate or to defect depends above all else on the circumstance of whether or not he is able to produce some part of the collective good on his own. In the second place, that, where a player is not able to do so, his decision depends on the expected costs of the sucker-payoff, and, if a player is able to produce a certain amount of the collective good on his own, on the expected costs of the outcome that neither of the players chooses to cooperate.

What definitely is not a player's main worry in the games I have discussed, is whether the other player might take advantage of his efforts. The oft-propounded proposition, by Michael Nicholson among others, that 'the core of the problem of collective goods, is the classic problem of the free rider', turns out not to be universally valid (Nicholson 1989, 1990ed., p. 131). The proposition does not apply to the players in the Prisoner's Dilemma, nor to the players in a coordination game like the Stag Hunt. These know full well that neither of them is able to produce some part of the collective good alone. In this situation, it is by definition impossible to take a free ride. For this reason it simply cannot be their chief concern that the other might become a free rider. What they worry about is that an unavailing contribution might lead to their ruin. Moreover, the proposition does not hold good for the players in a Game of Chicken who find themselves on the brink. These players are very much aware of the fact that the other might take a free ride, but this does not prevent them from choosing strategy C, since choosing D might result in an even worse outcome.

The proposition does not hold either in the situation (as depicted in Diagram 5.4) where the one player is able to produce some amount of the collective good on his own, and orders his preferences in respect of the outcomes in the same way as a player in the Game of Chicken does, while the other player is unable to produce some amount of the collective good on his own, and has the same order of preference with respect to the outcomes as a player in the Prisoner's Dilemma.

Diagram 5.4: Chicken Turns Sucker

		j	
		C	D
i	C	3,3	2,4
	D	4,1	1,2

It will be clear that in this situation also, despite the threatening 'exploitation of the great by the small' (Olson 1965, 1971ed., p. 29), the collective good will be produced. Player *i* will choose strategy C, even though he realizes perfectly well that player *j* will take a free ride on his exertions.

On the assumption that *i* is able to produce some amount of the collective good alone, while *j* is not, we can also envisage a situation in which the proposition does, however, apply. This is the situation where the difference in power between players *i* and *j* is such that the former is just able to produce a certain amount of the collective good on his own, and the latter only just not, and that *i* expects *j* to profit from his free ride to such an extent that *i*'s existing predominance would disappear. (See also Chapter 4, Section IV, where I have been arguing that Grieco's 'sensitivity to gaps in payoffs' increases in proportion as the power differential between individuals is smaller.) In these circumstances, it might indeed happen that *i* will in the end prefer the outcome that both players choose D over the outcome that *j* alone chooses D, and the proposition would hold that the problem of the free rider prevents the provision of the collective good.

NOTES

1.   Cf. Ordeshook: 'A strategy is a complete plan for playing a game that takes account of all possible contingencies, including the choices of other people' (Ordeshook 1986, p. 108). In this chapter I assume that the players only use *pure* strategies.

2.   An equilibrium outcome is an outcome in which none of the players will profit from shifting his strategy unilaterally.

3.   The transformation of the outcome or payoff matrix (which contains the four possible combinations of prison sentences) into the utility matrix that represents the Prisoner's Dilemma is, by the way, anything but straightforward. This transformation would lead to an entirely different result if both players, for whatever reason, would rather spend a year safely behind bars, than to be back on the streets after three months.

   The transformation from payoff matrix to utility matrix would also lead to a different result, if each of the players were to subordinate his own interests to the interests of the other. It is the convention, however, that the players are completely disinterested with respect to the payoff the other player receives (the value of the sensitivity coefficient λ is equal to 1). In the last section of this chapter I shall be discussing a situation in which this convention is abandoned.

4.   Both players prefer 'Tit-for-Tat' to 'Tat-for-Tit', since in a situation where both chose the latter strategy, the result would have been the same as if they had chosen 'all-D'. Moreover, it is inherent in the definition of the Prisoner's Dilemma that both players find a repeated Prisoner's Dilemma in which they take turns exploiting one another (as would result if one player were to play 'Tat-for-Tit' and the other 'Tit-for-Tat') less attractive than a repeated Prisoner's Dilemma in which both players choose to cooperate in every constituent game. For a more precise and formal exposition of the conditions under which the players in a repeated Prisoner's Dilemma will opt for conditional cooperation, see Taylor 1987, pp. 65–71 and Axelrod 1984, pp. 7–15.

5.   'La prévoyance n'étoit rien pour eux, et loin de s'occuper d'un avenir eloigné, ils ne songeoient pas même au lendemain' (Rousseau 1964ed., III, p. 166).

6.   It appears to me to be open to doubt whether states that find themselves in this situation will indeed prefer outcome (1) to outcome (2). Surely each state would prefer the outcome that it had a superiority in arms, to the outcome that all states find themselves in a state of equal disarmament? Even if the former outcome would be more costly than the latter? If one accepts this line of argument, then the preference order of the players would again be the same as that of the players in the Prisoner's Dilemma. George Quester comes to the same conclusion: 'The first choice of any nation may well be to sneak into a position of superiority even if deceit is required; compared with this, substantial disarmament may be only the second preference, ahead of a mutually continued arms race' (Quester 1977, p. 102).

7.   In the story of the Game of Chicken, the players could attempt to become a free rider by simulating drunkenness for example, i.e. by invoking a *threat that leaves something to chance* (Schelling 1960, 1963ed.). Taylor and Ward formulate the nature of such a threat, by the way, too absolutely. It is not necessary for a player to bind himself irrevocably to non-cooperation, if he wants his threat to be effective. It is sufficient that he manages to convince the other that his choice between cooperation or defection is not completely under his own control, so that there is a chance that he will choose defection, however disadvantageous this might be for him. In the words of Thomas Schelling: 'The key to these threats is that ... *the final decision is not altogether under the threatener's control*. The threat ... has an element of, "I may or I may not, and even I can't be altogether sure"' (Schelling 1960, 1963ed., p. 188, emphasis in original).

6. Change and its Consequences

I POLITICAL PROCESSES AND THEIR SOLUTION

The next step in my argument concerns the transition from the analysis of the behaviour of individuals in a system consisting of no more than two individuals, to the analysis of the behaviour of individuals in a system with more than two individuals. Moreover, in this chapter I shall be introducing the distinction between an anarchical and a hierarchical system, and shall briefly discuss some of the differences in the ways in which both kinds of systems react to changes in their environment. In this chapter I shall also be paying attention to the effects that geological, climatological, demographical and, in particular, technological changes may have on the existing affinities between individuals.

Assumption 1**:
More than two of the elements in the system under consideration are capable of behaviour that is governed by the mechanism formulated in the axiom.

The behaviour of groups of individuals is the result of the way in which the individuals involved influence one another's behaviour while they try to adapt to their environment (try to maximize their power). When I talk about collective behaviour in what follows, this does not then concern any random configuration of behaviour that individuals may exhibit. Collective behaviour presupposes a certain degree of order, a certain regularity, or, to put it another way, a certain division of labour. These patterns in the behaviour of individuals may come into being completely spontaneously, and they certainly need not be the result of invention or design. This is also true of human collective behaviour. This collective behaviour, too, is for the greater part, in the words of Adam Ferguson, the result of 'human action, but not the execution of any human design' (see Chapter 2, Section IV). Such patterns provide the individuals involved with 'information', and for this reason alone, the patterns will be valued by them. In the light of the above, I therefore define collective behaviour as follows:

Definition 12:
Collective behaviour is any configuration of behaviour by the individuals that are part of a system, that reduces the degree of entropy in the system.

From Thomas Hobbes's characterization of the state of nature, it can be deduced that a division of labour – and thus a certain amount of welfare – between individuals that are dependent upon one another can only be realized if these individuals do not use more than a part of their power in trying to influence one another's behaviour (cf. my definition of a harmony of interests), and, moreover, if they refrain from attempting to increase any further the weight of their demand behaviour towards one another (see further Section III of this chapter).[1] Individuals may only leave the state of nature behind if the *political process* between them, the expression that I shall be using from now on, has reached a *solution*. (For the sake of completeness, I should mention that a decrease in the weight of their demand behaviour towards one another – for example, because of a diminution in their power, which means that it becomes more difficult for the individuals to reach one another – will lead to a decline in the extent of the division of labour between them, and, consequently, their welfare.)

Definition 13:
A *political process* between individuals exists as long as these individuals are able and willing to increase the weight of their demand behaviour towards one another.

Definition 14:
A political process between individuals reaches a *solution* when these individuals refrain from applying still more of their power in order to increase the weight of their demand behaviour towards one another.

In this connection we should realize that, for a political process to reach a solution, it is not necessary for all individuals to be equally active. The solution of a political process is as much the result of the activity of some as of the passivity of others. We should also not lose sight of the fact that, after a solution has been reached, this does not imply that the individuals involved are subsequently free to reduce the weight of their demand behaviour towards one another. On the contrary, most of the time such behaviour would herald a new round in the political process. Generally speaking, the individuals concerned – and in any case the most powerful among them – will have to maintain their demand behaviour at the level of intensity reached. Although the solution may be such that it leaves room for compensating behaviour by other individuals in case some individuals – and, of course, not the most powerful among them – after a while, for whatever reason, do indeed reduce the weight of their demand behaviour towards the other individuals. The most extreme form of a system with such a *stable* solution constitutes the (surely completely hypothetical) market of perfect competition. In a perfectly competitive market, however, it is strictly speaking no longer possible for the individuals that are part of it to engage in demand behaviour towards one another, and, consequently, political processes cannot take place between them (see also Chapter 7, Section I and Chapter 8, Section III; cf. Russett 1968, pp. 460–61 and 464).

If an individual, i, tries to influence another individual, j, one cannot expect that i will be prepared to invest a large amount of its power in this attempt to influence j at the beginning of this political process. The following relationships appear to hold in this connection. The greater the power differential between i and j in favour of j, the greater the distance between i and j, the more (according to i) appears to be at stake (both with respect to what it hopes to attain and the risks it expects to run), and the less stable the system of which both individuals are a part (as this implies a decrease in i's information about the consequences of a possible intensification of its demand behaviour), then the greater the likelihood that i will invest too little of its power in an initial attempt to get j to act more in accordance with i's wishes. Whereas, conversely, the greater the power differential between i and j in favour of i, the smaller the distance between i and j, the less that appears to i to be at issue, and the more stable (predictable) the system of which both individuals are a part, then the greater the probability that i will invest too much of its power in an initial attempt to get j to act more in accordance with i's wishes. (I have already touched on the latter relationship in my discussion of credibility, in Chapter 4, Section II.)

The uncertainty about the consequences that might follow if an individual were to try to intensify its demand behaviour towards other individuals, means that the individuals involved in a political process will generally be inclined to solve the 'political' problem that has arisen between them as quickly as possible. To put it another way, they will be inclined to prevent the political process from escalating too far. However, the individuals are only able to find out by means of trial and error which behaviour or demand will lead to an escalation, and which will not. It is only by a process of error elimination that the individuals can discover what kinds of behaviour will be tolerated, and which demands will be met. Seen from this perspective, political processes are a means by which the individuals concerned gather information about one another.[2] It will be obvious that in the course of this process of error elimination many errors will be made, perhaps even fatal ones.

However great the individuals' need to solve a political problem as quickly and smoothly as possible, it will be clear that they will continue to try and intensify their demand behaviour towards one another, as long as they are of the opinion that the expected marginal utility of the outcome associated with this behavioural option will be higher than that of the other behavioural options subjectively available to them. With the result that, if this is indeed the case, they will invest more and more of their power in the political process. At a certain moment, the process will reach the point at which the individuals will begin to threaten one another with the use of violence, and will eventually actually use it. The objective of their violent behaviour is to damage the opponent's power, or perhaps even to destroy it, and in so doing to ensure that the opponent will behave itself more in accordance with their wishes (cf. my definition of a conflict of interests). The upper limit of a political process is reached when it leads to the physical destruction of some, or perhaps even all, of the individuals concerned.[3]

In the course of the political process, more and more of the individuals involved will separately reach the conclusion that it does not pay to intensify their demand behaviour any further. These individuals deem the outcome of the political process that has been reached thus far satisfactory enough (which is not to say that they are content with it), with the result that the probability increases that more and more individuals will attempt to induce the other individuals participating in the political process to refrain from intensifying their demand behaviour any further either. Whether, and how quickly, the exertions of the satisfied individuals (the satisfied powers) will be successful, depends on the preponderance of power they are able to build up against the individuals that are still dissatisfied (the dissatisfied powers). Or, to formulate it somewhat differently, the degree to which the satisfied powers are able to form a *dominant coalition*.

My characterization of the manner in which a political process reaches a solution, may give rise to the impression that a dominant coalition can only be realized if several individuals aim to bring this result about. Nothing is further from the truth, however. Most of the time, dominant coalitions will come into existence without the constituent individuals having consulted one another, or having entered into agreements with one another with that objective in mind. The phenomenon of a coalition government made up of several political parties may be a very good example of a dominant coalition, but the manner in which such a coalition comes into being, namely on the basis of an explicit agreement between two or more political parties about which they have been negotiating for a certain period of time, is in no way representative of the manner in which dominant coalitions usually come about. Besides, a dominant coalition may consist of a single individual (such as would be the case if in the international system a power were to manage to establish itself as a hegemon).

In this connection it is perhaps worth mentioning that the predictability of the environment (or a part of it) that is attendant on collective behaviour, constitutes a powerful incentive to the individuals taking part in it not to tolerate a challenge to the existing solution. This tendency will become even stronger as the predictability of the environment has induced (seduced?) the individuals involved to invest a greater part of their power in the realization of long(er)-term objectives.

Theorem 9:
A political process between two or more individuals will only reach a solution, where at least one of the participants in that political process is of the opinion that the expected marginal utility of the outcome that none of the participants intensifies its demand behaviour towards the other participant(s) any further, is greater than the expected marginal utility of the outcome that at least one of the participants increases the weight of its demand behaviour towards the other participant(s) still further, *and* that this individual has so much credibility in the eyes of the other participant(s) in the political process that they, in view of the promises and threats the individual holds out in prospect in order to prevent a further escalation of the political process, refrain(s) from intensifying its (their) demand behaviour towards this individual (and towards one another) any further.

The greater the power of a dominant coalition *vis-à-vis* the other individuals in the system, the quicker a political process will reach an outcome. This ability to end a political process quickly, I shall from now on refer to as the capacity of a system: the greater the power preponderance of the dominant coalition in a system, the greater the capacity of that system.

Definition 15:
The *capacity of a system* refers to the power preponderance of the dominant coalition in that system *vis-à-vis* the other individuals in that system. The greater this power preponderance, the greater the system's capacity, and the less of its total power the system will need to expend in order to have a political process between two or more individuals reach a solution.

The power preponderance of the dominant coalition may be realized in two ways. On the one hand, in a system in which there are either no, or only scarcely perceptible, differences in power between the individuals, because all, or almost all of them, are, for whatever reason, satisfied with the existing solution. On the other hand, in a system in which differences in power between the individuals do exist, because the only satisfied individual, or a small group of satisfied individuals, enjoys such a preponderance of power that it has the capability to impose the solution arrived at on the other individuals. In the latter situation the capacity of a system is a function of the polarity of that system.

Definition 16:

The *polarity of a system* refers to the differences in power that exist between individuals that are part of a system, and the number of individuals that belong to the dominant coalition. The greater the differences in power between the individuals in the system, and the smaller the number of individuals that constitute the dominant coalition, the higher the system's polarity.

A system with a high polarity always has a large capacity, but the reverse is not always true. A system with a high capacity does not always have a high polarity. Witness the case of a perfectly competitive market (see also Chapter 7, Section I). I shall also, by the way, be using the expression 'degree of integration of the system' as a substitute for 'polarity of a system' in the remainder of the book.

In the light of the above, I am now in a position to elucidate to some extent the distinction between an anarchical system and a hierarchical system that I shall be employing in the further development of my argument. Despite the reasons that Kenneth Waltz adduces in his *Theory of International Politics*, that this is a matter of a simple dichotomy (Waltz 1979, pp. 88 and 114–16), I am of the opinion that it is also impossible to draw a clear dividing line in the case of anarchy and hierarchy. An anarchical system and a hierarchical system must be placed on a continuum on which systems of collective behaviour are ordered on the basis of the polarity of these systems. A perfectly anarchical system and a perfectly hierarchical system constitute the two, inaccessible, extremes of that continuum (which implies that, in my approach, an anarchical system cannot be equated with a system in which complete chaos reigns). In proportion as the differences in power between the individuals in a system become greater and the number of individuals that are part of the dominant coalition declines, the system shifts on the continuum further and further in the direction of a perfectly hierarchical system, whereas, conversely, as the differences in power between the individuals become smaller and the number of individuals that make up the dominant coalition increases, the system shifts further and further in the direction of a perfectly anarchical system.[4]

II CHANGE AND ITS CONSEQUENCES

All societies are subject to the inexorable tendency to change. (Kennedy 1987, p. 536)

A. Introduction

Since in this book everything ultimately turns on the question of how international relations and foreign policy are interconnected, I shall be limiting my analysis of the ways in which individuals within anarchical and hierarchical systems react to changes in their environment, to the international system, as far as anarchical systems are concerned, and to organizations or conglomerates of organizations (in particular government organizations), as far as hierarchical systems are concerned. Here I assume that, in the case of the international system, the states that are part of it are the only elements in the system capable of behaviour that is governed by the mechanism formulated in the axiom, while, in the case of an organization, only the human individuals who participate in the organization are capable of such behaviour.[5]

When, in a system in which there exist differences in power between the individuals that are part of that system, the political processes between these individuals have reached a solution, while the environment of the individuals is stable, then the feedback mechanism I have been describing in the previous section means that the system will develop towards a state of 'equilibrium'. The capacity of the system will get larger and larger, and the likelihood of changes in the relationships between the individuals will become smaller and smaller (the rules and dividing lines within the system will become more and more rigid).[6] This development will repeatedly be interrupted because changes in the individuals' environment have consequences for their power positions and the distances between them. In consequence of these changes, the existing affinities between the individuals become either stronger or weaker. To put it another way, changes in the environment of the individuals that are part of a system (for the moment I shall put to one side the nature of these changes) strengthen or weaken the individuals' capability to engage in demand behaviour towards one another. Whether this will indeed be the case, and to what extent, naturally depends again on the capacity of that system. The larger a system's capacity, the less sensitive the individuals will be to changes in their environment (see also Chapter 7,

Section I and Chapter 8, Section IV). Besides, the consequences of these changes must become apparent both clearly and quickly. The individuals must notice that a change has taken place! The extent to which a certain change will have this effect, will, in its turn, vary with the power the individuals have at their disposal.

It will be clear that the effects of a change need not be the same for every individual in a system, and, moreover, that they need not affect every individual. These differences in effect have, in their turn, consequences for the ways in which the system will develop further. What is crucial here, is the effect of the change on the capacity of the system: is it weakened or strengthened by the change? If the latter, then the change constitutes an impetus for the development of the system towards an equilibrium. If the former applies, then the higher the degree of integration of the system at the moment the effects of the change become manifest, and the more these lead to a weakening of the power preponderance of the dominant coalition, the more profound the consequences of this change will be for the system. And, conversely, the less dependent the individuals in the system are on one another the moment the consequences of the change become noticeable, and the less these involve a weakening of the position of the dominant coalition, the less fundamental the consequences of this change will be for the system. Accordingly, an earthquake in a thinly-populated, isolated region with little economic or strategic value will have considerably fewer far-reaching consequences for the daily routine in a country, than an earthquake that leads to the collapse of a dam that is supplying the greater part of a country's electricity needs, while the tidal wave in the wake of the collapse of the dam partially destroys the government centre, and claims thousands of casualties. Likewise, to give another example, the bombardment of a region with a weak infrastructure has far less effect than that of a region with a highly developed infrastructure, in particular, if in the latter situation the bombardment were to lead to the destruction of the dominant coalition as well.

Individuals are continually confronted with changes in their environment. Usually these changes do not make life easier for them. At the same time, however, these changes are a source of progress. It is even the case, strictly speaking, that a system would herald its own destruction, if it were to succeed in isolating itself completely from its environment (see Chapter 4, Sections III and IV).

Change and its consequences may be classified on the basis of the period of time it takes for them to be realized and to become apparent. In his principal work, *The Mediterranean and the Mediterranean World in the Age of Philip II*, Fernand Braudel subsequently distinguishes between three kinds of changes. First, long-term changes (*la longue durée*), changes that have to do with geological characteristics, the climate and the composition of the population. Second, middle-term changes (*la conjoncture*), changes that concern the production process (such as the cultivation of grain, the construction of roads and the production of weapons). And, third, short-term changes (*les événements*), the 'historical' events that, while all-important in the eyes of contemporaries, nevertheless, according to Braudel, from the perspective of the historian appear most of the time to have been of an ephemeral nature (Braudel 1949, 1975ed.).

Change and its consequences can also be distinguished according to whether they are the intended or the unintended result of human action. In this case, too, three categories may be distinguished. In the first place there are 'natural' changes; that is to say, changes that occur irrespective of human action. This typically refers to changes that take place very gradually, and only become apparent after a long period of time, such as changes in the geological constitution of the soil, in the climate and in the composition of the population. But these changes can also occur suddenly and become obvious immediately, as in the case of earthquakes, volcanic eruptions, hurricanes and epidemics. The second category consists of 'technological' changes. These are changes that follow from the discoveries human beings make in the course of their search for the means that may enable them to transform the energy at their disposal even more efficiently into labour. These discoveries concern such things as tools, production techniques, the organization of the production process, and the settlement of transactions. The third category, finally, consists of 'natural' changes that are the result of 'technological' developments, as, for instance, mutations in the DNA of plants, animals and human beings, but also the encroachment of the desert on the countries of the Sahel and the greenhouse effect. In the remaining part of this section I shall, by the way, be paying attention only to the first of the two categories that can be identified in this way. It will become apparent that both are intimately connected with Braudel's *longue durée* and *conjoncture*.

B. Natural Change

The consequences of long-term natural changes manifest themselves in the first place in the ease with which individuals are able to reach one another. Geophysical processes cause an isthmus between two continents gradually to disappear beneath sea level, or the course of a river to change in such a manner that this river can now be navigated more easily and also further upstream. A change of climate turns what was once a prosperous and powerful empire into a piece of desert that can be little else than the natural frontier between other empires. A rise in temperature results in a mountain pass becoming more easily passable and for longer in wintertime. Moreover, changes of this kind have their repercussions on the power of individuals, because they have consequences for the *carrying capacity*, to use an ecological expression, of their environment. As a result of these changes the soil becomes more or less fertile, and the mining of ores more or less difficult.

A natural disaster that results in the resources on which many individuals in a system are dependent becoming inaccessible (and especially where it affects the resources of the individuals that are part of the dominant coalition), implies a shift in the affinities between the individuals in that system, and, accordingly, an intensification of the demand behaviour of these individuals (or some of them) towards one another. A natural disaster often heralds the downfall of an *ancien régime* (a dominant coalition whose power preponderance *vis-à-vis* the other individuals in the system has already been subject to erosion for a long time) as well. Because their power preponderance has been weakened further and further, the holders of power involved are no longer able to bring to a quick solution the political processes that arise in the wake of the natural disaster, or to prevent these political processes from escalating to such levels that they lose their power positions. The developments in France in 1788–89 are a good case in point. Hailstorms and a protracted period of drought in the summer of 1788 caused the failure of most of that year's harvest. Because the subsequent winter was unusually severe as well, the population's situation was exacerbated still further. The lack of food precipitated the so-called *Grande Peur* (Great Fear) in the spring of 1789, a series of peasant revolts and bread riots that led to the fall of the French absolutist monarchy within a matter of months.

If a state wishes to survive in the international system, then the size and composition of its population compared to those of other states constitute an important factor. Generally speaking, the proposition holds that, the greater the relative size of the population, and the larger the labour force as a proportion of that population, the greater the probability that the state will survive. If a state wants to be a great power, then the relative size and composition of its population are decisive. A state can only reach the status of a great power, and hold on to it for any length of time, if the size of its working population is very considerable in comparison to that of other states (and, of course, if this state is also able to mobilize this working population to a sufficient extent). The growth or shrinkage of the populations of states, or changes in the composition of the population (for instance, as a result of ageing), therefore constitute an important source of shifts in the relative power positions of states. When, as a result of an epidemic, the population of a certain state declines sharply, while the population in the surrounding states remains constant – and this decline is such that it is clear to the neighbouring states that the said state is no longer able to keep up its demand behaviour towards the other states at the same level of intensity – then this development implies that the neighbouring states will intensify their demand behaviour towards one another and towards the weakened state, and that a political process will get going between them. Conversely, a population explosion within a state that causes the *carrying capacity* of the state's environment to be considerably exceeded, has international repercussions if the surplus population attempts to settle somewhere else *en masse*.

Finally, it will be obvious that a strong growth in a state's population will lead to a strengthening of the mutual dependencies between the citizens of that state (if only because of the sheer rise in noise), which in its turn increases the likelihood of conflicts (possibly violent) between them. The larger the size of the population, and the greater the population density, the more extensive the machinery of coercion the state will have to have at its disposal in order to be able to stop political processes between its inhabitants at an early stage (and the less legitimate the state, the more extensive this machinery will need to be).

C. Technological Innovation

Technological developments constitute the second class of changes that I have identified. Through the ages, and with constantly increasing frequency, they have been a very important source of changes in the distances between states and between human individuals, and in their power positions *vis-à-vis* one another.

The rise of empires, the development of the present nation-state, and the establishment of Immanuel Wallerstein's modern world-system (Wallerstein 1974), are all inextricably bound up with innovations in the field of transport and communications. Thanks to these innovations, emperors, soldiers, bureaucrats and traders have been able to expand their activities over ever greater stretches of territory. In his famous article 'The geographical pivot of history', Halford Mackinder examines the shift in the balance of power that takes place at the end of the nineteenth century to the detriment of the powers of the *inner crescent* (Germany and Austria-Hungary), in favour of the power that dominates the *pivot area* (Russia), and attributes this shift to the construction of a railway network in Russia and the further development of the steam locomotive (Mackinder 1904, pp. 434–6). In the opinion of Robert Gilpin, reductions in the costs of transport constitute an important factor in the explanation of the dynamics of world history: 'In many instances the great social and political upheavals throughout history have been preceded by major advances in the technology of transportation and communication' (Gilpin 1981, p 56).

It goes without saying that inventions that increase the destructive power, the ease of operation and the availability of weapons, can have considerable repercussions for the relative power positions of states and human individuals. History abounds with examples of tribes, peoples and states that, because they have a new and superior kind of weapon at their disposal, are able to gain the ascendancy over their opponents, even though the latter are more numerous and more prosperous. Likewise, in the course of the sixteenth century, a rapid succession of innovations in the field of weaponry *and* means of transport laid the foundations of the European predominance in the world that was to last until the beginning of the twentieth century. In the period after the Second World War, a possible breakthrough in the field of nuclear armaments that would provide the opponent with a decisive advantage, either defensively or offensively, constituted the greatest threat to the bipolar balance of power between the United States and the Soviet Union. The nuclear arms race between both powers, which was so characteristic of their 'cold war', was also caused by their wish to prevent such a situation occurring at all costs.

According to Paul Kennedy, the rise and fall of the great powers in modern times is 'driven chiefly by economic and technological developments, which then impact upon social structures, political systems, military power, and the position of individual states and empires' (Kennedy 1987, p. 439), where again everything turns pre-eminently on the differences in repercussions that the technological developments have for the power positions of the powers involved. In Karl Marx's eyes, technological innovation is even the ultimate motive force for historical change. In his materialistic interpretation, new technologies lead to new production methods (a change in the productive forces), which, in their turn, cause changes in the social and political organization of a society (a change in the relationships of production): 'Technology discloses man's mode of dealing with nature, the process of production by which he sustains his life, and thereby also lays bare the mode of formation of his social relations' (quoted in Cohen 1978, 1979ed., p. 146; cf. also Kolakowski 1978, 1981ed., I, pp. 337–8).

Having reached this point in my argument, it would seem to be almost inevitable that I address myself briefly to the age-old debate about the conditions that are conducive to the invention of new technologies and their successful application. Many authors have studied this question, since it constitutes a constant bone of contention in the controversy between idealists and materialists over the correct answer to the question about the ultimate motive force in history: idea, or material interest. Whereas Friedrich Hayek defended the proposition that, 'Man has been impelled to scientific inquiry by wonder and by need. Of these wonder has been incomparably more fertile' (Hayek 1967, p. 22), Friedrich Engels, in a letter to Starkenburg, reached the conclusion that, 'If society has a technical need, it serves as a greater spur to the progress of science than do ten universities' (quoted in Carr 1939, 1964ed., p. 2). I am afraid that the answer to this burning question can be no other than that here, too, it is impossible to separate power from 'information', and that it is out of the question that the one would have primacy over the other. Inventions are the result of a creative process and therefore cannot be forced, not even by 'technical needs'. In that sense, inventions are chance-like events. At the same time, they can only be applied fruitfully when the social and economic circumstances are ripe. Franz Mehring pointed out that several of the inventions at the basis of the Great Industrial Revolution, such as those of the power loom and the steam engine, had been invented earlier, but had not at the time led to a social revolution, since under the prevailing social and economic conditions the potential application of these inventions was not obvious (Harmsen 1968, p. 88). Over two hundred years ago, the relationship between human creativity and materialistic need had already been strikingly put into words by Adam Ferguson:

Inventions, we frequently observe, are accidental; but it is probable, that an accident which escapes the artist in one age, may be seized by one who succeeds him, and who is better apprized of its use. Where circumstances are favourable, and where a people is intent on the objects of any art, every invention is preserved, by being brought into general practice; every model is studied, and every accident is turned to account. If nations actually borrow from their neighbours, they probably borrow only what they are nearly in a condition to have invented themselves. (Ferguson 1773ed., p. 282)

Innovations in the organization of labour relations can also have far-reaching repercussions for the power positions of states and human individuals. Many students of international relations and international economic relations, trying to find an explanation for the American decline in power *vis-à-vis* Japan since the beginning of the seventies, come to the conclusion that the difference in the way labour relations are organized in the United States and in Japan provides an important part of the answer. At this juncture in time, the once so successful American 'Fordist' model appears to be less efficient than the more recent Japanese 'Toyotist' model. Similarly, innovations in the ways in which armies are organized can also have far-reaching consequences for the power of states. The short-lived dominance of Greece by Thebes in the fourth century BC was based on the revolutionary manner in which the Theban troops were deployed before doing battle, the so-called oblique order of attack. For several years, Thebes' opponents, notably Sparta, had no defence against this innovation. The Roman hegemony, which lasted several centuries, was likewise the result of the (for that time) superior organization of the Roman legions.

A final category of innovations I should not fail to mention, relates to the techniques for raising loans to finance transactions and long-term projects (such as wars). According to Paul Kennedy, the decisive factor in the gradual rise of Great Britain as a great power in the course of the eighteenth century, at the expense of France, is that Great Britain, unlike France, was able to take advantage of the 'financial revolution' that took place in the same period (Kennedy 1987, pp. 76–86).

III COLLECTIVE BEHAVIOUR AND CHANGE

A. Anarchy and Hierarchy as Models of Collective Behaviour

As I have explained in my discussion of the concept of dependence, it pays the individual to give up a position of autarchy and to specialize. By a division of labour, two or more individuals are able to increase their individual and collective power. At the same time, specialization is always a risky affair and entails certain costs. The first and most existential risk concerns the fact that when an individual is occupied in performing a certain task – for example, growing grain – it will no longer be able to defend itself at all times against potential aggressors. The second risk is less life-threatening, but if things go wrong the consequences can be almost as disastrous for the individual. When, after a while (it will always take some time before the individual can reap the fruits of its decision to specialize), the individual offers the goods that are the result of its exertions to other individuals – in the hope of exchanging them for goods the individual itself needs – there is a risk that the other individuals may turn out not to be interested in the goods. The individual can reduce this risk by making forward (wholly executionary) contracts with other individuals, but this still leaves the risk that the other individuals will not perform their obligations at the agreed time, perhaps because of circumstances beyond their control. The individual can reduce this risk still further, by making enquiries about the reliability of potential contracting parties, but these enquiries are naturally not without cost. This also holds for the necessary negotiations with other individuals, and for drawing up and signing the contracts (together, these costs constitute the so-called 'transaction costs'). It will be clear that the risks and costs I have outlined will only increase as the individual specializes still further and has to enter into contracts more often.

One way to reduce the first, most existential, risk is that the individuals concerned decide to establish a collective security system. They agree from then on to regard an act of aggression against one of the members of the security system as an act of aggression against them all, and to assist the victim by all the means at their disposal (see also Chapter 7, Section III). The great disadvantage of a solution of this kind is that it immediately puts a brake on the process of further specialization, potentially so profitable to them all. Since every individual must at all times be ready to come to the defence of any other member of the system, the division of labour has to be confined to those projects that, if necessary, can be laid down at short notice without much difficulty.

A more profitable way for a group of individuals to reduce this fundamental security risk, is further specialization. A number of individuals within the group form a 'protective association' (Nozick 1974), which, in return for some recompense, is entrusted with the task of defending the individuals in the group against outside aggression. Such a solution can arise spontaneously (can be discovered), or can be imposed by some individuals that set themselves up as protectors, or can be the result of an agreement between the individuals concerned.

It stands to reason that, once a group of individuals has a protective association at its disposal, the individuals will also employ it to ensure that they fulfil their promises to one another. But this does not have to be the case. Especially not where the individuals set up an enterprise with a view to reaching a common objective, which requires them to specialize for some long time, and to carry out a mutually-contingent 'stream' of performances, as a consequence of which a large number of very diverse and very specific contracts would have to be entered into. In this situation, it is more efficient if the individuals involved reduce their transaction costs by 'organizing' this enterprise hierarchically. This means that some of them are charged with the task of ensuring, by means of rewards and punishments, that the other individuals fulfil their obligations to each other within the framework of the common objective as much as possible (cf. Williamson 1975 and 1985). Such a solution does not of course preclude the possibility that the individuals participating in this enterprise would employ the services of a protective association to deter potential aggressors, or that, should a dispute arise between them about the way they should fulfil their contracts with each other, they would enlist the services of a protective association to enforce these contracts.

Initially, several protective associations may establish themselves within a given geographical area. It will be clear that their chances of survival are determined by their ability to protect their clients against aggression from clients of other protective associations, and to enforce the fulfilment of contracts between their own clients. The more powerful a protective association is in comparison with other protective associations, and the more extensive the area over which it is able 'to project its protection', the greater the likelihood that this protective association will survive. Once one of these protective associations has gained ascendancy over the others (for instance, because it has superior weapons or means of transport, or is organized more efficiently), then it will gradually develop into the dominant protective association within that area. It is this dominant protective association that, by appropriating more and more tasks, especially regulatory tasks (naturally in return for revenue!), will develop further into a state. Up to now, there has been no protective association powerful enough to establish its dominance over the whole world. In the international system as it is today, many protective associations still exist, some 180 of which have developed more or less into states. The international system lacks, for the time being, an agency that can force states to fulfil the promises they may have made to one another. This situation is characteristic of an anarchical system. Of course, within an anarchical system, organizations can develop and flourish (witness the phenomenon and the success of multinational corporations), while, conversely, within hierarchical systems, anarchical systems can exist (for instance, corruption networks in bureaucracies).

Definition 17:
An *anarchical system* is a system with a comparatively low polarity that consists of two or more individuals, and that lacks an agency with the capacity to enforce the promises the individuals concerned may have made to one another. A *hierarchical*

system is a system with a relatively high polarity that consists of more than two individuals, and that does have an agency with the capacity to enforce the promises the individuals concerned may have made to one another.[7]

It is not the case that a system with a relatively high polarity is necessarily a hierarchical system, but an agency with the capacity to enforce the fulfilment of promises individuals may have made to one another can only be found in relatively highly integrated systems.

Theorem 10:
The higher the polarity of a system with more than two individuals, the more dependent the individuals involved are upon one another, and the more important their credibility is in their mutual relationships (in other words, the more extensive the division of labour in that system), then the greater the probability that this system has an agency with the capacity to enforce the promises the individuals may have made to one another.

In the first section of this chapter, I have already argued that an anarchical system ought not to be equated with a system in which complete chaos reigns. A division of labour is possible in an anarchical system too, and the individuals that are part of such a system are able to cooperate with one another in all kinds of projects. The cooperation between the West European powers in the context of the European Communities (now the European Union) constitutes a very good example of how far cooperation can go in an anarchical system. When Stephen Krasner defines a regime as a set of 'implicit or explicit principles, norms, rules, and decision-making procedures around which actors' expectations converge in a given area of international relations' (Krasner (ed.) 1983, p. 2), then such a regime comes under my definition of an anarchical system.[8]

To what extent individuals are prepared to specialize, regardless of whether the division of labour occurs in an anarchical or a hierarchical context, depends on their expectation as to how much that specialization will contribute to an increase in their power. The more effective they expect this form of collective behaviour to be, i.e. the more they expect specialization to yield, and the lower the expected risks, then the more individuals will be prepared to specialize. Of course, the individuals will have to learn whether, and to what extent, specialization will lead to an increase in their power in an anarchical or a hierarchical system. The expected effectiveness of a system, which I shall be calling the *legitimacy* of a system from now on, can only develop over time, and this implies that, during that time, the environment of the individuals concerned should not undergo too many violent changes. Therefore, legitimacy has less to do with the momentary interests of the individuals concerned, than with their long-term concerns (cf. De Vree 1982, p. 297).

> *Definition 18*:
> The *legitimacy* of an anarchical or a hierarchical system refers to the expectation on the part of the individuals in such a system that, to participate in a division of labour, and, consequently, to increase their mutual dependence, will lead to an increase in their power. The more these individuals expect further specialization, and, accordingly, stronger mutual dependence, to lead more probably to an increase in their power, then the greater the system's legitimacy.[9]

It will be clear that the credibility of an individual and the legitimacy of a system are, up to a certain point, equivalent concepts.

Regimes as well as organizations have rules that indicate things like, what acts are expected from the individuals taking part in those regimes or organizations, what goals they are supposed to pursue, in what ways they may influence one another, what kind of information is needed for the regime or organization to function successfully, and how that information has to be processed. As far as regimes are concerned, these rules need not be formulated explicitly. Organizations, on the other hand, always have a hard core of explicitly formulated rules. This feature follows from the multiplicity and specificity of the tasks the individuals concerned have to perform, in order to reach the stated objectives. A high level of communication is required for such a sophisticated system of division of labour: the participating individuals, if they are to be able to enter into agreements with one another and to judge whether these agreements are being complied with or not, must be capable of distinguishing true from false statements, and also of assessing the validity of statements. The high level of communication required also implies that organizations can exist only in social systems. That is to say, in systems of which human individuals are a part (Popper and Eccles 1981ed., pp. 57–60).

Not all the rules that govern the behaviour of human individuals in an organization are explicitly formulated, however. A great many will develop spontaneously, and will have to be discovered by the individuals involved through a process of trial and error. But these implicit rules cannot be separated from the hard core of explicit rules.

Another constant property of organizations, as opposed to regimes, follows from the fact that organizations, as hierarchical systems, have an agency with the capacity to enforce the promises the individuals participating in the organization may have made to one another. The hard core of explicit rules contains at least some 'enforcement rules' (Arrow

1971, p. 225). These are rules that state who, from what position, and with what authority, may command whom, and what sanctions may be imposed if the rules and commands are not complied with.

The above observations lead me to define organizations as follows:

Definition 19:
Organizations are hierarchical systems, consisting of human individuals, that provide these individuals with much more 'information' than other forms of collective behaviour, owing to the explicitness of the rules (or a part of the rules) that govern the behaviour of the human individuals who are part of it, among which rules there are at least some so-called 'enforcement rules'.

B. Anarchy, Hierarchy and Change: A Preliminary Assessment

For purposes of review, I shall conclude this section on collective behaviour and change with a preliminary assessment of the respective advantages and disadvantages of an anarchical system and a hierarchical system following from the fact that in an anarchical system the degree of polarity is relatively low, whereas in a hierarchical system this is relatively high. The degree of polarity of a system has far-reaching consequences for the facility with which the system can adapt to changing circumstances, and the ease with which the individuals in the system will use violence against one another. Whereas an anarchical system is open to change, a hierarchical system, in contrast, closes itself to new developments. In an anarchical system, violence (or the threat of it) looms large, while in a hierarchical system it remains far more in the background. In the next two chapters, I shall be analysing further the ways in which this particular distinction between an anarchical and a hierarchical system makes itself felt in things such as, what individuals find useful in their attempts to maintain themselves in the system, how they take decisions, how they attempt to cooperate with one another, how they try to solve problems and fight out conflicts. In the course of this preliminary assessment, I shall be returning to my earlier discussions, but I shall also be anticipating things to come. It will be shown that what is a relative advantage of a hierarchical system, is precisely a relative disadvantage of an anarchical system, and vice versa. My assessment, by the way, mainly concerns the pros and cons of anarchy and hierarchy as systems, and far less the pros and cons of those systems for the individuals that are part of it. For this reason, I shall also leave unanswered the question in what type of system the individual would be better off, if the individual, for whatever reason, displays the 'wrong' kind of behaviour for the type of system of which it is part.

The most important advantage of a hierarchical system is without doubt that, because of its high polarity, a very extensive division of labour can be implemented within such a system, and that, in consequence, the system has the capacity to carry out large, sometimes very lengthy and complicated, projects. In the context of this discussion, it does not matter whether this division of labour is imposed or arises spontaneously, although it has to be said that, the more such a division of labour is imposed, the lower the efficiency with which a project will be executed. Without organization, it would not have been possible to build pyramids, palaces and cathedrals, nor to construct large irrigation networks. Nor would it have been possible to wage war thousands of kilometres from home, in a hostile environment (hostile also in terms of physical and geographical conditions), as was the case in 1990–91 in the 'Desert Shield' and 'Desert Storm' operations, where a coalition of states under the leadership of the United States compelled Iraq to abandon Kuwait, which it had annexed only a few months earlier. Accordingly, Kenneth Arrow is of the opinion that: 'Truly among man's innovations, the use of organization to accomplish his ends is among both his greatest and his earliest' (Arrow 1971, p. 224). Perhaps one can even defend the proposition that the evolutionary success of the human species, such as it is, is attributable primarily to its capacity to organize itself.

Another great advantage of a hierarchical system is that its large degree of integration makes it easier for the individuals that are part of it to cooperate with one another. On the one hand, because the transaction costs will be lower. On the other, because the extensive division of labour reduces their sensitivity to gaps in payoffs. That this has to be true, follows from the following considerations. Individuals in a hierarchical system learn that it pays to specialize, and the more legitimate the system, the faster and more effectively they will understand this to be so. Specialization boils down to an investment in the future, and the more the individuals have invested in this way, the more they will be concerned about the 'absolute' outcome of their mutual cooperation, and the less they will worry about the 'relative' outcome of their cooperation (the value of the sensitivity coefficient λ approaches 1; see Chapter 4, Section IV). Thus it becomes less probable that conflicts will arise between them. Owing to the high polarity of hierarchical systems, it is already fairly unlikely that conflicts will lead to the use of violence. By no means the least of a hierarchical system's advantages is that peace and security are better guaranteed.

What amounts to the greatest advantage of a hierarchical system, that it is able to carry out extensive long-term projects, is at the same time that system's greatest disadvantage. The size of the investment that would be lost if a hierarchical system were to decide upon a change in policy, to embark on an entirely different project, means that a system of this kind is not very receptive to new developments and, as a result, that it is unable, or able only with the greatest difficulty, to adapt to new developments. It speaks for itself that this disadvantage will only weigh more heavily in proportion as the hierarchical system has been more successful in the past, and adaptation is the more vital for the system's survival. One of the factors to which Paul Kennedy attributes the phenomenon that such powerful empires as the Ottoman Empire, Ming China and the Mogul Empire were in the end no match for the cluster of internally divided states in Western Europe, is that these empires were over-organized.

At the beginning of the sixteenth century it was by no means apparent that the last-named region was destined to rise above all the rest. But however imposing and organized some of those oriental empires appeared by comparison with Europe, they all suffered from the consequences of having a centralized authority which insisted upon a uniformity of belief and practice, not only in official state religion but also in such areas as commercial activities and weapons development. The lack of any such supreme authority in Europe and the warlike rivalries among its various kingdoms and city-states stimulated a constant search for military improvements, which interacted fruitfully with the newer technological and commercial advances that were also being thrown up in this competitive, entrepreneurial environment. (Kennedy 1987, pp. xvi–xvii)

The second great disadvantage of a hierarchical system is that, although it is true that a high degree of integration decreases the likelihood that a conflict will get out of hand, at the same time it has the effect that, if, for one reason or another, this does happen on a particular occasion (a possibility that can never be ruled out), then this conflict will immediately turn into a very serious conflict indeed. Where a hierarchical system is not able to prevent the escalation of a conflict, then it is the consequence of the strong mutual dependence induced by the high polarity of the system, that much will be at stake for the individuals. For this reason, the individuals will be prepared to go to great lengths to defend their interests, and this increases the likelihood that the conflict will spread still further and, as a result, will become more and more 'total' in character.

Where a hierarchical system is thus at a disadvantage, an anarchical system has positive advantages. Thanks to the low level of polarity and the concomitantly low level of dependence, an anarchical system is better equipped to adapt to changing circumstances. The individuals that are part of an anarchical system will be less prepared to commit themselves to long-term projects, and will try to avoid specialization as much as possible. In consequence, the anarchical system retains the necessary flexibility. The system's low polarity and the limited mutual dependence between the individuals in the system also mean that the anarchical system has the advantage that the conflicts, which arise with great regularity between those individuals, will be more limited in character. Because less is at stake for a smaller number of individuals, conflicts can be isolated more easily.

The most prominent disadvantage of an anarchical system is, of course, that the individuals in such a system will be more inclined to settle possible conflicts by violent means. The lower the level of polarity in a system, the less individuals that have come into conflict have to fear from a dominant coalition, and the greater the probability that the conflict will escalate so far that they will try to settle it in their own favour by using violence. The second great disadvantage of an anarchical system relates to its unpredictability. This has a negative effect on the transaction costs. These may even rise so high that the individuals that are part of the system will no longer be prepared to enter into forward contracts with one another, and will limit themselves to the exchange of goods they can produce at negligible risk and costs. To be sure, if the transaction costs were actually to get this high, then we can no longer speak of an anarchical system. The individuals concerned would find themselves in the state of nature depicted by Thomas Hobbes, in which a division of labour is no longer possible.

NOTES

1.   According to Hobbes it is manifest that:

> During the time men live without a common power to keep them all in awe, they are in that condition which is called war; and such a war, as is of every man, against every man. For WAR, consisteth not in battle only, or the act of fighting; but in a tract of time, wherein the will to contend by battle is sufficiently known ... so the nature of war consisteth not in actual fighting; but in the known disposition thereto, during all the time there is no assurance to the contrary. ...
>
> In such condition, there is no place for industry; because the fruit thereof is uncertain: and consequently no culture of the earth; no navigation, nor use of the commodities that may be imported by sea; no commodious building; no instruments of moving, and removing, such things as require much force; no knowledge of the face of the earth; no account of time; no arts; no letters; no society; and which is worst of all, continual fear, and danger of violent death; and the life of man, solitary, poor, nasty, brutish and short. (Hobbes 1947ed., p. 82)

2.   I therefore agree with Jansen and De Vree that: 'In most cases power positions cannot be measured objectively in such a way that the members of a system could not but acknowledge them. In fact, the political process itself "measures" those relationships

experimentally; almost continuously the members of a system probe the others' willingness and ability to fend-off any changes which impair their position in the system' (Jansen and De Vree 1985, 1988ed., p. 3).

3. Cf. Carl von Clausewitz: '*War is thus an act of force to compel our enemy to do our will* ... Force, that is, physical force ... is thus the *means* of war; to impose our will on the enemy is its *object*. To secure that object we must render the enemy powerless; and that, in theory, is the true aim of warfare ... The thesis, then, must be repeated: war is an act of force, and there is no logical limit to the application of that force. Each side, therefore, compels its opponent to follow suit; a reciprocal action is started which must lead, in theory, to extremes. This is the *first case of interaction and the first "extreme"* we meet with' (Clausewitz 1989ed., pp. 75 and 77, emphasis in original).

4. It would appear that Waltz's claim that, if we wish to understand the effects of structure on the behaviour of individuals, it is sufficient to work with a simple dichotomy between anarchy and hierarchy, follows from his presupposition that anarchy and hierarchy are two opposite ordering principles (Waltz 1979, pp. 114–16). However, in the approach I have adopted, anarchy and hierarchy are seen as manifestations of the same ordering principle: the manner in which power is distributed between the individuals in the system.

5. Just to be perfectly clear, I wish to emphasize once again that it is purely a methodological question as to what the researcher will regard to be the individual, the environment or the system (see Chapter 2, Section IV). The researcher makes his choice in the light of the problems that interest him. From this it follows that, what in the context of one study may be seen to be 'the system' (for example, 'the state' in a study of foreign policy decision making within a certain country), may be seen in the context of another study as one of the individuals in a system (for instance, in a study of the effects of multipolarity on decision making in the international system).

6. In the vocabulary of thermodynamics, a development takes place in the direction of a situation of equilibrium. That is, an equilibrium defined in terms of a minimum of free energy. Cf. the manner in which Prigogine and Stengers describe the situation of the particles in a crystal. 'We can imagine each particle as imprisoned by its interactions with its neighbors' (Prigogine and Stengers 1984, p. 126).

7. It would be more precise to speak of 'an agency that claims to have the means at its disposal to enforce the fulfilment of the promises individuals may have made to one another'. After all, for various reasons, it will not always be possible to enforce the fulfilment of an agreement. Although more precise, this formulation is also more cumbersome, and therefore I use the more conventional formulation, 'an agency with the capacity to enforce the promises individuals may have made to one another' (see also the definition of non-cooperative games in the previous chapter).

8. The same applies to Robert Keohane's characterization of an institution: 'When we ask whether X is an institution, we ask whether we can identify persistent sets of rules that constrain activity, shape expectations, and prescribe roles' (Keohane 1989, p. 164).

9. In view of this definition, it would be even more exact (see note 7 above) to speak of 'an agency that claims to have the means at its disposal to enforce the fulfilment of the promises individuals may have made to one another, where this claim is accepted by a sufficient number of individuals in the system as being legitimate'. By the way, the greater the legitimacy of an anarchical system, the more it will have in common with Hedley Bull's anarchical society (see Chapter IV, Section II).

7. Decision Making and the Management of Conflict in Anarchical Systems

I WAR AS THE *ULTIMA RATIO*

It is war and the threat of war that help to determine whether particular states survive or are eliminated. (Bull 1977, p. 187)

A. Introduction

The polarity of the system in which individuals try to settle their differences and to resolve crises successfully, influences the ease with which these individuals are able to solve their common problems and succeed in managing crises in their mutual relationships, as well as the means they choose to employ in trying to do so. In this chapter, I shall be discussing what characterizes the ways such processes take place in anarchical systems.

As I have already explained in the previous chapter, the international system will serve as the example of systems with no agency capable of enforcing the promises that individuals in that system may make to one another. I shall also assume that states are the only elements in the international system capable of behaviour governed by the mechanism formulated in the axiom, but this assumption implies no denial of other actors and factors playing an important role in the international system. It *does* imply, that I assume, following Kenneth Waltz, that, 'when the crunch comes', in the international system everything turns on the behaviour of states and, especially, the behaviour of the great powers. It is the states, which 'remake the rules by which other actors operate' (Waltz 1979, p. 94).

My decision to take an approach to international politics that regards states as the central actors, is supported by the following argument. It is characteristic of anarchical systems, in contrast to hierarchical systems, that the individual members will more quickly try to solve conflicts by

112

violent means, and that these individuals in doing so will also employ violence on a larger scale. (This also explains why, in this chapter, conflict will be more in the foreground, while in the next chapter, in which I shall be dealing with decision making and the management of conflict in hierarchical systems, the emphasis will be on cooperation.) Moreover, the use of violence can be the most costly and unsettling kind of demand behaviour individuals can engage in towards one another. Since in the international system states are pre-eminently equipped to use violence against one another and against any other actors, it appears to be reasonable to assume that the best way to understand decision making and conflict management in the international system, is by assigning the explanatory principle to states.[1]

B. Violence and Subversion

First I have to make clear what I shall mean by violence and subversion in the context of this chapter. The definition I have chosen, is derived from the definition De Vree developed in his *Foundations of Social and Political Processes*, although I have slightly altered his wording.

Definition 20:
Violence and subversion concern the attempts by individual i to influence the behaviour of individual j by employing a part of its (i.e. i's) power to acquire the means that should give i the capacity to weaken or even to destroy the power of j, as well as by actually using these means. Whereby violence refers to the weakening or the destruction of the resources j has, and subversion to the weakening or destruction of the 'information' j has. (cf. De Vree 1982, p. 236)

It will be clear that this is a rather unusual definition. I shall use it nevertheless, because it enables me to emphasize three points of the utmost importance for understanding decision making and crisis management in international politics. In the first place, this definition makes clear that violence, like any other means of influencing the behaviour of other individuals, is a question of deploying scarce resources to reach a certain objective, and that, consequently, violent behaviour is not a special kind of behaviour, which would stand in need of a separate explanation. The probability that i will employ a part of its power with the aim of weakening or destroying the power of j, and in this way to bring about that j will behave itself more in agreement with i's wishes, will become higher in proportion as i expects that this behavioural option with a higher probability will lead to a greater number of things i values positively, and decreases in proportion as i expects this behavioural option to lead with greater likelihood to a greater number of things i values negatively. In the second place, the definition treats war as only one of the available forms of violence, so that there seems a priori to be no reason to study wars between states from a different perspective than revolutions, civil wars, piracy or riots. In the third place, finally, the definition indicates that the peaceful coexistence of individuals (states) can go together with high levels of investment in the means of violence, as when states try to prevent war by building up a credible defence or deterrence against one another (see my discussion of the 'security dilemma' further on).

A drawback of this definition is, it is true, that it does not admit violence as an aim in itself – the individual i behaving violently purely for the sake of the excitement that it brings, rather than as a means to persuade j to do certain things j otherwise would not have done, such as is the case with vandalism. John Keegan, for one, would strenuously object against this identification of violence with politics (witness his diatribe against Clausewitz, Keegan 1993, pp. 3–60). But in my opinion this drawback is more than matched by the advantages mentioned in the previous paragraph. Moreover, violence for the sake of violence only very rarely occurs in the world of states (which is not to say that it occurs very seldom in wars between states).

In the last paragraph of my introduction to this chapter, I have deliberately written that violence *can* be the most costly and unsettling kind of demand behaviour. Not every attempt by i to gain j's active cooperation with, or passive acquiescence in, the former's attempts to increase its power, needs to be very costly and unsettling for them. This is the case, for example, in the situation where i, as a great power, actually uses the means of violence at its disposal in order to 'correct' the behaviour of the small power j. There exists a relation of dependence between both powers that i at least wishes to continue – at any rate on its terms. The great power does not fight the small power in order to be in a better position to bargain about these terms, but as a means to punish it.[2] In such situations, the clearer relations are between i and j, the less likely it is that i's actual use of its means of violence against j will have far-reaching consequences. To be a little more precise, the more powerful i is compared to j, the lower the expected costs associated with the behavioural option of fighting j, the higher the expected effectiveness of actually using some means of violence at i's disposal against j, and, finally, the more predictable the environment i and j find themselves in, the less disruptive will be i's actual use of the means of violence at its disposal against j.

In the situation outlined in the previous paragraph, j is able to resist i's aggression, but with little expectation of success. In the next situation where the means of violence are actually being used, the difference in i and j's capacity for violence also leaves the victim little chance to defend itself successfully against the attacker. But this time this difference is due to the fact that the victim is insufficiently prepared for the attacker actually to use the means of violence it has, as is often the case with robbery and piracy, forms of one-sided violence that are not uncommon in the international system. It is characteristic of robbery and piracy (and of vandalism, by the way) that prior to the attack victim and attacker have no (strong) relationship of dependence, and that the latter expects its victim to pose little threat in the future. Individuals indulging in robbery and piracy are hardly affected by long-term considerations.

However, this definitely does not apply to states that end up fighting a war. In the case of war, it normally concerns the actual use of means of violence by parties that are more or less well-matched. The parties concerned will already have been dependent on one another for a considerable period of time, and expect this mutual dependence to continue in the future. The war between them constitutes a violent phase in an already long-established conflict with respect to the terms of their relationship of dependence. Each of the belligerents has decided at a certain moment that it is only by the use of violence that the opponent may finally come to realize that its interest is also served by active cooperation with, or passive acquiescence in, the other's attempts to increase its power. In such a situation, the use of force, and the manner in which it is being used, constitute elements of a bargaining process. War is always, in the words of Thomas Schelling, 'a bargaining process, one in which proposals, counterproposals and counterthreats, offers and assurances, concessions and demonstrations, take the form of actions rather than words, or actions accompanied by words' (Schelling 1966, p. 142). This implies that in the case of war, it is most of the time difficult to make a clear distinction between the state that commits aggression and the state that becomes the victim of it (even if there exists no doubt as to which state was the first to take up arms).

In the remainder of this chapter, I shall restrict my discussion to the phenomenon of war, because it holds the greatest dangers for the international system as a whole, and especially because this type of violence is the most difficult for the parties involved to keep under control by themselves. The poor manageability of war follows from the fact that it only strengthens the already existing relationship of dependence between the parties, which constitutes the basis of their conflict in the first place. It is true that, when either *i* or *j* will not actively cooperate with, or passively acquiesce in, the other's attempts to increase its power, both will in the first instance be reluctant to commit themselves too far – a reluctance that will increase, the more is at stake in their conflict, the smaller their difference in power, and the shorter the distance between them. But when neither *i* nor *j* is prepared to give in to the other, each of them, according to the importance of the issue and to bring about compliant behaviour, will in the course of time invest more and more of its power in means of violence, advancing the moment when at least one of them will come to the conclusion that only by the actual use of these means of violence will the other be persuaded to see the reasonableness of its demands. The probability that this moment will actually occur, increases in proportion as the environment in which *i* and *j* find themselves is more unpredictable. If it indeed comes to fighting, then this will be accompanied by the destruction of resources and 'information' on a large scale. It is the ever present possibility that an individual may get caught up in such a destructive conflict, that makes the individual's power rest ultimately on its ability to fight other individuals, either defensively or offensively. It speaks for itself that, seen from the perspective that war is a phase in a longstanding conflict between individuals about the terms of their relationship of dependence, the individuals' decision actually to use the means of violence at their disposal need not have much to do with their original motives – however high-minded or perfidious these may initially have been.

C. The Stability of the System

Assume that two more or less equally powerful states *i* and *j*, geographically rather isolated from the other states in the international system, have enjoyed for some time a strong, and mutually profitable, relationship of dependence. State *i* derives the greater part of its national income from the export of a certain raw material to state *j*. Without this raw material *j* would not be able to produce the semifinished product that, widely exported, makes such an important contribution to its national income. At a certain moment state *i* is under the threat of losing its monopoly in the raw material. Due to technological innovation, state *k* is now able to supply this raw material to state *j* as well. When state *j*, in view of this development, subsequently presses *i* for a revision of the terms of trade of their relationship to *j*'s advantage, a conflict of interest between both states arises. Such a conflict may eventually lead to a war between the two states. But of course this does not have to be the case.

Many factors are involved here. One of the most important relates to the degree of stability of the international system.

It may very well be that immediately it becomes clear that j's wish is not feasible, so that little else is left for j but to accept the existing situation, or that i has no other option than to give in to j's wishes, however disadvantageous this may be. After a disturbance of the existing relationships, the speed with which the individuals concerned accept either a continuation or a change of the status quo – and, accordingly, a decrease in the likelihood of a violent conflict between them – is a function of the stability of the system of which the individuals are a part. The more extensive the initial disturbance, the lower the level of intensity reached by the consequent political process, and the sooner the weight of the demand behaviour of the individuals concerned is back at the level before the disturbance – which is not to say that everything has stayed the same – the greater the stability of the system.

Definition 21:
The *stability* of a system S, in which there are two or more individuals, concerns the speed with which changes in the weight of the demand behaviour of the individuals towards one another – which are subsequent upon disturbances in the individuals' environment – are nullified. In proportion as greater disturbances in the environment of the individuals lead to smaller changes in the weight of the demand behaviour of the individuals towards one another, and these changes persist for a shorter period of time, the greater the system's stability.

Figure 7.1: Stability and instability

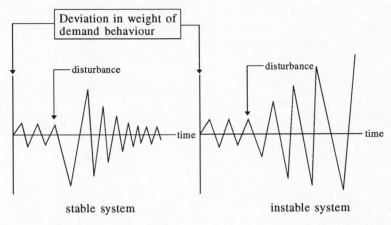

Source: Adapted from De Vree 1990.

There are two, hypothetical, forms of stable systems, which agree with my earlier characterization of a perfectly anarchical and a perfectly hierarchical system (see Chapter 6, section I). The first concerns a system in which all, or very nearly all, individuals are part of the dominant coalition, as is the case with the producers in a perfectly competitive market. Within this system, political processes cannot take place, since none of the individuals is able to engage in demand behaviour. Such a system is called an ultrastable or homoeostatic system. This is a system that is completely open to changes in the environment, and that is also able to react 'perfectly' to these changes. This system is based on the acceptance of change. The second form of a stable system concerns a system in which the dominant coalition consists of just one individual, which has such a preponderance in power that all other individuals in the system are subordinate to it. In this system also, political processes cannot occur, this time because there is only one individual that is able to engage in demand behaviour. Such a system is usually called an absolutely stable system. This is a closed system, based on the denial of change.

As I have explained, such systems are ideal-typical constructs, which have little to do with the realities of international politics. There everything turns on states attempting – in the light of changing circumstances – to persuade other states to behave themselves more in agreement with the former's wishes. In the international system, political processes are the order of the day. Whether these political processes will escalate to war, varies with the capacity of the international system. The greater its capacity, the greater the system's stability, and the lower the probability that war will actually break out.

The most important points in my argument in this chapter thus far, may be summarized in the following two theorems:

Theorem 11:
The smaller the capacity of the international system, the higher the probability that a state will value the marginal utility of an additional unit of resources that should strengthen its ability to weaken or even destroy the power of other states more highly than the marginal utility of an additional unit of credibility or of economic resources.

Theorem 12:
The greater the instability of the international system, and the more dependent states are upon one another, the greater the likelihood that a political process between states will escalate to such a high level that at least one of these states, call it i, actually decides to use the means of violence at its disposal in order to bring the other state (or states) involved in the political process to behave more in agreement with i's wishes.

D. The Security Dilemma

The greater the degree of instability in the international system, the more a state will view other states as posing a threat to its own security, and the more of its power it will expend in acquiring the capability for violence that should remove this threat. However, the unintended by-product of its quest for security is that the state, as a result of its greater ability to weaken or even destroy the power of other states, now poses a greater threat to the other states. The latter, in their turn, will attempt to remove this threat by strengthening their capability for violence. In consequence, they will again pose a greater threat to the first state, which subsequently decides to expend even more of its power on strengthening its capability for violence etc., etc. Through these stimulus–response interactions it becomes conceivable that, 'two states which support the status quo ... will end up, if not in war, then at least in a relationship of higher conflict than is required by the objective situation' (Jervis 1978, p. 182). John Herz has christened this phenomenon 'the security dilemma':

> Wherever ... anarchic society has existed – and it has existed in most periods of known history on some level – there has arisen what may be called the 'security dilemma' of men, or groups, or their leaders. Groups or individuals living in such a constellation must be, and usually are, concerned about their security from being attacked, subjected, dominated, or annihilated by other groups and individuals. Striving to attain security from such attack, they are driven to acquire more and more power in order to escape the impact of the power of others. This, in turn, renders the others more insecure and compels them to prepare for the worst. Since none can ever feel entirely secure in such a world of competing units, power competition ensues, and the vicious circle of security and power accumulation is on. (Herz 1950, p. 157)

Herz has emphasized the 'social character' of the security dilemma. It is not the aggressive motives of the states involved that makes them end up in a dangerous arms race. It is the consequence of the anarchical structure of the international system that they are caught up in this unhappy situation.[3] By the way, Herz did not realize that a 'real' security dilemma can arise only if the states concerned expect that, if they have to fight a war, offence will have the advantage over defence, and that, accordingly, it will be more attractive to be the first to attack, than to wait for the first attack. Only in this situation does the procurement of weapons by a certain state constitute a direct threat to the security of other states (cf. Wagner 1983, pp. 339–41, Christensen and Snyder 1990, pp. 144–7).

E. *Ultima Ratio* or *the* Ratio?

After having formulated in *Leviathan* his famous characterization of the state of nature (see the quotation in note 1 of Chapter 6), Thomas Hobbes admitted that there had perhaps never been a time when the situation as depicted by him, 'wherein particular men were in a condition of war one against another', had actually existed. But, as he continued, this did not mean that his depiction of the state of nature did not have any bearing on reality. Perhaps it did not apply to human beings, but it certainly did apply to states:

> Yet in all times, kings, and persons of sovereign authority, because of their independency, are in continual jealousies, and in the state and posture of gladiators; having their weapons pointing, and their eyes fixed on one another; that is, their forts, garrisons, and guns upon the frontiers of their kingdoms; and continual spies upon their neighbours; which is a posture of war. (Hobbes 1947ed., p. 83)

Nowadays, it is Kenneth Waltz who proclaims that the state of nature, the war of every man against every man, fully applies to the international system. According to Waltz, a state's foreign policy has only one objective: to try and prevent other states from actually using the resources at their disposal to weaken or destroy that state, given that 'in international politics force serves, not only as the *ultima ratio*, but indeed as the first and constant one' (Waltz 1979, p. 113).

However, as has become clear in the last chapter, the situation of states in the international system must not be equated with that of individuals in the state of nature, because in the state of nature, as Hobbes indeed argued, a division of labour is impossible. Waltz, who time and again stresses the point that anarchy is not the same as utter chaos, is therefore forced to claim that, in the international system, as far as the threat with, and the actual use of the means of, violence are concerned, no functional differentiation between states exists (Waltz 1979, pp. 93–7). However, in the international system it is also possible to have a division of labour between states in respect of the threat with, and the actual use of, the means of violence. A good example of such a kind of functional differentiation is seen in the relationship that was established between the United States and, respectively, the Federal Republic of Germany and Japan in the course of the Cold War. It was also because the United States were able and willing to provide a credible deterrent against the common threat of an attack by the Soviet Union, that the Federal Republic and Japan were able to focus their attention on strengthening their economic potential, and to develop into 'civic' powers of the first rank.[4]

At the same time, it cannot be denied that there are many states in the present international system that, by continually procuring more and more weaponry, indicate their hearty agreement with Waltz's characterization of that system. This difference between *welfare states*, such as the Federal Republic and Japan, on the one hand, and *power states*, like Iraq and Pakistan, on the other, follows from the fact that states so order their behavioural options lexicographically that they will give absolute priority to the procurement of the means of violence, and will do so until a certain level of security has been reached. (Whether this level is reached as a result of their own exertions, or of those of another state, or other states, is less relevant in this connection.) Only once the required level of security has been reached (which need not be the same for every state), will a state allow itself to pursue other goals as well. Contrary to Waltz's assertion, there is no difference in this respect between national and international politics. In international politics too, force is not *the* ratio, but the *ultima ratio*.

In the international system, peace and security are ultimately the prime considerations. Such a perspective on international politics emphatically does not imply that, in the words of Robert Gilpin, 'power and security are the sole or even the most important objectives of mankind'. It *does* imply, however, that 'more noble goals will be lost unless one makes provision for one's security' (Keohane (ed.) 1986, p. 305).

War 'lurks in the background of international politics' (Carr 1939, 1964ed., p. 109), and has retreated even further into the background after the Second World War, at least as far as the relationships between the two superpowers and their most important allies are concerned. This is the result of the rapidly accelerating technological revolution that has been taking place since that war with respect to the destructive power of weapons and the swiftness with which the opponent may be hit with these weapons. With the arrival of nuclear weapons and ballistic missiles, the military might of the United States and the Soviet Union has become geared more to destroying than to conquering. In such a situation, the power that is best able to exploit the fear for a possible catastrophe without war actually breaking out, has the advantage (cf. my discussion of a repeated Game of Chicken in Chapter 5, Section IV). It is for this reason that, also under these conditions, the deployment of military power remains the ultimate means for states to reach their objectives. To the states that find themselves in this situation, strategy is no longer the art of 'the use of engagements for the object of war', as Clausewitz described it (Clausewitz 1989ed., p. 129), but, as in Basil Liddell Hart's definition, 'the art of distributing and applying military means to fulfil ends of policy' (Liddell Hart 1954, 1967ed., p. 335).

In the relationships between the superpowers, strategy is no longer necessarily related to the actual use of the means of violence. As a matter of fact, the distinction between strategy and politics (diplomacy) has disappeared. In this way, the strategic relationship between the Soviet Union and the United States has gained the character of a 'psychological relationship'. As Morgenthau's student Robert Osgood has observed in his book *NATO. The Entangling Alliance*, 'Indeed, given the present inhibitions against the overt use of armed force ... the political and psychological consequences of the nature and disposition of armed forces may be the primary function, not just the by-product, of military strategy' (Osgood 1962, p. 5). All-important in this context is of course the credibility of the superpowers; that is, that they are able to establish the reputation *vis-à-vis* one another that they are able and willing to keep their promises and to execute their threats. In this sense their arms race, which continued till the end of the eighties, was indeed 'about politics'.[5]

II ESCALATION AND DE-ESCALATION

A. A Process of Positive Feedbacks

Assumption 5:
The environment of the states in the international system has experienced a disturbance, such that at least one of the states changes its behaviour to the extent that the weight of its demand behaviour towards one or more of the other states increases.

As I have already explained in Chapter 6, Section II, a political process between individuals is set in motion if changes in those individuals' environment have consequences for their relative power positions. The total amount of power available in the system need not increase or decrease as a result of these changes. The crucial point is that, because of these changes, from now on the available amount of power in the system will be distributed differently between the individuals that belong to it. Robert Gilpin has expressed this understanding as follows:

The most important factor for the process of international political change is not the static distribution of power in the system (bipolar or multipolar) but the dynamics of power relationships over time. It is the differential or uneven growth of power among states in a system that encourages efforts by certain states to change the system in order to enhance their own interests or to make more secure those interests threatened by their oligopolistic rivals. In both bipolar and multipolar structures, changes in relative power among the principal actors in the system are precursors of international political change. (Gilpin 1981, p. 93)

Where a conflict between states actually ends in war, the escalation process leading to it was triggered by a change in the environment of those states with possibly far-reaching consequences for the relative power positions of those states. While one state judges this change to provide it with a good opportunity to strengthen its position in the international system considerably, another state cannot see this change other than as posing a potentially serious threat to its position of power. Escalation takes place the moment one of the participants in the political process is able and willing to increase the weight of its demand behaviour towards the other participants to exploit this opportunity, or to eliminate this threat. It is characteristic of escalation that, the greater the amount of power the participants have invested in the political process at a given moment without result – and especially in resources that cannot be applied to other objectives (or only with the greatest difficulty), as is preeminently the case with weapons of heavy destruction – the more they will be prepared to let this political process escalate still further. Thus the escalation of a political process increases the likelihood that this political process will escalate still further. In this respect the process is self-reinforcing. It is therefore very doubtful that adversaries that have ended up in such a process of mutual escalation, will be able to keep the political process under control by themselves (as with every round the stakes are getting higher for them). This naturally applies *a fortiori* where war has actually broken out between them. Many authors have recognized this danger, beginning with Carl von Clausewitz, as in his treatise on the 'three cases of interaction' that feed war, and the 'three extremes' to which war 'in pure theory' must lead (Clausewitz 1989ed., pp. 76–7). Many of these authors subsequently invented constructions that ought to make it possible to avert this danger, such as, for example, the so-called 'strategies of stable conflict' (Freedman 1981, 1989ed., pp. 191–5). The designers of such strategies attempted to formulate rules that specify the ways in which the adversaries in a (nuclear) war are to react to one another's actions. In his *The Evolution of Nuclear Strategy*, Lawrence Freedman discussed the ideas of Amster and Sherwin, who devised rules:

For maintaining this steady state if threatened by accident, design or some expanding local conflict. The rules were only to engage in strategic bombing if attacked in this manner oneself, responding to attacks on cities with comparable attacks on the opponent's cities, and to attacks on bomb-carriers by sending off an equivalent number of carriers to those destroyed to bomb the opponent's cities. (Freedman 1981, 1989ed., p. 192)

The problem with agreements on the ways in which opponents are to react to one another's actions, is obviously that these will be kept only when the opponents have exactly the same amount of power and exactly the same resources in exactly the same proportions, or, at least, *think* that this situation obtains. That is to say, where, as far as the warring parties are concerned, a relationship of *essential equivalence* exists (Freedman 1981, 1989ed., p. 358). For, if this is not so – and we may safely assume that in reality both the 'hard' and the 'soft' condition will not be met – then the same move (e.g. the bombardment of a city) can have completely different consequences for the parties in the conflict, and be to the advantage of one party and to the disadvantage of another, so that the danger of further escalation is increased.[6] Another point is that, once the conflict has escalated to the level of war, it becomes even less likely that the opponents will be able to reach an agreement on the ground rules that should apply to their conflict, let alone on the interpretation of those rules. The higher the stakes get for the adversaries in an armed conflict, the smaller the likelihood that they will jointly be able to establish mutual and unequivocal 'saliences' or 'points-of-no-return' with respect to the course of their conflict, or that one of them will be able to impose these unilaterally. The constant threat that things will get out of hand means that the escalation process is far more akin to a 'homogeneous growth curve' than Richard Smoke would care for.[7] (Of course, this is not to say that escalation is not a matter of many discrete decisions – how could it be otherwise in view of David Hume's discovery (see Chapter 2) that nothing is inevitable in the empirical domain?) Thomas Schelling, too, emphasizes that the actual use of the means of violence diminishes the chances that the adversaries will be able to keep their conflict under control:

Violence, especially in war, is a confused and uncertain activity, highly unpredictable, depending on decisions made by fallible human beings organized into imperfect governments depending on fallible communications and warning systems and on the untested performance of people and equipment. It is furthermore a hotheaded activity, in which commitments and reputations can develop a momentum of their own. (Schelling 1966, p. 93)

The threat that an escalation process will get out of hand, only grows where the warring parties find themselves in a 'chicken'-like situation, in which there is a premium on 'dangerous' behaviour. Everything gets even more complicated, if the consequences of an 'all-out war' were to be so disastrous for the opponents that increasing the likelihood that it will actually break out becomes a means to force the opponent to keep the conflict limited (cf. again the repeated Game of Chicken).

B. Arms Races

Without doubt, arms races constitute the manifestation of an escalation process that appeals most to the imagination.[8] As I have also noted in the discussion of my definition of violence and subversion, an arms race between states need not necessarily end in their settling their conflict by actually using the means of violence they have. The states concerned are procuring arms with the aim of strengthening their position against the opponent to such an extent that the latter refrains from settling the conflict by the use of arms. An arms race, moreover, can undermine the economic capacity of an opponent to the degree that the latter feels forced to abstain from further investments in the means of violence, and to try and seek an accommodation. From this perspective also, an arms race is all about politics (see also my remarks at the end of the previous section).

It is characteristic of an arms race that, precisely as in every process of mutual escalation, as long as it goes on the exertions of the adversaries do not have the desired effect. To be sure, their own armament gets steadily bigger and more elaborate, but the threat this armament is intended to eliminate looms as large as ever. The biologist Leigh van Valen, inspired by what happened to Alice when she began to run with the Red Queen, has called this property of arms races the 'Red Queen effect'. However hard Alice and the Red Queen ran, however great their exertions, it would seem that they made no progress at all. When at last they stopped running, Alice discovered that they were indeed still under the same tree. When she exclaimed in great surprise that 'Everything's just as it was!', the Red Queen said:

'Of course it is, what would you have it?'
'Well, in *our* country,' said Alice, still panting a little, 'you'd generally get to somewhere else – if you ran very fast for a long time, as we've been doing.'
'A slow sort of country!' said the Queen. 'Now, *here*, you see, it takes all the running *you* can do, to keep in the same place. If you want to get somewhere else, you must run at least twice as fast as that!'. (Carroll 1871, 1975ed., p. 140, emphasis in original)

The participants in an arms race should be happy enough if all their exertions have the effect of them at least staying in the same place *vis-à-*

vis one another.

Arms races, partly as a result of the Red Queen effect, appear to be merely wasteful, but this is not the whole story. Arms races can also lead to a more successful adaptation to the environment. According to the biologist Richard Dawkins, it has largely been arms races, 'that have injected such "progressiveness" as there is in evolution' (Dawkins 1986, 1988ed., p. 178), while the historian Paul Kennedy is of the opinion (as I have already mentioned in Chapter 6, Section II) that arms races between the European powers in the course of the sixteenth century laid the foundation for European supremacy in later centuries (Kennedy 1987, pp. 22–5).

C. Escalation and Information

Changes in the environment of states make issues that appeared to be settled, suddenly seem no longer to be so. How far issues were in fact settled, what the status quo entailed precisely, always remains, by the way, somewhat uncertain (except when it concerns an ultrastable or an absolutely stable system). For, although a political process has reached a certain solution in an earlier phase, this does not signify that those that participated in that political process acquired an accurate understanding of one another's relative power positions, let alone that they grasped which factors and developments determined its solution (cf. Chapter 6, Section I). The main thing is that the participants, in the light of the information they had, and however incomplete, imprecise and unreliable this information may appear to be in the eyes of some 'disinterested spectator',[9] considered it no longer worth their while to invest more of their power in the political process.

Poor information, moreover, often heralds a new round in the political process. This relates to incorrect information about how significantly the power relationships within the system have changed, and, accordingly, how far the status quo has been undermined, as a result of changes in the environment. Erroneously, a dissatisfied power may conclude that, as a result of these changes, it is now in the position to make a satisfied power accept a change in the terms of their existing relationship of dependence to the advantage of the dissatisfied power. The fact that the dissatisfied power is indeed mistaken, can, by the way, only be established experimentally in the light of the way in which the satisfied power reacts (it will be clear that war is the ultimate test). We would wish that such misconceptions could be avoided one way or another, but a process of trial and error is the only method of finding out that it was a misconception after all. As Georg Simmel correctly observed, 'the exact knowledge of the comparative strength of the two parties [is] the most effective prerequisite for preventing struggle', but such exact knowledge can often be obtained only 'by the actual fighting out of the conflict' (quoted in Coser 1956, p. 133).[10] Besides, we should not lose sight of the fact that the more violent the changes in the states' environment, and the longer these continue, the more difficult it becomes for the states to obtain a more or less accurate understanding of one another's relative power positions.

Recent history has seen two clear examples of a state that mistakenly reached the conclusion that the power of an adversary in a conflict that had been dragging on for years, at a certain point in time had been so weakened, that the former could gain a decisive advantage over that adversary by further escalating the conflict, and thus that the latter would have no option other than to meet the former's wishes. The first example is Iraq's almost fatal miscalculation of the consequences for the power of Iran of the Shiite revolution that began in 1979. As a result, Iraq decided in September 1980 that the moment had at last arrived to settle the decades-old conflict with Iran about the sovereignty of the border river Shatt al-'Arab, by means of war. The second example is the erroneous Argentinian assessment in the spring of 1982 of the British ability and determination to reconquer the Falkland Islands after the Argentinians would have occupied those islands, and of the American willingness to support the British.

Poor information also plays an important role in the possible escalation of a conflict between a relatively powerful state and one relatively powerless. The greater the difference in power between both states, and, consequently, the less important the conflict appears to be to the powerful state, the less trouble the powerful state will take to obtain accurate information about its opponent (see also Chapter 4, Section II). As a result, the probability increases that an escalation of the conflict by the more powerful state will not have the desired effect, i.e. that the less powerful state decides to meet the former's wishes. This uncooperative attitude from the less powerful state brings the credibility of the more powerful state into play, which again increases the chances that the latter will invest more of its power in attempting to induce the less powerful state to behave itself in accordance with the powerful state's wishes.

To put it briefly, accurate information is indisputably of the utmost importance for the manageability of (violent) conflicts. At the same time, however, it is unlikely that the parties involved will have sufficiently accurate information available as long as the political process between them has not reached a solution, and this becomes even more unlikely, the more of their power the parties have invested in this conflict.

D. Escalation and Intervention

To judge from the foregoing, it is apparently rather difficult for two states, once they are caught up in a process of mutual escalation, to keep this process under control. As Clausewitz showed, they are driven to the extreme by the internal logic of the process. This may give rise to the impression that it is all to the good that two states involved in mutual conflict will not usually be so isolated from other states that their conflict will cause no inconvenience to those other states, and that, consequently, the latter will intervene in the conflict. Whereby intervention by other states becomes more probable, the wider the repercussions of the conflict (for instance, because the conflict threatens to spread to the territory of other states, or because the conflict threatens to cut off the other states' supply of vital raw materials, or because the conflict results in a massive stream of refugees to those other states). Nevertheless, this impression is only correct in part. Whether it is correct or not, depends on the degree of polarity of the international system. This impression is certainly correct where a hegemon exists, or a 'holder of the balance', that intervenes in the conflict with a certain show of strength at an early stage in the escalation process to punish the combatants (intervention-as-punishment); and, the greater the credibility of the hegemon, or the holder of the balance, the more limited this show of strength can be.[11] This impression is, however, wide of the mark, where other states intervene in the conflict on a limited scale by siding with one of the contending parties only after the escalation process has been going on for some time. Such intervention-as-interference precisely leads to a further escalation of the conflict, either because the intervening states wish to keep their involvement in the conflict limited, or because the combatants realize that this involvement can only be limited. In the first case, the power preponderance of the intervening states is not great enough *vis-à-vis* the combatants. In the second their power preponderance is potentially great enough, it is true, but the threat actually to deploy their power to end the conflict, is not credible in the eyes of the belligerents. In these circumstances, intervention by another state, or other states, merely contributes to the strengthening of the position of one of the combatants to a greater or lesser extent – and thus only encourages further escalation – and it certainly does not help to settle the conflict.

This does not alter the fact that the smaller the distances between the members of the system, the faster those members will experience the repercussions of a conflict, and the more likely they will be to get involved in the conflict one way or the other. The probability that this will indeed happen increases in proportion as the differences in power between the members of the system are smaller. In such a situation, the changes in the power positions of the contending parties consequent upon their conflict have direct repercussions on the power positions of the other members of the system. In these circumstances, escalation spreads like wildfire. Isaac Deutscher has described very aptly how this comes about, in a passage in which he tries to make his readers understand the terror exerted by the Bolsheviks after their takeover of power in Russia in 1917:

> Having accomplished a revolution, the Bolsheviks could not renounce revolutionary terror; and the terror had its own momentum. Every revolutionary party at first imagines that its task is simple: it has to suppress a 'handful' of tyrants or exploiters. It is true that usually the tyrants and exploiters form an insignificant minority. But the old ruling class has not lived in isolation from the rest of society. In the course of its long domination it has surrounded itself by a network of institutions embracing groups and individuals of many classes; and it has brought to life many attachments and loyalties which even a revolution does not destroy altogether. The anatomy of society is never so simple that it is possible surgically to separate one of the limbs from the rest of the body. Every social class is connected with its immediate neighbour by many almost imperceptible gradations. The aristocracy shades off into the upper middle class; the latter into the lower layers of the bourgeoisie: the lower middle class branches off into the working class; and the proletariat, especially in Russia, is bound by innumerable filiations to the peasantry. The political parties are similarly interconnected. The revolution cannot deal a blow at the party most hostile and dangerous to it without forcing not only that party but its immediate neighbour to answer with a counterblow. The revolution therefore treats its enemy's immediate neighbour as its enemy. When it hits this secondary enemy, the latter's neighbour, too, is aroused and drawn into the struggle. The process goes on like a chain reaction until the party of revolution arouses against itself and suppresses all the parties which until recently crowded the political scene. (Deutscher 1954, pp. 338–9)

At the end of this overview of the reasons why escalation tends to provoke further escalation, and why poor information and limited intervention appear only to strengthen this tendency, in a certain sense we can only regret that the parties between which the conflict started, did not fight it out (perhaps symbolically) in an early stage. Of course, such a method of keeping escalation under control is no longer achievable in the present-day international system, and would, moreover, be contrary to the prohibition of the threat or the use of force as was laid down in the Charter of the United Nations. All the same, it would have been less costly and less unsettling for almost all concerned, perhaps even for the loser of the fight.

E. De-escalation, Information and Intervention

As I have argued in the previous chapter, the fact that a certain political process has reached a solution does not mean that those that have taken part in it, are subsequently free to reduce the weight of their demand behaviour towards one another (except when this political process has led to the establishment of an ultrastable system). The political process comes to a standstill at a certain level of escalation (as is the case when belligerents conclude a cease-fire). De-escalation can only take place if at least one of the following three conditions is satisfied (or any combination of the three): 1) the power of the parties in the conflict decreases to such an extent that they are no longer able to maintain their demand behaviour at the level previously reached; 2) the difference in power between the contending parties increases, as a result of which the nature of their mutual relationship becomes clearer; and 3) the costs of maintaining their demand behaviour at the level reached previously become prohibitive – such as where another power or group of powers forces them to reduce the weight of their demand behaviour towards one another. (It will be obvious that when the first condition is satisfied, the third condition will usually also be satisfied, and conversely.)

The diminution of the adversaries' power may be caused by developments in the conflict that result in earlier investments in weaponry, in soldiers, but also in allies, being lost on a large scale, as well as by natural disasters, epidemics and technological innovations. Technological innovations can not only lead to the obsolescence of part of the belligerents' weapons arsenal, but can also undermine their economic basis. This loss in power implies, on the one hand, that any further investment in the conflict becomes more difficult to bear for the contending parties, and, on the other hand, that they do not have to take the difficult decision to write off a certain investment themselves. Together, these conditions make it more likely that the opponents will refrain from further investment in their conflict, and instead will reduce the weight of their demand behaviour.

Naturally, the smaller powers participating in the conflict will sooner be prepared to reduce the weight of their demand behaviour. Thus we have arrived at the second condition for de-escalation of a political process, namely if the differences in power between the adversaries increase. The relative power positions of the contending parties may diverge further because of the way the conflict develops. While one party enjoys success after success, the other experiences setback after setback. Again, technological innovations, natural disasters and epidemics may also cause this greater divergence in power between the adversaries. The greater the power preponderance of the one party becomes in the course of the conflict, the more often and more decisively the other is defeated, then the clearer the mutual relationships between the parties become. These relationships, by the way, have to be very clear indeed before the party that is on the losing side accepts that it has in fact lost. As Graham Allison observed, 'to have lost is not sufficient'. The loser will also have to understand that to continue the struggle is pointless, and 'only highly visible' costs can have this effect (Allison 1971, p. 262). For this reason, a last effort on the victor's part is often needed to make it clear to the loser that he really has lost.[12]

The increased difference in power between the contending parties, also means that something of a harmony of interests develops between them, which makes it easier for them to take the decision to de-escalate their conflict. The party that is on the losing side will, as a result of its relative decline in power, feel more inclined to behave itself in agreement with the wishes of the winning party, while the latter, in view of its relative rise in power, will be in a better position to treat the former leniently.

The third condition for de-escalation relates to the costs of maintaining the demand behaviour at the existing level (let alone of a further escalation) becoming prohibitive. Technological innovation can play a crucial role here too, as illustrated by the process of 'structural disarmament', which has been taking place with respect to the procurement of new generations of weapons in recent decades. Because the production costs of new weapons increase exponentially, a state can procure fewer and fewer of them. Naturally, a credible intervention in the conflict by another power, or a group of powers, can also induce the contenders to come to the conclusion that the costs involved in their conflict can no longer be sustained, and to start a process of mutual de-escalation.

The following theorem summarizes the most important aspects of my observations on de-escalation:

Theorem 13:
The probability that a political process between states de-escalates at a certain point in time (the probability that these states are able and willing to reduce the weight of their demand behaviour towards one another at a certain point in time), increases in proportion as, either their power diminishes more significantly, or the power differential between them becomes greater, or the costs of maintaining their demand behaviour at the level reached previously become higher (or any combination of the

three).

III THE STRATEGY OF ALLIANCES

A. Defence, Deterrence and Compellence

If two states, as a result of their mutual attempts to achieve a situation whereby the other will behave itself more in accordance with its own wishes, have ended up in a process of mutual escalation, then this escalation process will at a certain point reach such a level of intensity that the states begin to contemplate the possibility that their conflict may only be settled by the use of arms. Subsequently, each of them will attempt to avert the threat of war, or, in the unhoped-for event that it indeed comes to war, to avoid losing it. Each of them at least will aim to ensure that it is sufficiently well-armed to withstand a possible attack by the other, but would prefer to have sufficient weapons to deter the other from attacking, or to compel the other not to do so. The adversaries can achieve these objectives both by strengthening their own armaments and by concluding treaties with other states. Such a treaty can take the form of a non-aggression pact, which gives the state directly involved in the conflict the opportunity to deploy a larger share of the means of violence it has for the purpose of the conflict. It can also take the form of a treaty of mutual assistance, by which the signatories promise to come to one another's assistance should one of them become the victim of armed aggression by a third state, or promise jointly to attack a third state. (The diplomatic activities of the states involved in the conflict will naturally not be confined to concluding treaties with other states to strengthen their own position, but will also extend to trying to prevent their adversary from concluding such treaties.) In this section, I shall first be discussing the problems and uncertainties with which a state is confronted when it tries to conclude such a treaty of mutual assistance. Subsequently, at the end of this section, I shall be examining the complications that arise in executing a particular kind of a treaty of mutual assistance, a collective security system. These complications seem to undermine the credibility – and therefore the effectiveness – of this system beforehand.

Until the beginning of the 1930s, there existed only two ways to realize the aim, with the help of military means, that the adversary would refrain from armed aggression. One way meant that a state, with or without the assistance of allies, attempted to dissuade the opponent from attacking by building up a defence strong enough to convince the opponent that it would not be worth its while to attack. The other was aimed at persuading the adversary, again with or without the help of allies, to disarm itself. Thanks to a successful surprise attack on the adversary's territory (or by threatening to carry out such a successful surprise attack) a state could compel its enemy to reduce its weapons arsenal or its military forces.[13] The preparations for war by the opponents were geared to fighting a war on the ground. Everything turned on the conquest of territory, or, conversely, on the prevention of the conquest of territory. In the course of the 1930s, the development of the long-range bomber aircraft added a third method for preventing an adversary from attacking: deterrence. This means that a state threatens to bring its opponent to its knees by 'strategic bombardments' of its population and industries, rather than fighting it out on the ground. The aim of deterrence, just like defence, is to discourage a potential aggressor from attacking. Here, however, it does so not by ensuring that the state's defence is so strong that it would never pay the aggressor to attack, but by seeing to it that an attack will be answered with the large-scale destruction of the aggressor's resources.[14] The spectacular development of nuclear weapons and ballistic missiles after 1945, gave the United States and the Soviet Union so great a deterrent capability that this situation of Mutual Assured Destruction (MAD) became the dominating aspect of the 'cold war' that raged between them until the end of the 1980s (see Section I of this chapter).

Wallace J. Thies has pointed out that innovations in the field of communications (steamship, train, motor car and aeroplane), and improvement of infrastructure (docks, railroad network, road network and airports) meant that the manner in which, and the speed with which, allies could come to the assistance of a state that had become the victim of aggression, underwent a powerful transformation in the course of this century – and, after 1945, again a very dramatic transformation (cf. Thies 1987, pp. 325–30). Up to the end of the last century, the burden of defence rested almost completely on the shoulders of the state that had become the victim of aggression during the first phase of the hostilities. Its allies' contribution, even where these were neighbours, could initially be little more than minimal. The transport of the necessary troops, and the infrastructure that had to be put in place to facilitate this transport, inevitably took a considerable length of time. Where the allies were not immediate neighbours of the victim, they could render assistance only indirectly, by attacking the aggressor somewhere else. In these circumstances, allies were important, perhaps even decisively so, but a state that became the victim of aggression had largely to fend for itself as far as the defence of its territory was concerned. This situation altered drastically after 1945. Since then, because of the highly improved transport facilities and infrastructure, it has no longer been the case that the state that is the victim of an armed attack will most of the time also have to make the greatest contribution to the defence of its territory (this holds *a fortiori* for deterrence). If necessary, allies can be on the spot quickly to take part in the defence, even if they are not neighbours. (Whether the allies will be prepared to do so, is of course an entirely different matter.)

The development referred to above implies that, for the states taking part in an alliance in recent decades, the good 'a successful defence against a common enemy' has gained more of the character of a 'pure' collective good. Because the individual efforts of the allies can more easily be made to serve the common goal, the degree of jointness of supply, and the extent of non-excludability of the good have increased. However, defence will never become a really pure collective good, because too many private interests and considerations are also at stake in the production of this collective good – even though these private interests and considerations increase the likelihood that some amount of the collective good will actually be produced (see also Chapter 8, Section III). A better infrastructure for the defence against a common enemy, may also be profitable for the ally on whose territory these infrastructural improvements are carried out in peacetime. The development of new weapons may give a boost to the economy of the state in which these weapons are developed. Moreover, the better weapons, infrastructure and the stronger economy can also be employed to realize objectives that have nothing to do with the original alliance.

Deterrence, too, is not a pure collective good, even though it is easy to see that it is a more pure collective good than defence. However, in the case of deterrence, the allies are in particular concerned with the quality of this collective good (its degree of non-rivalness), which in its turn depends on the extent to which the allies *and* the common enemy deem it credible that the state in the alliance that has the deterrent will actually use it in order to punish aggression against one or more of its allies. The allies, as well as the common enemy, will take into account that congestion costs will arise, in the sense that, on the one hand, the greater the number of allies that state has, the less probable it becomes that it will use its deterrent for the good of each of them, and that, on the other hand, the less important an ally is to that state (strategically or economically), the more unlikely it becomes that it will actually employ its deterrent were that ally to become the victim of aggression.

B. 'Balancing' or 'Bandwagoning'

In his essay on the balance of power, David Hume argued that a state that aspires to hegemony will always find a confederacy of states against it that will try to prevent this from happening. He ascribed this law to the envy that a powerful state evokes in the other states. Hume readily admitted, by the way, that this understanding was anything but new. The maxim that one must preserve the balance of power, 'is founded so much on common sense and obvious reasoning', that, according to Hume, the ancient Greeks were already familiar with it. Hume, therefore, was mystified at the behaviour of Philip V of Macedonia. Instead of restoring the balance by siding with Rome, when defeat threatened for the latter in the second Punic War (218–201 BC), Philip 'most imprudently' formed an alliance with victorious Carthage (Hume 1985ed., pp. 333–6). Apparently, the pursuit of a balance of power is less a matter of course than Hume supposed. In this section, I shall be examining more closely (with the help of the perceptions gained in Chapters 4 and 5) the conditions under which a state will decide to create a counterweight against a state that threatens to establish a hegemony, that is to say, when a state will exhibit balancing behaviour, or, conversely, to attempt to join the potential hegemon on terms as advantageous as possible, in other words, when it will exhibit bandwagoning behaviour.

Assume an international system. Within this system three categories of states can be distinguished. The first category consists of the powers that make up the 'poles' of the system. In this case there are two poles, the states g and h. It holds for both superpowers that they can destroy one another, and that they also have the capacity to defend their territory in case of an attack by the other.[15] The second category of states consists of the great powers, which again is made up of two states, i and j. If the two of them were to manage to combine their power one way or another, then they would constitute a pole in the international system too. For the moment, however, the situation is such that neither i nor j has a sufficient deterrent or defence. If they were to succeed in conducting a common defence, then in time they would be able to defend their territory against the superpowers. Here, however, it is a question of all or nothing. They are not able to bargain about the level of their contribution to the common defence. Only if i and j dedicate all available resources to the common defence, can they succeed. The third category of states is made up of the small powers, k, l, m, etc., etc. These states experience the advantages and disadvantages of the activities the states in the other two categories develop in their attempts to strengthen their position in the international system, but they cannot significantly influence these activities.

Assume, moreover, that the distance between g, on the one hand, and the neighbouring countries i and j, on the other hand, is greater than the distance between h, on the one hand, and i and j, on the other hand. With the result that g is, as it were, the natural ally of i and j (see Chapter 4, Section I). Within the international system, h is the power in the ascendant, and if this trend continues, will begin to pose a threat for the continued independence of both i and j in the near future. The history of the relations between the neighbouring countries i and j is one of age-old rivalry and violent conflict. Now each of them faces the decision whether it will try to form a counterweight against h together with its old rival, or to join h on as advantageous terms as possible.

From the point of view of costs, the most attractive option for i and j by far would be to induce g to notify h that it would use its deterrent against the latter were it to commit aggression against either i or j. In view of the enormous financial advantages, i and j would be prepared to put up with the extreme degree of dependence on g that this development would entail. The insoluble problem with this option would be, however, that i and j could never be sure that g would attach so much importance to their continued existence that it would indeed be prepared to run the risk of its own destruction by using its deterrent against h in order to avenge the latter's attack on i and j. (This uncertainty would obviously only increase, the stronger h's position in the international system became.) To this must be added that g, as one of the poles in the international system, would be inclined to get itself mixed up in geopolitical adventures, which might hurt its credibility (see Chapter 4, Section II). The only thing i and j could really count on, is that g would be prepared to contribute to their defence if h were actually to attack. This contribution, however, would not be sufficient to enable either i or j, if need be, to withstand h's attack on its own.

In view of these considerations, i and j both reach the conclusion that it will depend on their own efforts whether they will be able to build up a credible defence against h. If they were indeed to succeed in doing so, then that would be the outcome they would value most. However costly such an undertaking may be, they at least preserve their independence. If, for whatever reason, they could not achieve a common defence, then the most attractive option for each of them would be to be the only one to reach a settlement with h. Not only on account of their long-standing rivalry, but also because, if only one of them were to reach an agreement with h, the conditions would no doubt be more favourable than if both were to conclude an agreement with *h*. But *i*, as well as *j*, strongly prefers this last outcome to the outcome of having to face *h* alone, since this would mean its reduction to the status of a client-state. In short, *i* and *j* find themselves in the same strategic situation as the hunters in Rousseau's Stag Hunt.[16]

In the Stag Hunt, it seems obvious that *i* and *j* decide to balance *h*. But this Pareto-optimal outcome is less natural than is supposed most of the time. As I have already argued in Chapter 5, the Stag Hunt can pose a problem of collective action too. This would be the case if incurring the sucker-payoff were to have disastrous consequences. It will be clear that, in the situation I have outlined above, this condition is satisfied. The costs attached to the outcome that either *i* or *j* alone tries to balance *h* are indeed considerable. In these circumstances, *i* and *j* will decide that it is more prudent to try and jump on *h*'s bandwagon, than to attempt to balance *h*. Only in the situation where *i* and *j* were to be very, very sure that the other would indeed decide to reach the Pareto-optimal outcome, would they be prepared to do so too. However, two factors that I have built into my story make it very difficult for them to acquire the necessary certainty. The first is the fact that there is a premium on the outcome of being the only state to reach a settlement with *h*. Combined with the age-old rivalry between *i* and *j*, this means that the situation in which *i* and *j* find themselves strongly resembles that of states caught up in a 'real' security dilemma. In the sense that mutual distrust leads to, as Jervis put it (see Section I), 'a relationship of higher conflict than is required by the objective situation', and so provides an incentive to reach an agreement with *h* as quickly as possible. The second factor that causes uncertainty, is that the stability of the international system is threatened by the rise of *h*. Both *i* and *j* realize that an important consequence of such an unstable environment is that the shadow of the future becomes shorter, while their common defence against *h* is precisely a matter that cannot be arranged from one day to the next. All in all, these uncertainties increase the probability that both *i* and *j* decide to join *h*, notwithstanding the fact that each of them places the highest value on the outcome that they both decide to balance *h*.

Assume now that *g* separately makes an offer to *i* and *j* to contribute to their defence to such an extent that, if necessary, either *i* or *j* would be able to undertake the defence of the territory of both states against an attack by *h* on its own. Assume also that *g* is prepared to commit itself in this in such a way (for instance, by giving hostages), that *i* and *j* can rely on *g* actually participating in the defence in case of armed aggression by *h*. Assume moreover that if an alliance between either *g* and *i*, or *g* and *j* is concluded, this will be sufficient to keep *h* from attacking *i* and *j*. In these circumstances, the most attractive outcome to *i*, as well as *j*, would be to succeed in somehow saddling the other with the defence against *h*, and not to contribute itself. Thanks to the efforts of *g* and the other state, it then could allow itself to adopt a policy of neutrality, and thus preserve its freedom of action. At the same time, *i* and *j* realize all too well that if both of them, in trying to become a free rider, reject *g*'s offer, this will lead to the worst possible outcome. In that case, each of them prefers the outcome that it alone accepts *g*'s offer, and with the help of the latter provides for the defence against *h*. But the outcome they prefer even more is that both accept *g*'s offer, and contribute to the defence against *h*. The preference order of the four possible outcomes by *i* and *j* accords with that of the players in the Game of Chicken, and just like the players in that game, *i* and *j* will choose to cooperate with one another (and *g*). They will choose to balance *h*, although each of them attaches a higher value to the outcome that it is the sole defector.

C. Collective Security

As I have already explained in my introduction to this chapter, the individuals that are part of an anarchical system, compared to individuals that belong to a hierarchical system, will more readily use violence against one another, and on a larger scale, when they attempt to settle their mutual conflicts. From the foregoing sections it may have become clear, too, that this property definitely holds good for the international system. It will come as no great surprise, therefore, that in the course of time several schemes have been advanced to reduce, or even to eliminate, the use of violence in the international system. A collective security system is generally regarded to be the most promising of these schemes.

A system of collective security is a special kind of treaty of mutual assistance. Special, because the members of a collective security system commit themselves to regard any act of aggression against a state that is a member of the system, as an act of aggression against themselves, and to come to the assistance of that state under all circumstances and regardless of who is the aggressor (equally so if the aggressor is a member of the system of collective security too). To the members of the collective security system the motto applies: 'one for all, and all for one'.[17]

States that set up a collective security system hope to ensure that a state contemplating committing an act of aggression against any one of them will refrain from doing so because it realizes that, were it actually to attack, it would automatically find a confederacy of states against it powerful enough to punish this act of aggression immediately. A properly functioning collective security system provides the participating states with the certainty that power political considerations no longer play a role with respect to matters of peace and security. How realistic is it, however, to expect that states will ignore the power political aspect in precisely those matters that really affect the core of their existence?

According to Hans Morgenthau, a collective security system can only be effective if the following three conditions are satisfied:

> (1) the collective system must be able to muster at all times such overwhelming strength against any potential aggressor or coalition of aggressors that the latter would never dare challenge the order defended by the collective system; (2) at least those nations whose combined strength would meet the requirement under (1) must have the same conception of security which they are supposed to defend; (3) those nations must be willing to subordinate their conflicting political interests to the common good defined in terms of the collective defense of all member states. (Morgenthau 1978ed., p. 418)

Morgenthau does not wish to preclude the possibility that, in a given situation, all three conditions would be satisfied, 'the odds, however, are strongly against such a possibility' (Morgenthau 1978ed., p. 418). But this is putting things in too charitable a light. The first condition implies that, at any rate, the states constituting the poles of the international system must belong to the system of collective security. Perhaps this condition may be realized, but it is impossible that this will also be the case with the second and third conditions. The latter, after all, imply that the poles of the international system must identify themselves with the status quo to a very large extent. This identification must also be so complete that, even where a pole belongs to the dissatisfied powers itself, it would nevertheless be prepared to defend that status quo, even at the expense of it relative power position – as where the burdens of the defence of the status quo would fall disproportionally heavily on the shoulders of the dissatisfied power.

The credibility of a collective security system stands or falls with the automatic and immediate punishment of possible aggression. However, the states participating in such a system will always attempt to keep their options open, and try to shift the costs of actual intervention on to one another, with the result that, time and again, one state or another will come to the conclusion that, in view of the dissensions between the members of the collective security system, its own attempt to settle a conflict with another state that has been dragging on for quite some time by means of arms, will not be punished by the members of the system, and consequently will actually proceed to do so.

As a matter of fact there is a fourth condition that has to be met if a collective security system is to function successfully. This condition does not make things easier either. Hans Morgenthau has pointed out that the states taking part in the collective security system ideally have to ask themselves only one simple question before proceeding to action, namely, 'who has committed aggression?' (Morgenthau 1978ed., p. 420). As I have, however, explained in the first section of this chapter, it is often not possible to give a simple answer to this simple question in situations that threaten to end in war, or actually do so. In this way also the automatism is undermined that would have to be the hallmark of a collective security system.

Myron Weiner concluded his article on irredentism in the Balkans during the first four decades of this century – which he dubbed the 'Macedonian syndrome' – with the observation that, 'the international community thus far [has not] been able to create an effective force capable of assuming the peace-keeping functions historically performed by hegemonic powers' (Weiner 1971, pp. 682–3). From the argument I developed in this section it will be clear that a system of collective security will also be unable to assume the peace-keeping functions of a hegemon, or, for that matter, a holder of the balance.

NOTES

1.　　Once again, this concerns a *methodological* question (see Chapter 2, Section IV, and Chapter 6, Section II). The decision to assign the explanatory principle to the state 'does not presume that (in international relations) states need always be the principal actors' (Gilpin 1981, p. 18).

2.　　Thomas Schelling calls this a situation in which 'pure violence' is being used. 'Pure violence ... appears, most conspicuously in relations between unequal countries, where there is no substantial military challenge and the outcome of military engagement is not in question' (Schelling 1966, p. 12).

3.　　More than two hundred years ago, Rousseau employed in his *A Lasting Peace through the Federation of Europe* the same kind of reasoning to explain why in an anarchical system wars occur. These are not the consequence of the wish to dominate the other (Morgenthau's *animus dominandi*), but of the fear of being dominated by the other:

It is quite true that it would be much better for all men to remain always at peace. But so long as there is no security for this, everyone, having no guarantee that he can avoid war, is anxious to begin it at the moment which suits his own interest and so forestall a neighbour, who would not fail to forestall the attack in his turn at any moment favourable to himself, so that many wars, even offensive wars, are rather in the nature of unjust precautions for the protection of the assailant's own possessions than a device for seizing those of others. (Rousseau 1761, 1917ed., pp. 78–9; cf. Waltz 1954, 1959ed., p. 180).

About 2100 years before Rousseau, the Athenian statesman Alcibiades went yet a step further. In the course of his speech in favour of sending an Athenian expedition to Sicily, he explained to the Athenian assembly that, 'the fact is that we have reached a stage where we are forced to plan new conquests and forced to hold on to what we have got, because there is a danger that we ourselves may fall under the power of others unless others are in our power' (Thucydides 1954ed., p. 379).

4. Japan and Germany have developed into so-called *trading nations*. Another possible specialization, which appears to be hardly profitable at all in the present international system, is that of the *warrior nation*. Joseph Schumpeter characterizes a *warrior nation* as follows:

> What *is* the crucial point is that in a warrior nation war is never regarded as an emergency interfering with private life; but, on the contrary, that life and vocation are fully realized *only* in war. In a warrior nation the social community is a war community. Individuals are never absorbed into the private sphere. ... For them, war was the only method for keeping alive, the only possible form of life in a given environment. (Schumpeter 1955 ed., pp. 25–6, emphasis in original; cf. also Keegan 1993, p. 189)

5. As is the title of an article by Colin S. Gray in *Foreign Policy* on the occasion of the SALT I treaty (Gray 1972/73).

6. With respect to the possible objection that in the longer term advantages and disadvantages would cancel each other out: it is not to be expected that, in such an uncertain situation as a war, the party that finds itself at a given moment in a disadvantaged position, will suffer this with equanimity, quietly confident that in the further course of the war, things will be set right again. Richard Smoke considered the asymmetries between states caught up in a conflict, an important cause of the escalation of this conflict. He identified possible asymmetries in respect of the power of the states involved (their capabilities), the behavioural options open to them, and the respective interests that are at stake (Smoke 1977, pp. 249–50).

7. See Smoke's definition of escalation, 'Escalation as the term is used in this book is not a homogeneous growth curve, nor a step of any foreordained magnitude, but *a step of any size that crosses a saliency*' (Smoke 1977, p. 32, emphasis in original – see also Dougherty and Pfaltzgraff 1990ed., pp. 359–60).

8. Arms races have been sub-divided into symmetrical and asymmetrical arms races (see, for example, Zinnes 1976, pp. 387–92). In the former, both parties attempt to increase their offensive capability, while in the latter, one party tries to improve its offensive capability, whereas the other attempts to weaken this offensive capability by improving its defensive capability. I shall not concern myself with this distinction any further.

9. As J.A. Hobson described himself at the start of his famous analysis of the causes of the imperialistic wars that took place at the end of the nineteenth and the beginning of the twentieth century (Hobson 1975ed., p. 48).

10. Cf. also the observation by Robert Jervis, 'The true state of the military balance can be determined only by war' (Rotberg and Rabb (eds) 1989, p. 107).

11. In his well-known essay 'Of the balance of power', David Hume argued that Great Britain could play the role of holder of the balance *vis-à-vis* the continental powers successfully, only if she showed herself to be moderate at all times, and constantly prepared to correct disturbances of the equilibrium (Hume 1985ed., pp. 339–41).

12. It is for this reason that, according to Schelling, 'pure' violence (see Section I) chiefly occurs at the end of a war, when matters are in fact already decided (Schelling 1966, p. 12).

13. Thomas Schelling is the first author who put this distinction between 'defence' and 'compellence' into words. In the case of defence, an individual attempts to prevent a certain kind of behaviour by the adversary. In the case of compellence, on the other

hand, an individual tries to force the opponent to behave in a particular kind of way (Schelling 1960, 1963ed.).

14.   Kenneth Waltz, too, has argued that the objective of deterrence, as well as of defence, is to dissuade the adversary from acting in a particular way. According to him, the difference between both strategies is that, 'in contrast to dissuasion by defence dissuasion by deterrence operates by frightening a state out of attacking, not because of the difficulty of launching an attack and carrying it home, but because the expected reaction of the attacked will result in one's own severe punishment' (Waltz 1981, pp. 4–5).

15.   Following John Mearsheimer's definition of a 'pole', 'to qualify as a pole in a global or regional system, a state must have a reasonable prospect of defending itself against the leading state in the system by its own efforts' (Mearsheimer 1990, p. 7).

16.   If the common defence against *h* had to be conducted almost entirely on the territory of one of the two states, say *j*, because it is nearer to *h*, then it becomes rather questionable whether *j* will indeed attach the highest value to the outcome of a successful common defence against *h*. In this situation, *j*'s first preference may very well be to accommodate *h*. Its preference order then becomes the same as that of a player in a Prisoner's Dilemma, with the result that both *i* and *j* will decide not to attempt to balance *h*, but to attempt to reach a settlement with the latter.

17.   Cf. Kissinger: 'Collective security defines no particular threat, guarantees no individual nation, and discriminates against none. It is theoretically designed to resist *any* threat to the peace, by whoever might pose it and against whomever it might be directed' (Kissinger 1994, p. 247, emphasis in original).

8. Decision Making and the Management of Conflict in Hierarchical Systems

I THE ESSENCE OF THE ORGANIZATION

A. Introduction

Since I shall be discussing decision making and the management of conflict in hierarchical systems in this chapter, and shall restrict my analysis to organizations or conglomerates of organizations (and then in particular government organizations), it seems to me to be a good thing to pause briefly at a strange inconsistency in the way in which the behaviour of people and that of organizations is talked about and evaluated, not only in small talk but also in scientific publications.[1] If people talk about the ways in which they take their decisions and process available information, then they are perfectly prepared to accept, indeed even to concur wholeheartedly, that these processes are regularly rather arbitrary in nature, and that they are accompanied by many failures of judgement. To put it somewhat differently, 'people' accept it as perfectly normal that 'people' act irrationally. For much the same reasons, many an economist or social scientist has rejected the rational actor model. This would leave no room for the irrational aspects of human behaviour. But then, it should surely be called remarkable that those very same people and scientists, with a few exceptions, as soon as they are discussing decision making and information processing by and within organizations – which, after all, can be little else than decision making and information processing by people within the context of organizations – apparently tacitly presume that there these processes could work out rationally. For, where organizations make mistakes – and 'everybody' knows that they make mistakes all of the time – then this is a source of amazement, of dismay, and even of outrage. Such a discrepancy in evaluation can point to little else than that they implicitly assume that, if organizations act 'irrationally', this must surely be an aberration. It would appear that they are under the impression that these mistakes and lapses could have been avoided one way or the other (usually meaning that the members of the organization ought to have refrained from subjugating the interests of the organization to their self-interest).

In this chapter, I shall attempt to demonstrate that organizations, groupings of human individuals, behave themselves just as 'normally' (in the sense used in this introduction) as 'ordinary' people. In the course of my argument, I hope to make clear that the behaviour of human individuals and that of organizations is subjected to the same mechanism – adaptation to the environment under conditions of uncertainty – and in this way to convey 'some feel for the confusion' that necessarily also accompanies decision making in the context of organizations (Allison 1971, p. 146).

B. The Essence of the Organization

In Chapter 6, Section III, I have explained that the explicit and implicit rules of the organization enable the human individuals taking part in it to decide what is the appropriate action in certain, mostly well-defined, circumstances. In this way, organizations provide 'information' to those taking part in them. By means of their rules, organizations structure the environment (or a part of it) of the human individuals concerned – internally, with respect to their mutual relations, as well as externally, with respect to their social and physical environment; where the amount of 'information' an organization contains, increases in proportion as the organization's capacity is greater. For, the greater the organization's capacity, the less attractive it becomes to the organization's members to increase the weight of their demand behaviour towards one another – for example, by breaking the existing rules of the organization – and, accordingly, the greater the predictability of their behaviour.

The 'simple' fact that participating in an organization increases the predictability of his existence, provides the human individual with a strong incentive to become a member of an organization. But, as I have pointed out before, predictability alone is not enough (see Chapters 2 and 3). In this respect 'information' cannot be considered apart from power either. In the end, the human individual's decision whether or not to participate in an organization, turns on his expectation whether the predictable environment offered by the organization will also lead to an increase in his power.

The foregoing observations on organizations as 'information' systems, do not imply that the moment a human individual joins an organization he trades in the viewpoints (theories) he has developed previously for those of the organization. They do imply that, the more the 'information' contained in the organization agrees with the perceptions the human individual has developed before joining the organization, the greater in his eyes will be the legitimacy of the organization, and, consequently, the greater his willingness to make himself familiar with (to internalize) the organization's system of explicit and implicit rules. The human individuals participating in the organization, *choose* to obey the rules of the organization, and, the greater the organization's legitimacy, the more probable it becomes that they will indeed do so, even if this would not agree with their immediate self-interest. As De Vree has observed:

> It is precisely the function of the rule's legitimacy to help ensure conformity even when such conformity would not agree with the agent's self-interest at a given moment. It should be emphasized here that no degree of legitimacy will ever be able to ensure complete conformity at any moment, for there will also be some agents to whom the costs of conforming to the rules at a given moment are so high that they cannot be neutralized by the rule's legitimacy, nor by sanctions. (De Vree 1982, p. 297)

To the degree that an organization's legitimacy is greater, the likelihood increases that the human individuals participating in it will be prepared to do things they would otherwise not have done. In proportion as the organization's legitimacy becomes greater, they will be more easily prepared to run the risk of specializing themselves, and, accordingly, the smaller will become their sensitivity to gaps in payoffs, with the result that they will be more readily prepared to cooperate actively with, or to acquiesce passively in, an attempt by another human individual belonging to the organization to increase his power. They develop, to put it another way, a certain degree of identification with, or loyalty to, the organization. This also means that, to the extent that the legitimacy of an organization is greater, the likelihood increases that the human individuals concerned will be willing to invest more of their power in the defence of the organization against external threats.

If I now, for the sake of clarity, for the moment leave out of consideration that the realization of the official goals of the organization can be considered to be a collective good, and that this implies that with respect to the provision of this good the organization's members exhibit a certain inclination to behave themselves as free riders (which inclination, by the way, decreases in proportion as the capacity and legitimacy of the organization are greater, see further Section III), and subsequently assume that the environment of the organization is stable, then the following positive feedback mechanism is implied by the argument developed in the previous paragraphs: the more the human individuals taking part in the organization are of the opinion that their participation contributes to an increase in their power, the greater the likelihood that they are prepared to invest still more of their power in the continued existence of the organization, and that the organization keeps on functioning effectively. Whereas, in the situation where the human individuals taking part in the organization regard it as being not very effective, the probability becomes higher that they are not prepared to invest even more of their power in the continued existence of the organization, and that, accordingly, it becomes less likely that the organization will function effectively in the future.[2] (In Section IV, I shall be going into the subject that things turn out to be completely different where the environment has experienced a drastic change).

Naturally, the extent to which the human individuals concerned will consider the organization to be legitimate also depends on the fact whether or not they are part of the organization's dominant coalition. It is the solution of the political process that previously took place between the members of the organization, which establishes what objectives may be pursued and what not, and what kinds of behaviour are permitted and what not.[3] This solution which, following Morton H. Halperin, I shall call the *essence of the organization* (Halperin 1974, p. 28), is by definition more valuable to the members of the dominant coalition than to the other human individuals taking part in the organization. The latter are at least uncommitted, and perhaps even hostile, to the existing solution. With the result that they will be more receptive to ideas about 'new' goals the organization ought to pursue, and about other rules that ought to be applied – in the expectation that through these innovations they will be able to strengthen their position *vis-à-vis* the members of the dominant coalition.

Theorem 14:
The lower the legitimacy of an organization in the eyes of the human individuals participating in it (or some of them), the higher the probability that these human individuals will be prepared to reject or change the existing goals and rules of the organization in favour of other goals and rules.

The essence of the organization, by the way, ought not to be equated with the official goals of the organization, as have been set down in charters of foundation, preambles, mission statements, etc., etc. While the essence of the organization relates to the actual functioning of the human individuals taking part in the organization, the official goals are about the ways in which their functioning may be justified. The latter refer to the ideological framework (the *discourse*, as this is called most of the time nowadays) of the organization. They provide the language in which the human individuals concerned may justify to one another, and to the outside world, their attempts to influence one another's behaviour with a view to increasing their power in the context of the organization.

II THE RESOLUTION OF 'POLITICAL' PROBLEMS

A. Introduction

The problems with which the human individuals participating in an organization are confronted, are of two kinds. On the one hand, there are problems for which there exist rules for solving them. On the other hand, there are problems for which there exist no such rules.[4] The last kind of problems I shall be referring to as 'political' problems. An important source of these political problems is the constantly recurring situation of a human individual taking part in the organization, in view of changes in his environment, being willing and able to increase the weight of his demand behaviour towards other human individuals participating in the organization. This situation can be the result of the human individual's realization that the policies of the organization have not been very successful thus far, of his perception that the organization's environment offers opportunities that have been insufficiently exploited until now, but also of his conception that he is inadequately compensated for his efforts compared to other human individuals. In this section, I shall be discussing the mechanism that provides the human individuals participating in the organization with the opportunity to resolve these political problems (and in this way are able to develop new rules).

B. Credibility as Criterion

In Chapter 7, Section I, I have explained that violence, because it can be so costly and unsettling, must be regarded to be the *ultima ratio* of power. From this it follows that the human individual, in view of the fact that the use of violence can be so costly and can lead to the large-scale destruction of 'information', will initially prefer to solve possible political problems in which other human individuals are involved, with the help of promises or threats of a non-violent nature (for instance, by holding out the prospect of monetary rewards or penalties, or of a gain or loss in credibility). Of course, the human individual's reticence to use violence will become greater to the degree that the system contains more 'information', and the legitimacy of the system is higher.

The foregoing implies that, in proportion as the capacity and the legitimacy of a system are greater, the human individuals participating in that system will go to greater lengths to protect the 'information' contained in the system. Another implication is that their preference for resolving political problems by relying on one another's credibility, instead of finding out whether these reputations for power are warranted or not, will also become stronger (putting to one side the question whether the pace with which the political process develops would leave them the time actually to do so; see also Chapter 4, Section II). The greater the capacity and legitimacy of a system, the more important credibility will be as a source of power to the human individuals belonging to that system. In this situation also the proposition applies – precisely as in a situation of mutual deterrence (see Chapter 7, Section I) – that, the more is in danger of being destroyed if a conflict gets out of hand, the more 'psychological' in character the relations between the adversaries will become. From this it follows, too, that the more 'theoretical' in character (as we may also call this) the environment will be in which human individuals have to solve their political problems, the more important guessing at the guesses of others will be to them, and the more likely that these guesses will begin to lead a life of their own, and, accordingly, the more tenuous will be the relationship between the human individuals' reputations for power and their 'real' positions of power.[5]

Theorem 15:
The greater the legitimacy of an organization, the higher the probability that a human individual participating in that organization will value the marginal utility of an additional unit of credibility *vis-à-vis* other human individuals taking part in the organization, more highly than the marginal utility of an additional unit of economic resources or of resources that should strengthen its ability to weaken or even destroy the power of those other human individuals.

Another implication of my argument is that, in proportion as the legitimacy of an organization becomes greater, the likelihood increases that the human individuals taking part in it will assess changes in the organization's environment, or in their existing relationships of mutual dependence, in the light of the possible consequences these changes may have for their credibility. As has become clear in Chapter 2, an individual is only able to observe things because it has 'theories' that tell the individual what is important, and what not. A human individual participating in an organization learns in the course of time, without having actually to be aware of this learning process,[6] that everything turns on his credibility *vis-à-vis* the other individuals taking part in the organization. In this way, the human individual's credibility gradually becomes *the* criterion with the help of which he assesses the changes in his environment – where the proposition applies that the greater the organization's legitimacy in the eyes of the human individual, the greater the likelihood that he will learn that his credibility *vis-à-vis* the other human individuals belonging to the organization, is the criterion by which to assess changes in his environment. He learns to determine his reaction to changes in his environment in the light of his answer to the question whether his credibility is threatened or, on the contrary, strengthened by these changes, or that these changes have no consequences for his credibility. If he reaches the conclusion that his credibility is indeed at stake, then he will in reaction attempt to increase the weight of his demand behaviour towards other human individuals participating in the organization. But if he decides that his credibility is not at stake, then he will not act on this information (he will ignore it).

From the foregoing argument, it can subsequently be deduced that, where a human individual participating in an organization needs the active cooperation or passive acquiescence of other human individuals participating in the organization (in other words: is dependent upon them) to resolve any problem relevant to the organization but not covered by its rules, this human individual will first have to acquire a reputation for fulfilling his promises and executing his threats for himself. It is irrelevant whether the human individual personally redeems these promises, or carries out these threats, or that others (perhaps inadvertently) do that for him. A human individual taking part in an organization will have to possess a certain degree of credibility himself, ever to be able to build a dominant coalition in order to solve a problem not covered by the rules of the organization.

In this connection, we should not lose sight of the fact that collective behaviour is as much the result of the passivity of many as of the activities of some (see also Chapter 6, Section I). A human individual participating in an organization, who succeeds in solving a problem not covered by the rules of the organization, without consulting anybody or without anybody challenging this solution, has also been able to 'build' a dominant coalition. Such a situation, by the way, will only come about in the case of very unimportant, 'technical' problems, that is to say, problems one dares to leave to the experts.[7] It will be clear that this kind of 'coalition' will be dependent on the dominant coalition that makes possible the functioning of the organization. It is also easy to see that, because the human individuals involved did not invest much in a solution of this kind, this 'coalition' will more easily be challenged in the event of changed circumstances, and that the political process following on these challenges will reach a solution more quickly.

The foregoing argument may be summarized as follows: whatever the objectives the various human individuals participating in the organization may wish to achieve – be it the satisfaction of the most vulgar self-interest, the realization of the loftiest of ideals, or the solution of a merely 'technical' problem not covered by the rules of the organization – none of them will ever be able to achieve these objectives without having first acquired the reputation of being able to fulfil his promises, and to execute his threats.

C. Five Factors Again

Assumption 5*:
The environment of the human individuals taking part in an organization has experienced a disturbance, such that at least one of those human individuals changes his behaviour to the extent that the weight of his demand behaviour towards one or more of the other human individuals participating in the organization increases.

The need to protect or to strengthen his credibility, provides the human individual participating in an organization with a viewpoint enabling him to decide how to react in the situation where he is confronted with a political problem. If the human individual decides that this political problem does not affect his credibility, then he will ignore it. If he reaches the conclusion that his credibility is indeed at stake (either positively, or negatively), then he will take action, either by trying to 'neutralize' the political problem (by passing it on to other human individuals in the organization, or, if this is not feasible, by shelving it), or by attempting to solve it. His decision whether to ignore the political problem, or to take action on it, appears to depend on the following five factors (cf. Chapter 3, Section III):

1. *The relevance of the political problem.* The greater the relevance of the political problem to the human individual's credibility, the higher the probability that he will take action; and, conversely, the less important the political problem, the greater the likelihood that he will ignore it.
2. *The expected (alternative) costs involved.* The higher the anticipated costs of taking action on the political problem (in terms

of gaining access to other human individuals taking part in the organization, and inducing them to cooperate actively with, or to acquiesce passively in, the human individual's attempt to maximize his credibility), compared to the expected costs of ignoring it, the greater the likelihood that the human individual will indeed ignore it. Conversely, the lower the expected costs of taking action, compared to the anticipated costs of ignoring the political problem, the more likely it becomes that he will take action.

3. *The power of the human individual vis-à-vis the other human individuals taking part in the organization, and the extent to which he is familiar with the existing explicit and implicit rules of the organization.* The more powerful the human individual believes himself to be compared to the other human individuals participating in the organization, and the more familiar he believes himself to be with the rules of the organization, the higher the probability that he will take action on the political problem. Whereas, conversely, in proportion as he believes himself to be relatively less powerful, and to be more unfamiliar with the rules of the organization, the likelihood increases that he will ignore the political problem.

4. *The amount of non-reusable power the human individual has invested in the existing solution (in relation to the amount of power the human individual has compared to the other human individuals taking part in the organization).* The more non-reusable power a human individual has invested in the existing solution (for example, by having specialized himself further and further), the higher the probability that he will ignore the political problem; and, conversely, the less the human individual has thus invested, the greater the likelihood that he will take action on it.

5. *The legitimacy of the existing solution.* The greater the legitimacy of the existing solution (the more the human individual believes the existing solution to have contributed to his power), the higher the probability that the human individual will ignore the political problem. Whereas, conversely, the smaller the legitimacy of the existing solution, the greater the likelihood that he will take action on it (cf. theorem 14).[8]

D. A Typology of Reaction Patterns

On the basis of the argument I have been expounding in this section thus far, the following typology of reaction patterns to a political problem may be constructed (see also Figure 8.1).

A human individual who has worked his way up in the organization, and now belongs to its most powerful members (regardless whether he belongs to the dominant coalition or not), and who has invested relatively much of his power in the existing solution, will adopt a noncommittal attitude if he is confronted with attempts to resolve a political problem.[9] In proportion as he has acquired more power within the organization in the course of the years, the probability becomes higher that he will reach the conclusion that the marginal addition to his power that would be entailed by the possible successful solution of a political problem, will not outweigh the expected costs and risks. Only in the case where he expects that solving the political problem involves almost no costs and hardly any risks, will he be prepared to put a part of his credibility on the line in an attempt to resolve this political problem.

Figure 8.1: A typology of reaction patterns

	Investment in existing solution			
	high		low	
	Legitimacy		Legitimacy	
Power	high	low	high	low
high	U	U	I	
middle	U	I	E	D
low		D	E	D

Key
U = uncommitted behaviour
I = ideological behaviour
D = disinterested behaviour
E = enthusiastic behaviour

The reaction pattern I have outlined above, does not so much apply to a human individual who occupies a powerful position in the organization, but who has invested little in the existing solution (someone who, in Dutch civil service lingo, has been 'parachuted' in the top of the organization). The latter's behaviour will be more in accord with that of a human individual taking part in the organization who has invested much of his power in the existing solution, but who still does not belong to the most powerful individuals in the organization. To such a person, the gains of investing part of his credibility in an attempt to achieve the resolution of a political problem, will more readily outweigh the costs and risks that may be involved in trying to do so. He will try to maximize his credibility by championing a particular solution to a certain political problem, naturally in the expectation (the hope?) that the solution advocated by him will be successful. Whether it concerns large or small political problems is of less relevance. In a certain sense, such an individual behaves himself as an 'ideologist'. He is continually busy propagating the solution advocated by him, and vehemently denouncing the 'fatal' consequences of a 'wrong' decision; all this, of course, in terms of the official goals of the organization.[10]

As far as the behaviour of a human individual belonging to the powerless members of the organization is concerned, the crucial variable is his assessment of the legitimacy of the organization. Everything turns on the extent to which he expects that trying to solve a political problem, and to make the necessary investments, may contribute to an increase in his power. A human individual who has not managed to leave the bottom ranks of the organization's hierarchy in all the years of his participation in the organization, and a human individual who expects, when joining the organization, that he will not be able to leave these ranks, will adopt an attitude of disinterestedness with respect to attempts to solve problems relevant to the organization but not covered by its rules. He has either learned, or realizes, that it will be useless to try and solve such a problem. The only exception being, to a certain extent, political problems that touch upon his personal well-being, such as a rise in wages, or his dismissal.[11] Such disinterested behaviour will also be exhibited by a human individual who finds himself in the lowest ranks of the hierarchy, and who has been forced to participate in the organization (such as, for instance, a conscripted soldier). As opposed to this, a human individual at the bottom of the hierarchy who expects that taking part in the organization will increase his power, in his enthusiasm will be prepared to invest a part of his power in attempts to solve problems not covered by the rules of the organization. (Although this human individual, because he is still rather powerless *vis-à-vis* the other human individuals participating in the organization, will as yet not allow himself ideological behaviour).

In the light of the above, it becomes conceivable that it may happen that all the human individuals taking part in an organization support a particular policy that is supposed to resolve a problem relevant to the organization but not covered by its rules, although all of them entertain objections to this policy. The reason for this is that all of them expect to increase their credibility by supporting this, in their eyes objectionable, policy. This implies that this phenomenon, which already has been observed so many times and censured in the fiercest of terms, need not be a reflection of a frivolous, unthinking attitude of *après nous le déluge* on the part of the human individuals concerned, but may equally well be the manifestation of their efforts to protect their reputation for power, precisely with an eye to the future! In the latter case, they merely have fallen into, what the historian James Thomson has named, the 'effectiveness trap'.[12]

E. The Power of Argument

As I have regularly been emphasizing in the course of this book, in the empirical domain 'information' is inextricably linked up with power. This implies that in daily life human individuals will not be interested all that much in, what Bolzano has called, *statements-in-themselves* (see Popper 1982ed.b, pp. 180–82). They will not only be interested in the message, but also in the messenger who brings it; the messenger gains in importance at the expense of the message, to the degree that according to the human individuals more seems to be at stake. This also holds true for human individuals who participate in an organization. The more relevant they consider a particular political problem to be, the less value they will attach to arguments as a means of solving this problem. They will only be prepared to resolve a political problem solely by means of argument in the case where they consider it to be a comparatively unimportant, esoteric, 'technical' question. In all other cases, arguments mainly serve to legitimize the positions they take up with respect to the possible solutions of this political problem. This means that in the majority of cases in which the human individuals taking part in an organization are confronted with a problem not covered by the rules of the organization, they will be less interested in the arguments that are advanced to solve the problem than in the reputation of power of those who bring them up. Another implication is that the greater the messenger's credibility, the less important the quality – in terms of internal and external consistency (see Chapter 2, Section III) – of his arguments. This signifies as well that – in the situation where there exist conflicting proposals how to resolve a particular political problem – the higher the level to which a conflict within the organization will escalate with respect to the solution of this problem, the less value the adversaries will attach to arguments as a means to resolve it.

In contrast to the less powerful members of an organization, the most powerful members need to invest less of their power and time in inventing arguments in support of the solution of a political problem advanced by them. Moreover, they need to pay comparatively less attention to the quality of their arguments. It is easy to see that, in contrast to the less powerful members of the organization, they would also have less time available to do so. In the context of organizations, too, demand behaviour is focused on the most powerful members of the system (see Chapter 4, Section II). After all, these are the ones with the reputation for getting things done, and their amount of available time will only become less to the extent that the pace of the political processes in which they take part becomes faster. Conversely, it will be clear that, comparatively speaking, the organization's less powerful members have more time to invent arguments for or against a particular solution of a political problem, and to pay attention to the quality of these arguments.

Theorem 16:
Working under the assumption that in an organization various human individuals advance more or less contradictory proposals for the resolution of a problem relevant to the organization but not covered by its rules, then the following applies: the less powerful the proponents of a particular proposal for the solution of this problem *vis-à-vis* the other human individuals participating in this political process, the more of their power, as compared to the latter, they will employ in inventing arguments in support of the solution advanced by them, and the less likely it becomes that this solution will be adopted.

In an unfinished note on his plans for revising *On War*, presumably written in 1830, which was found among his papers, Carl von Clausewitz, in a certain passage between the lines, gave expression to his expectation that in the future greater weight would be attached to the quality of argument with regard to discussions on strategy. He wrote:

Yet when it is not a question of acting oneself but of persuading others in discussion, the need is for clear ideas and the ability to show their connection with each other. So few people have yet acquired the necessary skill at this that most discussions are a futile bandying of words; either they leave each man sticking to his own ideas or they end with everyone agreeing, for the sake of agreement, on a compromise with nothing to be said for it. (Clausewitz 1989ed., p. 71)

The purport of the argument I have developed in this section, is that Clausewitz's expectation will never be fulfilled as long as decisions on strategy may decide the fate of nations.

III THE LOGIC OF BUREAUCRATIC ACTION

A. Success as a By-Product

The picture of the organization that should emerge on the basis of my observations in the foregoing sections, is one of the organization as a collection of human individuals all attempting to maximize their power in the context of the organization, without concerning themselves too much with the realization of the official goals of the organization while doing so. Also, it should be clear from my discussion that their concern for this collective good only decreases in proportion as more human individuals participate in the organization. The latter proposition is in agreement with the conclusions that follow from Mancur Olson's *logic of collective action* (Olson 1965, 1971ed.). In the first part of this section, I shall briefly be going into the relationship between the general behavioural theory I have been expounding in this book, and Olson's logic of collective action.

Olson defines a collective good purely on the basis of non-excludability. In his view a collective good is 'any such good such that, if any person X_i in a group $X_1,..., X_i,..., X_n$ consumes it, it cannot feasibly be withheld from the others in that group' (Olson 1965, 1971ed., p. 14). It is easy to see that the realization of the official goals of an organization, as the common interest of the human individuals taking part in it, is covered by this definition. The core proposition in Olson's book is that in proportion as the number of human individuals in a group increases, it becomes less likely that they spontaneously will act to achieve their common interests. This holds true *even* in the situation that there is 'unanimous agreement in a group about the common good and the methods of achieving it' (Olson 1965, 1971ed., p. 2). In the context of organizations, this proposition implies that, to the degree that the number of human individuals taking part in an organization increases, the probability becomes lower that each single one of them will be prepared to contribute spontaneously to the realization of the official goals of that organization. The latter will only be the case in organizations with a very limited membership. In all other cases, the human individuals concerned will only be prepared to contribute to the realization of the organization's official goals if the organization also provides them with *selective incentives*. That is to say, that the organization holds out to each of its members the prospect of rewards and punishments from which other members can be excluded (Olson 1965, 1971ed., p. 51).[13] (It will be clear that, in the terms I have been using in this book, the greater the capacity and the legitimacy of the organization, the more powerful these selective incentives can be.) In this way, the realization of the official goals of the organization becomes a *by-product* of the various actions performed by its membership.

But first I shall have to address the problem that Olson himself believes that his logic of collective action does not apply to the behaviour of the employees of an organization (Olson 1965, 1971ed., pp. 6–7). To my mind, this belief follows from the fact that Olson is not sufficiently alive to the possibility that the production of collective goods can be the unintended social consequence of purposeful individual behaviour. Like so many authors on this subject, Olson reduces collective behaviour, unknowingly (and unintentionally?), to *political* collective behaviour. That is to say, to collective behaviour aimed at influencing government policy, for instance in order to receive certain subsidies, to promote particular legislation, or to protect existing negotiation positions. Only if we adopt such a narrow interpretation of collective behaviour, it may possibly make sense in certain cases to restrict the group of human individuals profiting from the collective good, to those who have set up the organization to further their common interest through government intervention, and to exclude that organization's employees from that group. However, if we do not wish to make this reduction – and I do not see any reason why we should make it – then this distinction appears to be irrelevant.

An important implication of my more general approach to collective behaviour, is that the production of collective goods need not always be so costly and problematical as is usually supposed in the literature on collective behaviour. Human individuals, including those who participate in an organization, daily produce collective goods, without a hitch, and more or less as a matter of course, often without their being aware of doing so (this happens, for instance, when they play their radio too loudly, or when they pollute the environment, but also when they lay out a garden, the sight of which can be enjoyed by neighbours and passersby).

With regard to the collective good 'the realization of the official goals of the organization', the following appears to apply. The most powerful members of the organization, it is true, are too occupied with protecting their credibility to busy themselves with its production, and many members at the bottom of the hierarchy will show no interest in producing it, but the 'ideologists' and 'parachutists', as well as the organization's new members for whom the organization's legitimacy is (still) high, will occupy themselves with the question what policies the organization ought to adopt to produce this collective good. However, it applies to them, too, that they are not concerned about the organization's fate because of their attachment to its official goals (although this possibility cannot be excluded in the case of new, enthusiastic members), but because they expect to be able to increase their credibility by exhibiting this behaviour. It also holds true for them that the realization of the common interest is a by-product of their attempts to adapt to their environment as successfully as possible.

The logic of bureaucratic action I have outlined above, implies also that an organization, exactly like all kinds of collective behaviour, can be successful – in this case in terms of the official goals of the organization – without any of the human individuals participating in it making it his aim to realize these official goals. To paraphrase Adam Smith's famous passage on the workings of the invisible hand:

> The members of an organization intend only their own gain, and they are in this, as in many other cases, led by an invisible hand to promote an end which was no part of their intentions. Nor is it always the worse for the organization that it was no part of it. By pursuing their own interests they frequently promote that of the organization more effectually than when they really intend to promote it. (cf. Smith 1979ed.b, I, p. 456)

B. An Instable Solution

An organization can be regarded as an oligopoly with leaders and followers. In an oligopoly of this type, the most powerful members of the system, the market leaders, determine the price – in the terminology I have adopted in this book, the solution of the political process – but within the bounds of this solution the less powerful members are free to pursue their own policies. Moreover, the most powerful members of an organization behave towards one another like oligopolists would do.

The solution of a political process leading to an oligopoly is not stable, in the sense that, as far as the market leaders are concerned, there is little room for compensating behaviour (see Chapter 6, Section I). For this reason an oligopoly is, what Michael Nicholson has called, an 'actor-dominant system' (Nicholson 1989, 1990ed., p. 116). If one of the oligopolists manages to increase or to decrease the weight of his demand behaviour, then a new round in the political process is on. It is for this reason that, in the words of Mancur Olson:

> each firm warily watches other firms for fear they will attempt to drive it out of the industry. Each firm must, before it takes any action, consider whether it will provoke a 'price-war' or 'cut-throat' competition. This means that each firm ... must be sensitive to the other firms in the group and consider the reactions they may have to any action of its own. (Olson 1965, 1971ed., p. 42)

But this will not come as a surprise. After all, it is precisely the most powerful members of a system who are the most dependent upon one another.

In this way too, it becomes apparent that the stability of the existing solution influences the probability that an individual will be able and willing to increase or to decrease the weight of its demand behaviour towards other individuals in the system, as well as the likelihood that the individual's behaviour will induce those other individuals, in their turn, to strengthen or weaken the intensity of their demand behaviour. As the above quotation taken from Olson has already indicated, in an oligopoly there is room for the market leaders to bargain about the conditions under which they will be prepared to continue their mutual cooperation in the field of prices and market shares. In a perfectly competitive market, however, it is out of the question that the firms operating in it could ever bargain about the terms of their mutual cooperation. The latter find themselves in, what Nicholson has dubbed, a 'parametric' system; a system in which 'no single actor can significantly alter his environment' (Nicholson 1989, 1990ed., p. 116).

An oligopolist exhibits 'strategic behaviour'. He realizes that an increase or a decrease in the weight of his demand behaviour towards the other oligopolists will have consequences for the intensity of their attempts to influence him, and by means of negotiations about prices and market shares he attempts to achieve a result that is as favourable as possible. As opposed to this, a producer in a perfectly competitive market adopts the same attitude as the powerless individuals in an organization who do not expect to leave the bottom ranks of that organization. Such a producer exhibits so-called *Cournot*-behaviour (after the mathematician Augustin Cournot, who was the first to characterize this behaviour). He considers the behaviour of the other producers to be fixed, and expects that an increase or a decrease in the weight of his demand behaviour towards them will have no effect on the weight of their demand behaviour towards him. In an environment like this, there is little use in bargaining about prices and market shares. As Buchanan and Tullock have observed: 'Insofar as markets are competitive, little scope for bargaining exists ... The individual buyer or seller secures a "net benefit" or "surplus" from exchange, but the conditions of exchange, the terms of trade cannot be influenced substantially by its own behavior' (Buchanan and Tullock 1962, 1965ed., pp. 103–4).

Whether there will be room for the individuals belonging to a particular system to bargain about the conditions of their (continued) cooperation, has everything to do with the fact whether this (continued) cooperation could also be established with other individuals belonging to the system without too much difficulty. This depends on the degree of stability of the existing solution. The less stable the existing solution, the smaller the number of individuals with which cooperation is possible, and the more room there is for bargaining about the terms of cooperation. This result agrees with the proposition I have formulated in Chapter 4, Section II, that, to the extent that the number of possible contracting parties decreases, credibility will play a more important role in the relations of the individuals concerned. Where are reputations more useful than in negotiations? The result is also in agreement with my conclusion in Chapter 4, Section III, that the more individuals are dependent upon one another, the more they will try to influence one another's behaviour.

From the foregoing it follows that, as far as a market of perfect competition is concerned, there exists no room for the producers to bargain about the conditions of their mutual cooperation. On the other hand, in an organization, as a result of the far-reaching division of labour, there is plenty of room to bargain for the human individuals taking part in it (which is not to say that all will do so, see my typology of reaction patterns), not only because of the degree of specificity of the tasks the human individuals perform in the organization, but also, and mainly, because of the indispensable system of explicit and implicit rules that establishes this division of labour – the purport of which is often to indicate who has to cooperate with whom in order to reach what objective. It will go without saying that these ample opportunities for strategic behaviour constitute an added inducement for the 'psychologization' of the relations between the human individuals belonging to the organization.

IV THE ADAPTABILITY OF ORGANIZATIONS

A. Adapting to a Stable Environment

In my discussion of the behaviour of human individuals who participate in an organization, I have until now assumed that their environment is not too volatile. I have only in passing noted in Section III that the extent to which their environment is experiencing disturbances greatly influences the likelihood that they – and, consequently, the organization – will be able to adapt to that environment successfully. The relationship between the stability or instability of the environment, and the possibility of successful adaptation, is the topic of this section. In this connection, I shall be examining two situations. The first relates to an organization that has only recently been set up, and where the human individuals belonging to it try to maintain themselves in an environment that experiences only minor disturbances. The second situation relates to an organization that has been successful, and where the human individuals taking part in it are unexpectedly confronted with a fundamental change in their environment. In my analysis, I shall be dealing mainly with the implications of my earlier conclusion (see Section II) that the criterion by which the members of an organization assess the relevance of disturbances in their environment is the possible effects of these disturbances on their own credibility, for the way in which, and the extent to which, an organization is able to change its policies.

First I have to emphasize, however, that it is perfectly possible that an organization will not be successful, that is to say, that it will not be able to increase the power of the human individuals taking part in it. On the one hand, because these human individuals simply lack the correct information to bring to a successful conclusion, by means of trial and error, the process of adapting to the environment (firms that go bankrupt because nobody wants to buy their products, clubs that are dissolved because of a lack of interest, etc., etc.). On the other hand, because the environment is to such an extent unpredictable that it becomes impossible for the human individuals concerned to structure it (putting to one side the fact that, in proportion as the environment is more unpredictable, the likelihood decreases that they will want to specialize themselves for the benefit of the organization).

Assumption 6:
The (physical and social) environment of the human individuals participating in the organization under consideration, experiences only minor disturbances.

Assume that an organization has recently been established. Within this organization a dominant coalition has come into being that has imposed a particular policy on the other individuals participating in the organization. Then the proposition holds that, to the extent that this policy has led to a more successful adaptation to the environment according to the human individuals taking part in the organization, the credibility of the members of the dominant coalition will be strengthened. Apparently, they are able to fulfil their promises. At the same time, the success of the policy of the dominant coalition involves a loss of credibility for the human individuals who have previously opposed this policy. This means that it becomes more likely that this policy will be continued. Also, the probability becomes higher, if the members of the dominant coalition were to advance proposals to solve other political problems, that these proposals will be accepted.

Conversely, if the human individuals participating in the organization consider this policy to be a failure, then this means a loss of credibility for the members of the dominant coalition, whereas the credibility of those who previously opposed this policy, becomes greater – perhaps even to such an extent that the latter are able and willing to increase the weight of their demand behaviour to a level of intensity leading to the disintegration of the dominant coalition. Afterwards a new dominant coalition may come into existence, which initiates a new policy that, in its turn, may or may not lead to a successful adaptation to the environment.

Such a change of power will more easily take place, the smaller the amount of non-reusable power the human individuals concerned have invested in the existing solution. Naturally, the latter is also a function of the speed with which the failure of the existing policy becomes apparent. The sooner this becomes clear, the less non-reusable power the human individuals taking part in the organization will have invested in the existing solution. The faster it becomes clear that a particular policy is unsuccessful, the less numerous the group of human individuals who would stand to lose comparatively much of their power, if the organization were to pursue another policy, and who, for this reason, would be prepared to defend the existing solution. In the very beginning, this group for the greater part consists of the (political) entrepreneurs who have spontaneously provided the collective good 'the organization' to the human individuals who have subsequently joined the organization. It will be true of the latter, the free riders, that the proven ineffectiveness of the organization will make it a not very attractive proposition to use part of their power to attack or defend the existing solution.

Generally speaking, the proposition holds that the sooner it becomes evident that the existing solution is not very successful, the higher the probability that the human individuals concerned – including those who have invested a relatively large amount of non-reusable power in this solution – will become indifferent with respect to the fate of the organization. Their indifference will only increase in proportion as it takes longer before a successful policy is found, and eventually will be so great that the organization will cease to exist for lack of interest.

We should take into account that it is entirely irrelevant whether the success or failure of an organization is 'really' being caused by the policy imposed by the dominant coalition. Success and failure may very well be the result of developments that are completely missed by the human individuals taking part in the organization. Moreover, it is often a very costly and lengthy affair to find out what are the 'real' causes of this success or failure, provided that these could be established unequivocally. All that matters is that a particular policy appears to be a success or a failure.

The process of adaptation by means of trial and error, which I have outlined above, will of course take its time. It will always take some time before it becomes clear to the human individuals concerned (or some of them) that a particular policy is not successful and ought to be revised, and this learning process will take longer in proportion as the environment is more favourable (see Chapter 3, Section I). Moreover, it will take some time to build a dominant coalition powerful enough *vis-à-vis* the other human individuals participating in the organization, to carry through a revision of policy. This process of coalition building will take longer in proportion as the current dominant coalition has invested more non-reusable power in the existing solution, and the legitimacy of the organization is greater. This is why an environment that experiences only minor disturbances – simply because it allows them more time – increases the likelihood that the human individuals taking part in the organization, by means of this process of error elimination, in the course of time, but not at any one moment, will hit upon the policy that will increase their power, and, accordingly, their chances of survival.

Theorem 17:
The fewer disturbances the (physical and social) environment of the human individuals participating in the organization under consideration experiences, the higher the probability that these human individuals, in the context of the organization, will be able to adapt successfully to this environment.

B. Adapting to a Drastically Altered Environment

Before I start my discussion of the most probable reaction to strong and sudden changes in the environment by the human individuals taking part in an organization that has been successful until then (in terms of an increase in their power), I should not fail to mention that the mechanism I have outlined above does not preclude the possibility that these human individuals remain completely oblivious to these changes, however violent and obvious these may appear to be to a Hobsonian 'disinterested spectator'. It is possible, although not very likely, that the human individuals concerned remain entirely ignorant of the great changes taking place in their environment (however important these changes appear to be 'objectively' for the continued existence of the organization), because these changes just do not fit in their existing system of information. It is conceivable, therefore, that the human individuals participating in the organization, in spite of drastically altered circumstances, will continue to exhibit their 'normal' behaviour, even though this behaviour has for the greater part become irrelevant, or even self-destructive.

Assumption 6*:
The initially stable (physical or social) environment of the human individuals participating in the organization under consideration, has experienced a fundamental change.

Although it is possible that a drastic change in their environment is not noticed by the human individuals belonging to the organization, it is, however, not very likely that this will indeed happen. Precisely because an organization is made up of a number of human individuals, the probability becomes higher that at least one of them will discover that the environment has experienced a fundamental change, with far-reaching consequences for the organization. In this respect the organization has the advantage over a single human individual trying to adapt to his environment successfully. This advantage is, however, more or less nullified by the greater amount of time and power the human beings concerned will have to invest before they will be able to change the organization's policies in view of the changed circumstances – where this amount will only become greater to the extent that the capacity and legitimacy of the organization are greater. For, the upshot of the argument I have developed thus far can be no other than that the more successful an organization has been in the past in the eyes of the human individuals taking part in it, the less likely it becomes that this organization will also function successfully in a drastically altered environment.

This negative relationship between successful specialization and poor flexibility is the result of three, self-reinforcing, tendencies. In the first place, that the more successful the dominant coalition's policy has been previously, the greater the credibility of the members of the dominant coalition *vis-à-vis* the other human individuals participating in the organization, and the more improbable it becomes that the latter will be able to topple the dominant coalition. (In the situation that the change only becomes manifest by degrees in the course of the years, the probability becomes higher that the dominant coalition, because of a gradual loss in credibility, can be overthrown and replaced by a new dominant coalition; see also Chapter 6, Section II.) In the second place, that the greater the organization's legitimacy, the more the human individuals taking part in it will have specialized themselves, and the more expensive it will become for them to adapt their behaviour to a changed environment.[14] In the third place, we should not forget that the greater the successes of the dominant coalition's policies have been, the more these will have increased the predictability of the environment of the human individuals belonging to the organization. This increase in predictability will have encouraged them to invest more of their power in long-term projects aimed at increasing their power (of course, in the context of organizations, these projects are aimed particularly at strengthening their credibility). This means that they will stand to lose more in the case of a change of policies, and, accordingly, it becomes more improbable that they will allow others taking part in the organization to change the existing policies.

The consequence of these tendencies is that the more successful an organization has been in the past, the more likely that the human individuals taking part in it will react to strong and sudden changes in their environment by continuing to do things in the ways they are used to do them, however pertinent these changes are in respect of the successful functioning of the organization. Of course, the organization's lack of success in this new and unfamiliar environment will not go unnoticed (as opposed to the, not very probable, situation that they fail to notice possible changes in their environment), but because the human individuals concerned have invested so much of their power in the existing solution that cannot be reused – in relation to the amount of power they have – they do not see how they may change the organization's existing policies.[15]

Theorem 18:

The higher an organization's legitimacy, the higher the probability that the human individuals taking part in it will react to a fundamental change in their environment by continuing to behave in the way they are used to.

If I subsequently preclude the possibility that the drastic changes in the environment lead to a more favourable environment – the human individuals concerned need to expend less effort in order to be able to maintain themselves – then the failure to adapt themselves will in the end result in the destruction of the organization. Likewise, the chances of a successful adaption to a 'new' environment are greater for an organization that has until then been less successful. The probability that the dissatisfied members of the organization will be able to replace the dominant coalition, and to initiate a new policy, becomes higher in proportion as the credibility of the members of the dominant coalition is lower, the human individuals taking part in the organization have specialized less, and have invested less in long-term projects.

C. The Adaptability of Government Organizations

After the foregoing, it will be clear that organizations are relatively insensitive to changes in their environment, and that this insensitivity only increases to the degree that these changes are of greater relevance to the existing solution making the organization's functioning possible (as I have pointed out before, small, 'technical' adaptations can take place without too much difficulty). Only after lengthy procedures, and with much difficulty, are organizations able to change policies, or to initiate new ones – and this will take more time and be more difficult in proportion as the organization's legitimacy is greater, and the human individuals taking part in the organization are more convinced that more of their power is at stake in the case of a change in policy. Also, the possibility cannot be precluded that previous successes will prevent the organization from adapting with some degree of success to a changed environment, however unsuccessful (irrelevant) current policy has become.

The latter conclusion is especially relevant for the 'behaviour' of organizations belonging to the set of organizations that succeed in maintaining themselves, one way or the other, to a greater or lesser extent, more or less explicitly, through involuntary exchange. Because of the worldwide, spectacular rise of the state as the regulatory agency of social and economic life at the national level during the nineteenth and twentieth centuries, government organizations without doubt make up the most conspicuous part of this set. On the basis of the state's monopoly of the legitimate use of violence, the human individuals taking part in government organizations, whether they are aware of this or not, have at their disposal a very effective instrument to increase their power, namely the levying of taxes.[16] If I further assume that the competition for available financial resources between government organizations will be just as fierce as the competition between firms for a share of the market, then the human individuals participating in government organizations will be less concerned with the dictate of reality (at least in the short term, eventually they will also not be able to ignore this dictate with impunity), than the human individuals taking part in organizations who are not able to fall back on the use of violence in their attempts to increase their power. Because government organizations have a *soft budget constraint*, as the economist János Kornai has called it, they will go bankrupt less quickly than private organizations (Kornai 1986, pp. 1697–8).

Thanks to the levying of taxes, and the sanctions connected with it in case the citizens of the state were to attempt to evade paying these taxes, the environment of human individuals participating in government organizations is more favourable than that of human individuals taking part in private organizations – leaving to one side, of course, the human individuals who are members of protective associations that have as yet not succeeded in establishing themselves as the dominant protective association in a given territory (as is the case with organized crime). To the latter the same situation applies in principle as to human individuals taking part in government organizations.[17] Although, naturally, there is the important difference that any member of the mafia, precisely because he does not participate in a dominant protective association, is less sure of his life than any government official, and, accordingly, is inclined to consume more and to invest less than a human individual belonging to a government organization.

The capability of levying taxes also implies that the human individuals participating in government organizations, compared to human individuals taking part in private organizations, have to expend less effort in trying to maintain themselves. If a consumer is not satisfied with the quality of a product of a particular firm, then he can go to another firm, or, in the case of a monopoly, decide not to buy the product (to boycott it). Things are different with the majority of the products of a government (it will be clear that this does not apply to the selective incentives government organizations provide to their employees). Even though the customer is dissatisfied with the quality of those products, he must, under the threat of violence, buy them. Albert Hirschman's *exit*-option is only rarely available to the customers of a government.[18]

The relative certainty of tax income implies that, generally speaking, the legitimacy, and, consequently, the capacity, of government organizations is higher than that of organizations having to acquire their income by means of voluntary exchange. The concomitant greater predictability of the (organizational) environment, means that government officials are even more prepared, compared to human individuals participating in private organizations, to specialize themselves, and willing to invest an even greater part of their power in long-term projects with a view to strengthening their credibility. The result is that they are even less prepared to tolerate challenges to the existing solution than human individuals taking part in private organizations. To put it briefly, government organizations are even more insensitive to changes in their environment, are even more inner directed, than are private organizations. (With the result that something like *fine tuning* the national economy is about the last thing that can safely be entrusted to government organizations.)

From the foregoing, it can also be deduced that the more of the national income is claimed by the government, the less the society in question is able to react successfully to drastic changes in its environment. In proportion as the government takes on more and more tasks, and provides more goods to its citizens, not only 'pure' collective goods – defined in this connection, following Rawls, as goods that are supplied to all citizens in the same amount, irrespective of their wishes (internal and external peace and security are the classic examples of a good of this kind) (Rawls 1971, pp. 266–7; see also Hirschman 1970, pp. 101–2) – but also all kinds of other collective and private goods (such as the wages of the government's employees), the less likely it becomes that a society is able to adapt successfully to a changed environment.

D. The Rent-Seeking Society

The conclusion I have drawn above, namely that to the extent that a government's hold on society is stronger, this society is less able to adapt to changed circumstances successfully, can also be derived in another way. In this case the argument is based not only on the behaviour of the producers, the human individuals taking part in the government organizations, but also on the behaviour of the consumers, the citizens of the society in question. In this approach, which has been named the theory of the *rent-seeking society*,[19] the developing rigidity is explained by the ways in which producers and consumers react to the government's monopoly on the legitimate use of violence.

In the theory of the rent-seeking society, the state is seen as a source of revenue that, compared to the market, can relatively easily be tapped, because of the state's monopoly on the legitimate use of violence (although it will speak for itself that here also congestion costs will occur). The theorists of the rent-seeking society will no doubt heartily endorse the statement by the well–known eighteenth–century publicist Samuel Johnson, that 'Politicks ... are now nothing more than means of rising in the world. With this sole view do men engage in politicks, and their whole conduct proceeds upon it' (Powell (ed.) 1934, p. 369). Because of its monopoly on the legitimate use of violence, government can enforce that the competition for jobs, permits, subsidies and social benefits will remain restricted to those prepared to support the government. In this perspective, the monopoly on the legitimate use of violence is the instrument by which the power holders in a country (it does not matter whether they are generals, colonels, politicians or bureaucrats) attempt to strengthen their own position. At the end of his analysis of the persistent failure of post-independence agricultural policies in Africa, Robert Bates reaches the conclusion that this failure can only be explained by the perception that:

> States have their own objectives. They want taxes and revenues and intervene actively in their economic environments to secure them. Politicians want power. And they use the instruments of the state to secure and retain it by manipulating the economy to political advantage. In Africa, as we have seen, political elites have rendered economic markets instruments of political organization. (Bates 1983, pp. 146–7)

According to James Buchanan, the theory of the rent-seeking society is based on the understanding that 'the unintended results of competitive attempts to capture monopoly rents are "good" because entry is possible; comparable results of attempts to capture artificially contrived advantageous positions under government enforced monopoly are "bad" because entry is not possible' (Buchanan, Tollison and Tullock (eds) 1980, p. 8). The central theme in the theory is that, in proportion as the government's hold on the national economy becomes stronger by means of more extensive and far-reaching controls, social life will become more and more politicized, and this will have great, adverse, consequences for the welfare and the well-being of the citizens. In the words of Peter Bauer:

> In closely controlled economies, the decisions of politicians and civil servants take the place of private decisions in production and consumption. Economic life is extensively politicized. Official directives replace voluntary transactions. The

decisions of the rulers largely determine people's incomes and employment opportunities. Indeed, these decisions often determine the economic or even the physical survival of large sections of the population ... The attention, energies and resources of many people are then diverted from productive economic activity to the political arena, whether from choice or necessity; and this diversion of people's activities necessarily affects not only their own personal fortunes, but the economic performance and progress of the whole society as well. (Bauer 1984, pp. 27–8)

Bauer's reasoning shows that greater state intervention in the national economy not only causes rigidities since, as I have argued above, government organizations are pre-eminently inflexible, but also because the pressure on the government increases on the part of individuals and groups trying to secure or to better their position through the government. The knowledge that the government controls their well-being to a far-reaching extent, induces the citizens to direct their efforts more and more at the government. The more government intervenes in social life, the more attractive the, more political, *voice*-option becomes in comparison to the, more economic, *exit*-option. Webber and Wildawsky have observed in this connection:

Big government breeds bigger pressures. Each new program creates interests who organize around it. More people make demands on politicians. Decisions must be made to satisfy them and to cope with the consequences of prior policies. Politicians find themselves busier than before with less room to maneuver. (Webber and Wildavsky 1986, p. 493)

It is almost ironic that the power holders' attempts to increase their hold on the population by bringing more and more social and economic processes under their control through an increasingly elaborate system of rules (naturally backed up by their monopoly of the legitimate use of violence), produce the unintended and unwanted by-product that they are almost completely powerless *vis-à-vis* this population if they wish to carry through policy changes. The 'grace and favor state', as Wade has called such a state (Wade 1985, p. 486), the 'intervention state', as Van Doorn has named it (Van Doorn 1988, pp. 116–22), is doomed to inertia. The very limited room for manoeuvre available to the power holders in the former command economies of the Soviet type, when they tried to carry through the, also in their eyes, necessary economic reforms, and their great reluctance to take policy measures that would involve an increase in the prices of the basic necessities of life, constitute a striking illustration of this conclusion.[20] The foregoing also makes clear that the continuing debate between students of underdevelopment with respect to the question whether the states suffering from it, are *hard states* or *soft states*, is really based on a misconception. In proportion as the state dominates social life more – designs more rules, grants more permits and exemptions, fixes more prices, and takes more initiatives – opposition in society against policy changes will become greater. The *hard state* is necessarily also a *soft state*.

The approach I have developed in this book, as well as that of the theory of the rent-seeking society, leads to the conclusion that a 'small' government – a government that confines itself to the provision of 'pure' collective goods in the sense defined in this section, however powerful this government may be *vis-à-vis* its citizens with respect to the means of violence it has (Hobbes's *Leviathan* can very well be reconciled with the night-watch state) – increases the likelihood that the citizens of that state will (collectively) be able to adapt successfully to a changed environment. Whereas, conversely, it is also true that, to the degree that the government claims a greater part of the national income, the probability decreases that the citizens will (collectively) be able to adapt successfully to a changed environment.

NOTES

1. I wish to thank Don F. Westerheijden for pointing out this inconsistency to me.
2. Cf. also Albert Hirschman's 'Theory of Loyalty' (Hirschman 1970, pp. 77–98).
3. Cyert and March expressed themselves in a similar vein, when they argued that 'organizational goals are a series of independent aspiration-level constraints imposed on the organization by the members of the organizational coalition' (Cyert and March 1963, p. 117).
4. The distinction made by Katz and Kahn between types of decision tasks, with 'problems' on the one hand, and 'dilemmas' on the other, rests on the same idea. Problems are those questions that 'can be solved in the frame of reference suggested by [their] nature, by past precedents for dealing with [them], or by the application of existing policy', whereas dilemmas refer to all those questions in which it is not immediately clear how to deal with them (Longley and Pruitt 1980, p. 78 and Janis 1982, p. 299).
5. Cf. Kenneth Boulding's observation, that 'There is a great deal of evidence that almost all organizational structures tend to produce false images in the decision-maker, and that the larger and more authoritarian the organization, the better the chance that its top decisionmakers will be operating in purely imaginary worlds' (Boulding 1966, p. 8).
6. And did not A.N. Whitehead notice already, that 'civilization advances by extending the number of important operations we can perform without thinking about them' (quoted in Hayek 1952, 1979ed., p. 154)?
7. Remember the saying, attributed to the great French diplomat Talleyrand, that war is far too important a matter to leave it to the military ('la guerre est chose trop sérieuse pour être laissée aux militaires').
8. Strictly speaking, yet another factor is involved, the period of time the human individual expects it to take before the political problem will be solved. Since the

length of this period will mostly be a function of the costs that are involved in a solution, I shall put this factor to one side.

9. This individual will exhibit, in Steinbruner's terminology, 'uncommitted thinking' (Steinbruner 1974, pp. 128–31).

10. In this connection, Steinbruner uses the expression 'theoretical thinking' (Steinbruner 1974, pp. 131–6; see also Halperin 1974, pp. 22–3 and Snyder and Diesing 1977, pp. 337–8).

11. In Steinbruner's terms the individual exhibits 'grooved thinking' (Steinbruner 1974, pp. 125–8).

12. 'The "effectiveness" trap [is] the trap that keeps men from speaking out, as clearly or often as they might, within the government ... The most important asset that a man brings to bureaucratic life is his "effectiveness", a mysterious combination of training, style, and connections. The most ominous complaint that can be whispered of a bureaucrat is: "I'm afraid Charlie's beginning to lose his effectiveness"' (cited in Halperin 1974, pp. 90–91 – see also Janis 1982, pp. 114–15).

13. This conclusion does not imply that De Jasay is wrong in arguing that, strictly speaking, every selective incentive also exhibits a certain degree of 'publicness' (De Jasay 1989, pp. 130–31). If a member of an organization finds out that another member is more generously rewarded for doing what is, in his eyes, the same kind of work, then he will, invoking the principle of equal treatment, try to ensure that he is equally well rewarded, while the punishment of a member of the organization, for instance by demotion, will have an effect on the behaviour of the other members of the organization.

14. The negative relationship between successful specialization and poor flexibility is, by the way, completely general. To give an example, it also applies to organisms. With respect to the latter, Garrett Hardin has observed that:

> Each of these specializations probably gives its possessor an advantage over other, less-specialized organisms but in so doing it places the species in, or near, an evolutionary cul-de-sac. For it is one of the few rules of evolution that extreme specialization results in eventual extinction. Environmental changes are inevitable, and the specialist-species is too strongly committed to one way of life to be able rapidly enough to 'back up' genetically and take off in another 'direction'. ... Conspicuous success in evolution, as in human affairs, is all too likely to be the prelude to extinction. (Hardin 1960, p. 320)

15. The so-called 'groupthink' syndrome, which has extensively been studied by the psychologist Irving Janis, is one of the ways this phenomenon can manifest itself. Witness his finding that groupthink typically occurs in the situation whereby an originally successful group of decision makers cuts itself off from the outside world in the face of adversity, and contents itself with immunizing pertinent information in order to protect their consensus (Janis 1982).

16. Cf. Theda Skocpol, 'Any state first and fundamentally extracts resources from society and deploys these to create and support coercive and administrative organizations' (Skocpol 1979, p. 29).

17. Undoubtedly, some will be shocked by the proposition that in certain respects government can be classed with organized crime. Perhaps it may soften the blow a bit to know that an approach like this can hardly be called revolutionary. For instance, Charles Tilly has argued in his essay 'War making and state making as organized crime', that the way in which organized crime operates, offers fruitful leads to understanding the ways in which the modern nation-state was established (Evans, Rueschemeyer and Skocpol (eds) 1985, pp. 169–91). Thomas Sowell, too, has emphasized the similarity between the government and the criminal regarding the manner in which they acquire their income:

The fact that actual violence does not usually occur in no way undermines the crucial importance of violence in the outcome. Most armed robberies also do not lead to actual violence: common sense usually causes the victim to turn over his money without a fight and causes the robber to take the money and go. Yet no one would deny that the prospect of violence is central to armed robbery, even if in retrospect it turns out that there is seldom actual violence in the commission of that crime. The government's threatened violence ... is violence in the same sense in which armed robbery is violence. The power of the government is so overwhelming to the private individual or institution that it is seldom necessary to add that defiance of the government rulings will cause policemen or soldiers to forcibly drag the offender away to jail. (Sowell 1980, p. 74)

18.   With respect to Hirschman's possible objection that an individual who is in this way 'securely locked in', will more effectively use his *voice*-option in order to improve the government's products, I wish to point out that, generally speaking, *voice* will be more costly to the individual than *exit*, and that this increases the chances that the individual will reconcile himself to the unsatisfactory state of affairs. Hirschman acknowledges this point, it is true, but he does not realize its implications, because he is more interested in the importance of *voice* and *exit* for the capacity of government organizations to correct themselves, than in the interests of the individual customers of those organizations. Another point that Hirschman overlooks all too easily, is that the corrective power of *voice* diminishes in proportion as a greater part of the government organizations' revenue is assured through the levying of taxes.

19.   After Anne Krueger's 1974 article 'The political economy of the rent-seeking society' (Krueger 1974).

20.   As Valerie Bunce has observed with respect to the one-party states of the Soviet type, 'the Party functions as a political monopsony as well as a political monopoly. Such states, in short, must be understood not simply as powerful but also as besieged' (Bunce 1985, p. 29).

9. International Politics and Foreign Policy

I INTERNATIONAL STRUCTURE AND FOREIGN POLICY

A. Three Images, One System

In his *Man, the State, and War*, Kenneth Waltz has argued that authors attempting to formulate an answer to the question why it is that war has been unavoidable in the international system until now, can be classified into three categories according to the images they employ in giving their answer. The proponents of the *first image* assume that 'the locus of the important causes of war is found in the nature and behavior of man' (Waltz 1954, 1959ed., p. 16). In their view, war results from the aggressive impulses, the selfishness and the obtuseness inherent in human nature. To be sure, those employing the first image differ sharply among themselves in respect of the issue whether this sorry state of affairs can be ameliorated or not. Whereas the 'utopians' are of the opinion that war can eventually be eliminated, provided the world's population is reared and educated in the proper way, the 'realists' maintain it is impossible to change human nature, and that mankind will never be delivered from the scourge of war. The authors who employ the *second image* hold the view that 'the internal organization of states is the key to understanding war and peace' (Waltz 1954, 1959ed., p. 81). According to them, the relationships between states are determined by the internal structure of those states. War would be a thing of the past if all states possessed the correct internal structure. Those using the *third image* consider the anarchical structure of the international system to be the principal cause of war, 'with many sovereign states, with no system of law enforceable among them, with each state judging its grievances and ambitions according to the dictates of its own reason or desire – conflict, sometimes leading to war, is bound to occur' (Waltz 1954, 1959ed., p. 159). War could only be abolished if a world government were established.

174

However, the protagonists of the third image do not give much for the chances that this indeed will happen.

Waltz acknowledges that his categorization is a bit artificial in the sense that authors who according to this scheme are adherents of one of the three images – and certainly not the least among them – regularly make use in their analyses of war and peace of perceptions not consistent with that image, and that actually belong to the intellectual heritage of the other two images. Although, from the point of view of the applicability of his classification scheme, this habit is regrettable, according to Waltz it is nevertheless conducive to a better understanding of international politics. The fact is that the three images are not mutually exclusive. On the contrary, only if the three images are related to one another is it possible to understand why international relations develop the way they do:

> The third image describes the framework of world politics, but without the first and second images there can be no knowledge of the forces that determine policy; the first and second images describe the forces in world politics, but without the third image it is impossible to assess their importance or predict their results. (Waltz 1954, 1959ed., p. 238)[1]

In *Between Anarchy and Hierarchy*, I have adopted Waltz's point of view, and I have been employing all three images in the course of the book. It will be clear that my analysis of bureaucratic decision making in the preceding chapter ought to be placed in the tradition of the second image. It will also be obvious that the arguments I developed in Chapters 4 and 7 accord with the third image. That Chapter 3 contains an exposition in line with the first image is perhaps a little less evident. For, in that chapter I have argued that the axiom of the utility-maximizing individual is an empty formalism, which must not be equated with a negative image of human nature, whereas researchers adhering to the first image, as I have said, take an explicitly dim view of human nature. Still, the principle of explanation and the first image have one, decisive, characteristic in common. They are both tautologies. To both the first image and the principle of explanation the following applies: in themselves, they cannot explain anything at all. As Waltz observes, 'While human nature no doubt plays a role in bringing about war, it cannot by itself explain both war and peace, except by the simple statement that man's nature is such that sometimes he fights and sometimes he does not' (Waltz 1954, 1959ed., p. 29). This 'simple statement' implies that the first image provides just as much understanding of international politics, as the meteorological theory predicting that tomorrow it will rain or not, does of the weather (see

Chapter 2, Section IV). Another point of agreement, is that both in the first image and in the principle of explanation it is assumed that the behaviour of the actors in the (international) system is goal-oriented.

By emphasizing that an explanation of international politics is only possible if one takes the relationships between the three images into account, Waltz in his *Man, the State, and War* in fact argued in favour of a systemic approach to international politics, which he elaborated and specified in his later *Theory of International Politics*.[2] Central to his approach is the distinction between, on the one hand, the international structure, and, on the other hand, the properties of the interacting units, *in casu*: the states. According to Waltz, 'any approach or theory, if it is rightly called "systemic", must show how the systems level, or structure, is distinct from the level of interacting units' (Waltz 1979, p. 40). Until now, I have not explicitly satisfied this demand. It is true that in Chapter 3, Section II, in an attempt to throw some light on the relationship between resources and 'information', I have made a distinction between the operational and the psychological environment of the individual, but this is not the distinction Waltz is referring to. In his approach, a state's operational environment is split up into an external environment and an internal environment, whereby he considers the state's psychological environment to be part of its internal environment too. The external environment (external structure) corresponds with the third image. It has to do with the ways in which states are dependent upon one another. It relates to such matters as: the degree of polarity in the international system, the degree of stability, the extent of the division of labour, the state of technology, etc., etc. The internal environment (internal structure) coincides with the second image. It refers to the properties of the state itself: its power, its geographical position, the amount of available resources, the extent to which these resources may be mobilized, etc., etc. In a systemic approach of this kind, which is also employed by Theda Skocpol, 'states necessarily stand out at the intersections between domestic socio-political orders and the transnational relations within which they must maneuver for survival and advantage in relation to other states' (Evans, Rueschemeyer and Skocpol (eds) 1985, p. 8).

As I have noted already, Waltz considers the psychological environment also to be part of a state's internal structure. In his approach, the psychological environment refers to the adaptability of a state, in other words, the extent to which changes are possible in a state's behavioural repertoire. In particular, it relates to the way in which a state processes information about its environment, the quality of the 'theories' it has at its disposal, and its capacity for collective decision making.

Only if it may be assumed that the individuals are situated in a parametric system, such as a perfectly competitive market (see Chapter 8, Section III), is the researcher well-advised to ignore the individuals' internal structure in his explanations of their behaviour. Such a system, however, is not dynamic. Whenever a researcher attempts to get a grip on the behaviour of individuals participating in a system evolving in the course of time – for example, the behaviour of states in an international system changing from bipolarity to multipolarity – it is imperative that he develops an eye for, what Snyder and Diesing have called, 'the external–internal dimension': the interaction between external and internal environment (Snyder and Diesing 1977).

How the process of adapting to the requirements set by the external environment affects the states' internal structure, and how the results of this adaptation process, in their turn, have consequences for the external structure, is the subject of this chapter, the last of *Between Anarchy and Hierarchy*. In the present section, I shall be paying attention to the way in which a state's external structure operates on the behaviour of that state, influencing in this way its internal structure, while in the next section, I shall be dealing with the question how a state's internal structure acts on the behaviour of that state, and in this manner affects its external structure.

The key to a proper understanding of the evolution of the international system, and the behaviour of the states constitutive of it, is the perception that states, too, can only discover the nature of the external structure by means of trial and error, and that, because of differences in the states' internal structure, this learning process in every state will proceed in a different way, and that, moreover, states in the course of this process of error elimination will inevitably make mistakes that can have consequences for the external structure. In order to explain the behaviour of states, it is not enough to know – to use a well-known analogy – that states *are* billiard balls. States must also view one another as billiard balls (see also Chapter 4, Section II). What matters in particular, is how states learn that they will be better off treating one another as if they were billiard balls, and that this learning process can only proceed by means of trial and error. In the international system there indeed exists a certain 'dialectic between subjectivity and objectivity' (Keohane 1989, p. 42).

The reasons why states make mistakes, misjudge the international environment, have regularly been discussed in the previous chapters. States err in the first place, because the external structure changes more rapidly than states are able to learn. This situation can be the result of the fact that the pace with which changes take place in the international environment is simply too fast to allow states to adapt themselves successfully, as well as of the slowness with which states are capable of executing the process of error elimination, or of a combination of both. In the second place, errors result from changes in the states' internal structure. Here it concerns both changes having consequences for the resources a state has – as changes in the production structure following upon the discovery or the depletion of supplies of raw materials and technological innovation, demographic developments and natural changes – and changes in the existing solutions of the internal political processes having repercussions on the states' capacity for (collective) decision making, and on the 'theories' in respect of the nature of the international system the states have at their disposal. Those who come to power after a violent revolution, or peacefully conducted elections, hold a totally different view from their predecessors as regards the how and why of international politics. Leon Trotsky's expectation that the Bolsheviks, after they had seized power in the October Revolution of 1917, could dispense with foreign policy, is a rather famous case in point. After he had been appointed People's Commissar of Foreign Affairs, Trotsky explained to a colleague that he saw it as his task to 'issue a few revolutionary proclamations to the peoples of the world and then shut up shop' (Carr 1953, 1966ed., III, p. 28).

In this section I shall, by the way, concern myself only with the effects on the behaviour of states of changes in, what Susan Strange has called, the international 'security structure' and the international 'production structure' (Strange 1988). I shall not pay special attention to the effects of changes in the international financial structure. This limitation should not be interpreted to mean that I think researchers like Strange and Gilpin are wrong in maintaining that, in the words of the latter, 'international money matters' (Gilpin 1987, p. 118). It follows from the fact that the general phenomenon that in the states' external environment, developments occur that are barely under their control, of which some states may profit more, some states less, and some states not at all, may sufficiently be illustrated on the basis of the security and production structures, the two structures that have figured most prominently in the previous chapters. Moreover, it applies to the financial structure, as well as to the security structure and the production structure, that because of all kinds of innovations a process has been set in motion in the course of this century that, on the one hand, provides the state with more and more instruments to increase its hold on society, but that, on the other hand, increasingly undermines the importance of the state's *raison d'être*, its territoriality.

B. The Security Structure

As I have explained before, structures do not determine the behaviour of individuals. Unfortunately, common parlance is not really equipped to accommodate this understanding. Usually we speak loosely of structures or structural developments causing a particular kind of behaviour to happen (see also Chapter 1, Section I). In Chapter 6, Section II, I, too, by the way, have made use of this way of expressing things, where I discussed the effects of natural and technological changes on the behaviour of states. Few will have noticed this inconsistency at the time. But here, immediately after my exposition of the importance of learning behaviour on the previous pages, sentences in which I refer to the effects of bipolarity or multipolarity on the behaviour of states, no doubt will sound rather less matter-of-course. Nevertheless, I shall again be following common parlance in the remainder of this section. Although I realize full well that, strictly speaking, the sentence 'in a multipolar system the majority of states will learn that it is only prudent not to specialize themselves too much', is more correct than the sentence 'the most important effect of multipolarity is that states do not specialize themselves too much'. My approach in this section is also not altogether correct in another respect. As I have explained in this section's introduction, it will be concerned with the effects of the external structure on the behaviour of states. At the same time, however, I have pointed out that, except for the situation in which it is assumed that the international system is a parametric system, it would be a mistake to analyse the effects of the external structure on a state's behaviour without taking into account that state's internal structure, in particular its power. In this section, I shall adhere to the latter position. Although this procedure is perhaps not completely defensible from the point of view of transparency, at least it once again demonstrates how fruitless studying international relations and foreign policy apart from one another would be.

A system with a multipolar structure contains less 'information' than a system with a bipolar structure. In a multipolar system, the power relations between states are less clear than in a bipolar system.[3] A state in a multipolar system will constantly ask itself which states it can count as its friends, and which states it must regard as its enemies. Moreover, it will continually worry about the question whether, when the crunch comes, its allies will honour their obligations. These worries hold for great powers as well as for small powers. At the same time, the great powers in a multipolar system try to shift the burdens of changing or defending the status quo on to one another. The great powers' attempts to become a free rider, and so to profit from the others' efforts, merely increase the always present danger of a possible fatal miscalculation. Because the great powers in a multipolar system feel themselves less responsible for maintaining the status quo, the opportunities for small powers becoming a free rider are correspondingly smaller. The latter have to bear the greater part of the costs of defending their territory themselves. In a multipolar system, specialization among small powers occurs less frequently, and is more limited in character, than among small powers in a bipolar system. Free ridership is also not the role of the superpowers in a bipolar system. To be sure, it is very attractive for each superpower to become a free rider, and to saddle the other with the costs of defending the existing solution, but if both powers would do so, then this would have disastrous consequences – for them, and for the international system. The superpowers in this way feeling themselves responsible for the status quo, the small powers in a bipolar system have to rely less on their own efforts in defending their territory than the small powers in a multipolar system, and they will be more prepared to participate in the international division of labour. Notwithstanding the fact that a small power in a bipolar system can never be sure that the superpower it is allied with will actually honour its obligations – in view of the interests that might become at stake for the latter – if that small power becomes involved in a (violent) conflict in which the other superpower is somehow involved too.

Because they matter less in the overall balance of power, small states in a bipolar system have a greater freedom of action than small powers in a multipolar system. Nevertheless, they, too, will have to put up with interventions in their (internal) affairs by the poles of the system. However, the superpowers' interventions in a bipolar system are completely different in nature from the great powers' interventions in a multipolar system. To the latter, interventions in the affairs of third states are a part of the bargaining process continually going on between them. A great power in a multipolar system cannot allow itself not to intervene, for if it would not do so, another great power may gain a decisive advantage. At the same time, however, its intervention will be on the lowest possible level, in the hope of preventing a reaction by the other great powers. Since the other great powers also wish to keep their intervention limited, the effect of their interference in the affairs of third states will be an escalation of the conflict in question. Interventions in the affairs of small powers by the superpowers of a bipolar system result from an attempt to correct the behaviour of the small powers concerned through a certain show of strength. As far as the superpower is concerned, the intervention is not a part of an ongoing bargaining process, neither with the small power(s) in question, nor with the other superpower. If a superpower actually does intervene, then initially not much is at risk, precisely because of the small powers' secondary importance in the balance of power between the superpowers, and the superpower's intervention need not lead to further escalation. This picture drastically changes the moment the intervention does not produce the desired effect. If that happens, the very thing is at stake that a superpower – in view of the psychological nature of the relationship between the superpowers – values more than anything else: its credibility. If this does in fact occur, then the superpower is prepared to escalate the conflict to very high levels in order to protect its credibility, however small the initial importance of the whole affair.

A war of intervention by a superpower, on however large a scale, need not lead to a war between the superpowers themselves. Perhaps because of this intervention the psychological 'war' between them will reach very great heights, but in view of the disastrous consequences of actual war between them, they will continue treating one another with the greatest circumspection. The probability of war breaking out between the superpowers in a bipolar system, is smaller than the probability of war breaking out between the great powers in a multipolar system. At the same time, however, the proposition holds that, if war does break out between the superpowers – and this possibility can never be excluded – that war's consequences will be far more fundamental than those of a war between the great powers in a multipolar system.

Indeed, there exists only one method to banish war from the international system, and that is by establishing a world government. A world government leads, however, to ossification, and possibly tyranny. Moreover, it is out of the question that a world government will always be able to prevent civil war. For these reasons, for many people the price that has to be paid to make war a thing of the past, will be too high. Immanuel Kant is one of them. In his *Perpetual Peace*, he observed that normally we have nothing but 'profound contempt' for 'savages' who are so much attached to 'their lawless liberty ... that they would rather be at hopeless variance with one another than submit themselves to a legal authority constituted by themselves' (Kant 1992ed., p. 130), but that he does not agree with this viewpoint. Admittedly, the situation in which exist a number of independent states 'is in itself already a state of war', but nevertheless, 'according to the Idea of Reason':

this is better than that all the states should be merged into one under a power which has gained the ascendency over its neighbours and gradually become a universal monarchy. For the wider their sphere of jurisdiction, the more laws lose in force; and soulless despotism, when it has choked the seeds of good, at last sinks into anarchy. (Kant 1992ed., pp. 155–6)

Hedley Bull, too, is convinced that a genuine choice is involved here:

The classical argument for world government is that order among states is best established by the same means whereby it is established among individual men within the state, that is by a supreme authority ... The classical argument against world government has been that, while it may achieve order, it is destructive of liberty or freedom: it infringes the liberties of states and nations ... and also checks the liberties of individuals who, if the world government is tyrannical, cannot seek political asylum under an alternative government. (Bull 1977, pp. 253–4)

Until the middle of this century, war consisted of one state attempting to conquer another state's territory, and the latter trying to prevent the former from achieving its aim. A clear relationship existed between military capacity and territory. The power of a state increased or decreased in proportion as it succeeded in establishing its authority over a greater or smaller piece of territory through military actions. As I have already explained in Chapter 7, Section III, this relationship has become far less self-evident with the development of the long-range bomber, ballistic missiles, and conventional and nuclear weapons with great destructive power in the last fifty years or so. As far as the superpowers and their allies are concerned, war is now in the first place about the capability to destroy the enemy, and only in the second place about the ability to conquer territory or to defend it. The most far-reaching implication of the situation of mutual assured destruction is that, if the holders of the balance of terror were to decide to go to war against one another, this could never be in the expectation that their territory would be spared the horrors of war (as, for example, was the case with the United States in the First and Second World Wars). This traditional assignment of the state has also been undermined by technological innovations in the military field in another way. The costs of the development and procurement of new weapons have risen exponentially in the course of the last decades, so that it is no longer possible for states (the United States are perhaps the only exception) to have at their disposal the whole range of weapons necessary for successful deterrence and defence. Through this process of 'structural disarmament' a process of reluctant specialization has taken place. States have only some kinds of weapons at their disposal. In the case of a bipolar system, this development towards increasing military dependence is not really posing a threat to peace and security in the international system, but this would definitely be so if these military dependent states were suddenly to end up in a multipolar system.

C. The Production Structure

The globalization of the international economy, the constantly expanding division of labour between individuals living at ever greater distances from one another, would be impossible without the revolution in the means of transportation and communication that was set in motion several centuries ago and that continues unabated to this day. However, the modern world-system would also be impossible without the simultaneous distribution and multiplication of market relations between individuals in all corners of the world. On this such diverse writers as Immanuel Wallerstein and Friedrich Hayek are at least agreed. According to Wallerstein, the market has accomplished what no (political) empire would ever be able to accomplish (Wallerstein 1974, pp. 15–17), and in the eyes of Hayek, 'that interdependence of all men, which is now in everybody's mouth and which tends to make all mankind One World, not only is the effect of the market order but could not have been brought about by any other means' (Hayek 1982ed., II, p. 112).

'The market', viewed as an institution, has three characteristic properties. In the first place, the market is based on voluntary exchange. Transactions between parties are effected without any of the parties having recourse to violence or the threat to use violence. In the second place, the parties are bound in their transactions by several universal rules of good conduct, especially with respect to ownership and good faith. In the third place, the parties have to bear the negative consequences of wrong decisions themselves. Parties are not capable of shifting the possible negative consequences of their decisions – when these come to light – on to others. To put it somewhat differently: the parties are faced with a 'hard budget constraint'. According to Hayek this last property is crucial, 'the whole system rests on providing inducement for all to use their skill to find out particular circumstances in order to anticipate impending changes as accurately as possible. This incentive would be removed if each decision did not carry the risk of loss, or if an authority had to decide whether a particular error in anticipation was excusable or not' (Hayek 1982ed., II, p. 125).

The relationship between market and state is anything but simple. It is both symbiotic and antagonistic, in precisely the same way as the relationship between information and power. Market and state are interwoven to a large degree, but they are also opposed to one another.

Although a market without a state can be conceived of, this does not hold for a state without a market. At the same time it is true that a market will function more successfully in the presence of a state. However, the more successful a market is, the greater a threat it poses to the state's *raison d'être*. The contrast between market and state boils down to the contrast between an anarchical system, which is open to change, and a hierarchical system, which is bent on eliminating change as much as possible – and this contrast comes to the fore most strongly with respect to territoriality. As Robert Gilpin has noted, 'for the state, territorial boundaries are a necessary basis of national autonomy and political unity. For the market, the elimination of all political and other obstacles to the operation of the price mechanism is imperative' (Gilpin 1987, p. 11).

The complicated relationship between state and market finds expression also in the following phenomenon. In the long term a state can considerably increase its power – and, accordingly, its chances of survival in the international system – if it furthers as much as possible the national economy's adaptability. In the short term, however, the situation obtains that, because of the state's monopoly on the legitimate use of violence, it is more attractive to a state to improve its relative power position *vis-à-vis* the other states by undermining as much as possible the operation of the market by shifting on to other states the costs of the process of continual adaptation caused by the market, through the levying of import and export duties, the introduction of a quota system and the manipulation of the national currency ('beggar-my-neighbour' policy). This policy's attractiveness is not diminished by the knowledge that the other states will reason in precisely the same way. This 'struggle for relative efficiency' between states (Mackinder 1904, p. 422), can at any one moment get a disastrous process of unilateral measures and counter-measures going, which in the end causes all states to be worse off. The analogy with the security dilemma is obvious. It also speaks for itself that, because the great powers will succeed in shifting the costs of this process of adaptation more easily than small powers, the outcome of their considerations is decisive in determining whether this constant threat of a trade war becomes reality or not. To the small powers economic change is far more, in the words of Peter Katzenstein, 'a fact of life. They have not chosen it, it is thrust upon them. These states, because of their small size, are very dependent on world markets, and protection is therefore no viable option for them' (Katzenstein 1985, p. 24). Of course, small powers would like to have it otherwise, however great the advantages of an open economy in the long run. They, too, would prefer shifting the costs of adaptation on to other states, and will regularly not be able to resist the temptation to give in to this preference, notwithstanding the adverse consequences in the long term. But generally speaking the proposition applies that, as far as small powers are concerned, 'the fear of economic retaliation by larger and less vulnerable states inhibits protectionist instincts' (Katzenstein 1985, p. 40). It is far more true of small powers than of great powers, that there is little else for them than to adapt themselves to the demands of the market as well as possible. On the other hand, it equally holds for great powers that they cannot permanently ignore the working of the market. If they were nevertheless to try to do so, then this implies that at a given moment they would no longer be able to continue the 'struggle for relative efficiency', and would be destroyed.

Until about the middle of the 1950s, there existed a simple criterion to establish which state had won a war, and which state had lost it: the winner enlarged his territory with the regions the loser had to give up. Territory and production structure were interwoven to such an extent that a state's acquisition of territory was synonymous with an increase of that state's (economic) power. In recent decades, because of the advancing division of labour and technological innovations, the relationship between territory and production structure has become considerably more loose. At present, production is less tied to a particular country or a particular region, and can be transferred without too much trouble to an area where conditions are more advantageous. The upshot of this is that states have nowadays to compete with one another in respect of the conditions under which production may take place on their territory. The present-day situation is more that states have to *make* concessions to entrepreneurs than that they, as in the past, *grant* concessions to entrepreneurs (cf. Strange 1992, pp. 6–7). Because of this development, the importance of success in the struggle for relative efficiency has substantially increased as far as a state's chances of survival in the international system are concerned. The importance of this struggle has also increased in another way. The global division of labour implies a high level of mutual dependence between the states in the international system, where this system still lacks an agency that may authoritatively settle possible conflicts between them. Admittedly, for as long as the states – and at least the poles of the system – manage to avoid mutual 'dependence as vulnerability', this high level of mutual dependence does not necessarily pose a threat to the international system's peace and security. Unfortunately, however, the higher the level of the division of labour in the international system, the more it encourages specialization, and, in this way, the more it strengthens dependence as vulnerability.[4] In addition to this, the pace with which the technological revolution takes place, means that it becomes more and more difficult for states to discover what measures they could possibly take to promote relative efficiency, and that, in consequence, wrong decisions become more likely. It will speak for itself that this development will lead to violent conflict more readily in a multipolar system than in a bipolar system.

II NATIONAL STRUCTURE AND INTERNATIONAL POLITICS

A. Introduction

An important reason why the iterated Prisoner's Dilemma developed by Michael Taylor appeals so much to the imagination, is without doubt that, notwithstanding the 'negative' attitude of the players, something 'nice' grows up between them. However, the empirical credibility of this hopeful result ultimately does not depend on the fact that we would like to believe such a positive result, but above everything else on the answer to the question whether the assumptions Taylor introduced to reach this result are consistent with the basic assumptions of game theory – which are the same as the ones that form the basis of the general behavioural theory developed in this book. It is very doubtful whether this is indeed the case with the assumption that the value of the discount parameter w remains constant during the course of the game (see Chapter 5, Section II). One of the assumptions Michael Taylor calls into question himself in his discussion of the results of his analysis of the two-person Prisoner's Dilemma supergame, is the assumption implying that a player is able to react immediately to possible changes in the other player's behaviour. If necessary, the decision to change strategy can instantly be taken and executed. In Taylor's view, it is doubtful whether this assumption of 'perfect flexibility' is a realistic point of departure, in view of the way in which most collective goods are produced. Once it has been decided to contribute to the production of a collective good, it will normally take some time before this collective good will actually be produced. Moreover, the investments being made during that period, mean that a player will not immediately revise his earlier decision, even if this would be required by the other player's behaviour. These, what we may call, second-image processes induce in the players' attitudes a certain measure of rigidity that, according to Taylor, increases the likelihood that players finding themselves in a repeated Prisoner's Dilemma, nevertheless choose not to cooperate with one another (Taylor 1976, pp. 95–6; cf. Gowa 1986, p. 183).

Taylor's observations are a nice illustration of the proposition that it is vital for a proper understanding of the evolution of the international system, and of the behaviour of the states belonging to it – why they cooperate with one another, or why, on the contrary, they come into conflict with one another – to take into account the existing differences between states with respect to their ability to adapt to changes in their external structure. The development of the international system can be understood only if we realize full well that, in the words of Peter Gourevitch:

> the international system, be it in an economic or politico-military form, is underdetermining. The environment may exert strong pulls but short of actual occupation, some leeway in the response to that environment remains. A country can face up to the competition or it can fail. Frequently more than one way to be successful exists ... Some variance in response to external environment is possible. The explanation of choice among the possibilities therefore requires some examination of domestic politics. (Gourevitch 1978, p. 900)

If we are interested in understanding the dynamics of international politics, which, after all, remains 'the ultimate goal of the trip' (Gourevitch 1978, p. 881), we must realize that a state's foreign policy takes shape in the context of domestic structures. This means that we ought to have an eye for the way in which the process of collective decision making works out inside states, in particular in respect of the way 'through which values are allocated authoritatively'. Not only as regards security policy – the activities that are undertaken to protect a state's territory from armed aggression – the subject of the studies by Allison (1971), Janis (1982) and Steinbruner (1974), but also with regard to, what for brevity's sake I shall call, economic policy – the measures that are taken to adapt the national economy to the demands of the market. Economic policy relates to such diverse matters as the speed with which the economy takes advantage of technological changes, the quality of the labour force and labour relations, the size of the government, etc., etc. These matters figure prominently in the works of international political economists like Gilpin (1987), Katzenstein (1985), Krasner (1985) and Strange (1988) (cf. also Stopford and Strange 1991). I shall be discussing both kind of policies in the remainder of this chapter.

B. Security Policy

In Chapter 7, Section I, I have argued, following Thomas Schelling, that a proper understanding of the *ultima ratio* of international politics – war – requires that it is regarded as a part of a negotiation process between states about the terms of their relationships of dependence. Each state uses violence to convince its adversary that it is in the latter's interest to behave itself more in agreement with the former's wishes in the future. In the following paragraphs I shall be giving a general characterization of how a state's internal structure of decision making in respect of this bargaining process affects the ways in which a state prepares and makes a 'move' in that bargaining process – without, by the way, explicitly paying attention to the way in which these moves are executed.

The departments of foreign affairs of the states concerned have a central position in this bargaining process. It would seem to go without saying, therefore, that a department of foreign affairs is strongly oriented towards the outside world, has also a good grip of it, and that, of all departments of state, it is the least inward-looking. This first impression is nevertheless wrong. Indeed, the very opposite appears to be the case. This follows in the first place from the fact that, compared with the other departments of state, a department of foreign affairs is pre-eminently confronted with 'political' problems. This understanding was put into words rather nicely by Gosses when, in the framework of his study of the management of British foreign policy before the First World War, he made a comparison between the nature of the work of the Foreign Office and that of the other British departments, 'elsewhere it was often a question of the application of settled statutory principles to concrete instances; at the Foreign Office, however, they were chiefly occupied with isolated cases which continually varied' (Gosses 1948, p. 78). But this is not all. At the same time the proposition holds that 'each step in the domain of foreign policy might, in theory at least, have far-reaching results. For such work only the highest authority, the minister himself, could as a rule bear the responsibility'. From this it follows that the Foreign Secretary 'is continually overwhelmed with work, with much unimportant work too, which his colleagues left to their officials'. But where, Gosses wonders, 'was the boundary between important and unimportant at the Foreign Office? What had the chief to reserve for himself and what could he safely entrust to others' (Gosses 1948, p. 79)? Because potentially each of the many political problems may be of great importance to the decision makers concerned, they are more strongly inclined to play it safe and to try and pass these political problems on to other decision makers, or to shelve them.

Together the greater amount of political problems, and the potential importance of those problems for the credibility of the decision makers, cause the decision-making process in the department of foreign affairs to proceed even more sluggishly than it, because of the soft budget constraint, already does in government organizations. They also mean that a decision maker at a department of foreign affairs has to go through even more trouble than his colleagues in other departments if he wishes to solve a political problem, either by himself or with the help of others. Which fact, in its turn, increases still further the attractiveness of a cautious attitude.[5] Although from a certain viewpoint this circumspection is all to the best – after all, it does no harm not to rush into making decisions that may determine between war or peace – at the same time it will be clear that it sharply reduces the possibilities of a successful adaptation to changes in the external structure, as where the latter changes from bipolarity to multipolarity. The most important consequences of this mechanism are that, compared to other government departments, in the department of foreign affairs the messenger is even more important than the message, the quality of arguments matters even less, the relationship between 'objective' reality and the ideas existing about it in the department is even more tenuous, and the relationships between the decision makers are even more psychological in character.

The 'ideologists' and 'parachutists' who attempt to solve a political problem nevertheless, and who, in order to be able to effect this solution need the active cooperation or the passive acquiescence of other decision makers, are forced by the sluggishness of the process into defending this solution in no uncertain terms, however great their own doubts about its merits. If they were to give expression to these doubts, then this would provide the other decision makers with a very good excuse not to take action on these proposals (the so-called 51–49 principle, Allison 1971, p. 178).[6] This excessive sluggishness, by the way, also means that the ideologists and parachutists may with an easy conscience put their credibility on the line. The likelihood that their proposed solution will actually be implemented and that, consequently, their credibility becomes at risk, is because of this sluggishness after all rather small.

Moreover, these political problems are often such that it cannot be very clearly established who would be in the right and who would be in the wrong. It is characteristic for decision making in these circumstances that ideologists and parachutists split up into two factions, who fight one another's viewpoints and solutions with fervour. A good example of such a development is the conflict that raged in the American security community during the first few years after the Second World War between, what Daniel Yergin has called, the proponents of the Riga-axioms on the one hand, and the supporters of the Yalta-axioms on the other, which conflict was definitely settled in favour of the former early in 1950 (Yergin 1977). In this case the conflict turned on the correct answer to the question how the Soviet Union's foreign policy ought to be interpreted, and what, in the light of this answer, would be the best attitude to adopt for the United States towards the Soviet Union. Whereas the supporters of the Riga-axioms employed a second-image approach, and saw Soviet foreign policy as a reflection of the totalitarian character of the Soviet state and of the ideology it propagated, the proponents of the Yalta-axioms used a third-image approach, leading them to regard Soviet foreign policy as a foreign policy that any 'normal' great power in the Soviet Union's place may adopt.

The above example demonstrates also very clearly that important problems usually lie at the root of the departmental trench warfare, the bitter disputes and the political machinations. Important, however, always in two respects: not only with regard to the survival of the state, but also in respect of the credibility of the decision makers involved, and the possibility cannot be excluded that, even in questions where the state's very survival is at stake, the decision makers' own credibility will nevertheless weigh more heavily in their considerations. This hardly reassuring proposition is one of the central themes in Allison's *Essence of Decision* (1971).[7] His analysis of the Cuban missile crisis in the autumn of 1962, on the basis of his organizational process model and governmental politics model, shows that, in spite of the evident irrationality of a nuclear war of destruction, we can never disregard the possibility that through the execution of organizational routines, or the fighting out of bureaucratic conflicts, states nevertheless somehow end up in such an irrational war, 'the process of crisis management is obscure and terribly risky ... the interaction of internal games, each as ill-understood as those in the White House and the Kremlin, could indeed yield nuclear war as an outcome' (Allison 1971, p. 260).

I shall conclude my observations on security policy with a brief discussion of two further issues that I, for the sake of methodological correctness, was not able to discuss in Chapter 7, Section II, and that once more illustrate how important it is to have an eye for the 'external–internal dimension'. The first relates to a state's decision whether it has indeed lost a war. It will be clear by now that more is involved in this decision than the prospective costs the adversary threatens to inflict on the state if it continues the war. More important in any case is how the progress of the war has affected the power positions of the supporters and the opponents of the war effort inside that state. The stronger the opponents' position has become, the higher the probability that the state, in view of the threatening catastrophe, resigns itself to defeat. Whereas the stronger the supporters of the war have become, the more likely it is that the state, despite the possible disastrous consequences, decides to continue the war.

The second matter relates to my analysis in Chapter 7, Section II, of the tendency of states to intervene in conflicts between other states. In that section, my analysis had to be limited to the effects of the international structure. My general conclusion was that, in proportion as the polarity of the international system decreases, the probability increases that such intervention will take place only after some time, will moreover be limited in nature, and, because of this, will have only an escalationary effect. In the context of the present discussion I am in the position to introduce the following refinement, which I take from an article by Thomas Christensen and Jack Snyder (1990). It relates to the behaviour of the members of an alliance that find themselves in a multipolar system with, what Christensen and Snyder have called, a 'checker-board geography' (as obtained in Europe before the First and Second World Wars). These allies will, in the situation that one of them is under threat of attack, either react too precipitately (as in the run-up to the First World War), or, on the contrary, too reluctantly (as in the period before the Second World War). The first kind of behaviour they have dubbed 'chain-ganging', and the other 'buck-passing'. Which of these two characteristic reaction patterns allies will in fact display, depends according to Christensen and Snyder on the perceptions that exist within the countries involved with respect to the relative advantages of the offence versus the defence – which perceptions are based on the lessons they have learned from the past – and of the fact whether the defence establishment is under civilian control or operates relatively autonomously (Christensen and Snyder 1990, pp. 144–7). Chain-ganging will occur if decision makers are of the opinion that the attack has the advantage and the military establishment is more or less autonomous. Buck-passing will be the reaction if decision makers think that the defence has the advantage and the civilian authorities have a firm hold on the military.

C. Economic Policy

A state's economic policy could be the unintended consequence of the purposeful behaviour of that state's citizens. The measures that are taken to adapt the economy to the demands of the market, need not necessarily be designed by the state. Such a detached approach to economic policy might even be the most successful one with an eye to the state's chances of survival in the long run. Nevertheless it will only very rarely happen that a state chooses this approach. It is in the state's nature to attempt to steer the national economy through specific economic policies – at least partially and sometimes even completely. (Whether the state will succeed in doing so, is naturally quite another matter.) The state's almost uncontrollable inclination to intervene is a consequence of its monopoly of the legitimate use of the means of violence, not only as an instrument through which the state acquires the financial means to strengthen its position, both internally and externally, but also as a means by which the state's citizens, united in pressure groups or not, may shift on to others the negative effects of the errors they made in their attempts to adapt to the dictate of the market.

Before everything else, a state is concerned with protecting its power position, with respect to other states, and with respect to groups inside the state dissatisfied with the distribution of rights and duties, advantages and disadvantages, resulting from the existing solution. From this perspective, economic vulnerabilities, which grow up in consequence of the way in which the international division of labour develops – for instance, the national economy becoming extremely dependent on the import or export of a single product, or strongly oriented towards a single trading partner – or that threaten to materialize, pose a great danger to the state's chances of survival. Not only in respect of the possible loss of economic power that would result if the import or export of the product in question were to fall away, or the trading partner were to cease to exist, but also with regard to the revenue the state would stand to lose itself. By intervening in the market the state intends, if not to eliminate this danger, then at least to reduce it.

It will speak for itself that a state's inclination to intervene in the economy, at least to mitigate the negative consequences of these vulnerabilities, becomes stronger only to the degree that this state, because of its limited capacity internally to collect taxes, is financially more dependent on revenue generated through trade with foreign countries, in the shape of import and export levies, licences, concessions, etc., etc. Speaking more generally, the extent to which a state will attempt to remove the negative effects of existing or threatening vulnerabilities through intervention, depends above all on the extent to which the state in question has already developed into an intervention state in the past. The more a state already has the character of an intervention state, the higher the probability of this state trying to remove the negative consequences of vulnerabilities by steering the economic activities of its citizens in a direction that would seem to diminish these vulnerabilities. Intervention induces further intervention in the same way that escalation induces further escalation. An intervention process, too, is difficult to keep under control. A good case in point is the development of the modern welfare state in Western Europe in the course of this century. The two world wars were the most important spurs to this process. The conduct of these wars demanded from the states involved that they acquired an, until then, unprecedented hold on their economies and societies, which was, however, only partially loosened after the end of these wars. (This withdrawal process was undertaken most reluctantly in almost all Western European states after the Second World War, and only in order not to jeopardize the economic aid the United States held out in prospect if the former reduced state intervention.) But this time the acquired capacity for intervention, which has expanded even further in recent decades, is no longer used in the conduct of a world war, but in the battle against things such as poverty, sickness, illiteracy and inequality in income, 'the warfare state ... paved the way for the modern welfare state' (Gilpin 1987, p. 128). Another example illustrating that intervention induces further intervention, relates to the consequences of, what Peter Bauer has called, 'the living legacy of dying colonialism' for the West African states that were part of the British Empire (Bauer 1984, pp. 90–105). The British authorities developed in West Africa during 1930s and 1940s a system of 'marketing boards' – government monopsonies for the purchase of cash crops and food crops – which was initially established to protect the producers of agricultural products from the vicissitudes of the market, but which, after these states had gained their independence, turned into the most important instrument for the new elites to strengthen their hold on the economy and society.[8]

An unintended negative by-product of the state's attempts at steering the economy, is that these create new vulnerabilities through the security of income they appear to offer to those who adjust their behaviour to the state's economic policies. On top of that, because the citizens of the state learn that the best way of maintaining or improving their position is to secure state intervention on their behalf, the state's interventions lead to increased pressures on the state, and a further restriction of its room for manoeuvre. Accordingly, the state's economic policy develops more and more into an income transfer policy. The upshot of the state's interventions in the national economy and society, which were undertaken to reduce the negative effects of existing or threatening vulnerabilities, is a diminished capacity of the national economy and society to adapt to the requirements of the market. Through its interventions, the state eventually achieves an even greater vulnerability, the very opposite of what it set out to achieve.

It is not only the dynamics of the external structure – the development of the modern world-system – which leads to an increase of dependence as mutual vulnerability between states in the course of this century, but also the dynamics of the internal structure – the rise of the intervention state. Together these processes mean that the probability increases of states getting into conflict with one another while trying to maintain themselves in the international system. This development is not sufficient to endanger peace and security in the international system in itself, provided that the capacity of that system increases correspondingly. However, if the latter does not take place – the capacity of the international system stays the same, or becomes even smaller, as when there is a shift away from bipolarity to multipolarity – then the likelihood increases that a state, in the case of a conflict with another state, at a given moment reaches the conclusion that only through the actual use of the means of violence at its disposal, will the adversary come to see the reasonableness of its demands.

NOTES

1. Cf. Peter Gourevitch, 'the international system is not only a consequence of domestic politics and structures but a cause of them. Economic relations and military pressures constrain an entire range of domestic behaviors, from policy decisions to political forms. International relations and domestic politics are therefore so interrelated that they should be analyzed simultaneously, as wholes' (Gourevitch 1978, p. 911).

2. Accordingly, it would be a mistake to regard Waltz as someone who is of the opinion that the structure of the international system determines international politics. As Waltz has observed himself, 'Structure, however, does not by any means explain everything. I say this again because the charge of structural determinism is easy to make' (Waltz 1979, p. 174).

3. Cf. the way in which Waltz treats this subject in his *Theory of International Politics*, chapter 8 'Structural causes and military effects', Section II (Waltz 1979, pp. 163–70).

4. It is also in this context that Mackinder introduces the struggle for relative efficiency:
    From the present time forth ... we shall again have to deal with a closed political system, and none the less that it will be one of world-wide scope. Every explosion of social forces, instead of being dissipated in a surrounding circuit of unknown space and barbaric chaos, will be sharply re-echoed from the far side of the globe, and weak elements in the political and economic organism of the world will be shattered in consequence ... Probably some half-consciousness of this fact is at last diverting much of the attention of statesmen of all parts of the world from territorial expansion to the struggle for relative efficiency. (Mackinder 1904, p. 422)

5. To be sure, bipolarity ought to reduce this 'political' atmosphere as regards issues

having to do with the relationships between, on the one hand, the superpowers and, on the other, the small powers, and the relations among the small powers themselves; whereas in respect of issues concerning the relationships between the superpowers, on the contrary, it ought to reinforce this political atmosphere.

6.   The 51–49 principle appears to offer a fruitful point of departure for explaining the phenomenon pointed out by Daniel Yergin, that policy makers dealing with international affairs tend 'to exaggerate the policy coherence of an adversary' (Yergin 1977, p. 36).

7.   The same theme also figures prominently in John Steinbruner's *The Cybernetic Theory of Decision*. In this book Steinbruner refers to the work of Richard Neustadt, who found in his analysis of the foreign policies of the United States and Great Britain during the Suez crisis of 1956, and of the Skybolt controversy of 1962, that these policies were fundamentally shaped and determined by 'domestic political games', and that, 'foreign policy outcomes in both these cases were in many ways by-products of other concerns' (Steinbruner 1974, p. 141). Moreover, Steinbruner's so-called cognitive paradigm makes plausible that foreign policy disasters need not be the result of 'an error in calculation'. According to this paradigm these can very well be 'the consequence of the normally functioning decision process' (Steinbruner 1974, p. 148).

8.   I should not fail to mention the effect recorded by Bauer that the greater the part of a state's revenue deriving from foreign aid (bilateral or multilateral), the more it intervenes in the economy and in society (Bauer 1984, pp. 43–7).

Appendix I: List of Definitions

Definition 1:
A *system* consists of a set of elements that are somehow interrelated, that is to say, the conduct or state of any one of the elements is influenced by the conduct or state of the other elements.

Definition 2:
An *individual* is the only element within a system that is capable of behaviour governed by the mechanism formulated in the axiom.

Definition 3:
The *environment* of an individual consists of all the other elements in the system (individuals or otherwise) of which the individual is a part.

Definition 4:
Information concerns everything that reduces the degree of entropy in a system (everything that reduces disorder and uncertainty in a system).

Definition 5:
The *expected marginal utility* of the outcome (o) of a certain behavioural option consists of the sum of the marginal utility of (o) at time t, and the marginal utilities of all the other outcomes to which the individual expects (o) to lead at times $t+1$, $t+2$, ... , $t+n$, multiplied by the subjectively estimated probability that these outcomes will be realized.

Definition 6:
Energy ('power') refers to everything that makes it possible to bring about a change in the state of a system.

Definition 7:
Material resources refers to everything in the 'operational environment' of the individual that makes it possible for the individual to bring about a change in the state of the system of which it is a part.

Definition 8:
Demand behaviour is any kind of behaviour by an individual *i* that has the effect that it induces a change in the attractiveness of the behavioural options subjectively available to another individual *j*.

Definition 9:
The *credibility* of *i* refers to *j*'s expectation that *i* is able and willing to execute the threats and to fulfil the promises that, according to *j*, seem to be involved in *i*'s behaviour.

Definition 10:
Individual *j* is *dependent* on individual *i* in some form or other where the latter disposes of sufficient power to strengthen or weaken the power of *j*.

Definition 11:
In a situation in which it is not possible for individual *i* to realize the outcome of a certain behavioural option without the active assistance or passive acquiescence of individual *j*, then there exists a complete *harmony of interests* between individuals *i* and *j* with respect to the realization of this outcome if *j* behaves itself in accordance with *i*'s wishes without *i* having to expend any amount of its power, however small, to bring *j*'s behaviour about; whereas, conversely, there exists a complete *conflict of interests* between individuals *i* and *j* with respect to the realization of this outcome if *i* is unable to persuade *j* to behave itself in accordance with (or more in accordance with) *i*'s wishes, even if *i* would expend all of its power to bring about this change in *j*'s behaviour.

Definition 12:
Collective behaviour is any configuration of behaviour by the individuals that are part of a system, that reduces the degree of entropy in the system.

Definition 13:
A *political process* between individuals exists as long as these individuals are able and willing to increase the weight of their demand behaviour towards one another.

Definition 14:
A political process between individuals reaches a *solution* when these individuals refrain from applying still more of their power in order to increase the weight of their demand behaviour towards one another.

Definition 15:
The *capacity of a system* refers to the power preponderance of the dominant coalition in that system *vis-à-vis* the other individuals in that system. The greater this power preponderance, the greater the system's capacity, and the less of its total power the system will need to expend in order to have a political process between two or more individuals reach a solution.

Definition 16:
The *polarity of a system* refers to the differences in power that exist between individuals that are part of a system, and the number of individuals that belong to the dominant coalition. The greater the differences in power between the individuals in the system, and the smaller the number of individuals that constitute the dominant coalition, the higher the system's polarity.

Definition 17:
An *anarchical system* is a system with a comparatively low polarity that consists of two or more individuals, and that lacks an agency with the capacity to enforce the promises the individuals concerned may have made to one another. A *hierarchical system* is a system with a relatively high polarity that consists of more than two individuals, and that does have an agency with the capacity to enforce the promises the individuals concerned may have made to one another.

Definition 18:
The *legitimacy* of an anarchical or a hierarchical system refers to the expectation on the part of the individuals in such a system that, to participate in a division of labour, and, consequently, to increase their mutual dependence, will lead to an increase in their power. The more these individuals expect further specialization, and, accordingly, stronger mutual dependence, to lead more probably to an increase in their power, then the greater the system's legitimacy.

Definition 19:
Organizations are hierarchical systems, consisting of human individuals, that provide these individuals with much more 'information' than other forms of collective behaviour, owing to the explicitness of the rules (or a part of the rules) that govern the behaviour of the human individuals who are part of it, among which rules there are at least some so-called 'enforcement rules'.

Definition 20:

Violence and subversion concern the attempts by individual i to influence the behaviour of individual j by employing a part of its (i.e. i's) power to acquire the means that should give i the capacity to weaken or even to destroy the power of j, as well as by actually using these means. Whereby violence refers to the weakening or the destruction of the resources j has, and subversion to the weakening or destruction of the 'information' j has.

Definition 21:

The *stability* of a system S, in which there are two or more individuals, concerns the speed with which changes in the weight of the demand behaviour of the individuals towards one another – which are subsequent upon disturbances in the individuals' environment – are nullified. In proportion as greater disturbances in the environment of the individuals lead to smaller changes in the weight of the demand behaviour of the individuals towards one another, and these changes persist for a shorter period of time, the greater the system's stability.

Appendix II: The Structure of the Argument

Assumption 1:
Only one of the elements in the system under consideration is capable of behaviour that is governed by the mechanism formulated in the axiom.

Axiom:
Individual behaviour comprises overt behaviour, a change in the relationship between the individual and its environment, as well as covert behaviour, which behaviour entails changes in the nature and the quality of the information the individual has at its disposal. It follows from the individual's choosing of a certain behavioural option from a subjectively available set of such options; where the probability that the individual will choose a certain behavioural option is a function of the marginal utility of the outcome (the payoff) associated with this particular option, in the sense that, the greater the expected marginal utility of the outcome associated with a certain option, the higher the probability that the individual will choose that option.

Auxiliary assumption 1 (the assumption of asymmetry):
Where the individual's set of subjectively available options consists of two behavioural options, o_1 and o_2, the individual either strictly prefers o_1 to o_2, or o_2 to o_1, but not o_1 to o_2 *and* o_2 *to* o_1.

Auxiliary assumption 2 (the assumption of negative transitivity):
Where the individual's set of subjectively available options consists of three behavioural options, o_1, o_2 and o_3, and working under the assumption that the individual strictly prefers o_1 to o_2, the individual either strictly prefers o_3 to o_2, or o_1 to o_3, or both relationships hold.

Assumption 2:
The marginal utility that the individual expects at time t from the future realization of an outcome (o) associated with a certain behavioural option

will decline monotonically and fall below zero, in proportion as the total utility of that outcome realized in the past is greater.

Assumption 3:
The marginal utility that the individual expects at time t from the future realization of an outcome (o) associated with a certain behavioural option will become smaller, the longer the period of time the individual expects it to be before this outcome is realized.

Assumption 4:
The system of which the individual is a part is governed by the laws of thermodynamics.

Theorem 1:
The individual will choose, from the set of behavioural options subjectively available to it, the behavioural option with which is associated the outcome with the highest expected marginal utility in terms of power.

Theorem 2:
The individual is only able to acquire new information, if it is able to relate this information to the information already at its disposal.

Theorem 3:
The individual will value information in proportion to the contribution the individual expects this information to make to the maximization of its power.

Theorem 4:
If the individual detects that recently observed phenomena or newly acquired understanding are inconsistent with the information already at its disposal, it will either try to ignore the inconsistency (deny that an inconsistency exists), or try to remove it. Which behavioural option the individual will choose (and to what extent) is dependent on the marginal utility, in terms of power, the individual attaches to ignoring or resolving this external or internal inconsistency.

Theorem 5:
The marginal utility of the outcome attached to the behavioural option of ignoring an inconsistency (denying that it exists) will increase, the less threatening to its power the individual expects this inconsistency to be,

the higher the (alternative) costs of removing this inconsistency are (compared to those of ignoring the inconsistency), and the less power and information the individual has; *and* the greater the amount of non-reusable power invested in the information that has turned out to be inconsistent the individual believes there to be, and the more it believes this investment to have contributed to its power up to now.

Whereas, conversely, the marginal utility of the outcome associated with the behavioural option of trying to remove an inconsistency will increase, the more threatening the individual expects this inconsistency to be to its power, the lower the (alternative) costs of removing this inconsistency are (compared to those of ignoring the inconsistency), and the more power and information the individual has; *and* the smaller the amount of non-reusable power invested in the information that has turned out to be inconsistent the individual believes there to be, and the less it believes this investment to have contributed to its power up to now.

Assumption 1*:
Only two of the elements in the system under consideration, i and j, are capable of behaviour that is governed by the mechanism formulated in the axiom.

Auxiliary assumption 3:
The power relationship between individuals i and j is such, that either i is more powerful than j, or j is more powerful than i, or i and j are equally powerful.

Theorem 6:
The smaller the distance between i and j, and the greater their respective power, the greater the likelihood that they will engage in demand behaviour towards one another.

Theorem 7:
The more power i has at its disposal, and the shorter the distance between i and j, the more j is dependent on i.

Theorem 8:
The extent to which i and j are dependent on one another increases in proportion as both individuals are more powerful, the distance between them is smaller, and their credibility greater; and, conversely, the extent to which both individuals are dependent on one another decreases in

proportion as *i* and *j* are less powerful, the distance between them is greater, and their credibility less.

Assumption 1**:
More than two of the elements in the system under consideration are capable of behaviour that is governed by the mechanism formulated in the axiom.

Theorem 9:
A political process between two or more individuals will only reach a solution, where at least one of the participants in that political process is of the opinion that the expected marginal utility of the outcome that none of the participants intensifies its demand behaviour towards the other participant(s) any further, is greater than the expected marginal utility of the outcome that at least one of the participants increases the weight of its demand behaviour towards the other participant(s) still further, *and* that this individual has so much credibility in the eyes of the other participant(s) in the political process that they, in view of the promises and threats the individual holds out in prospect in order to prevent a further escalation of the political process, refrain(s) from intensifying its (their) demand behaviour towards this individual (and towards one another) any further.

Theorem 10:
The higher the polarity of a system with more than two individuals, the more dependent the individuals involved are upon one another, and the more important their credibility is in their mutual relationships (in other words, the more extensive the division of labour in that system), then the greater the probability that this system has an agency with the capacity to enforce the promises the individuals may have made to one another.

Theorem 11:
The smaller the capacity of the international system, the higher the probability that a state will value the marginal utility of an additional unit of resources that should strengthen its ability to weaken or even destroy the power of other states more highly than the marginal utility of an additional unit of credibility or of economic resources.

Theorem 12:
The greater the instability of the international system, and the more dependent states are upon one another, the greater the likelihood that a

political process between states will escalate to such a high level that at least one of these states, call it i, actually decides to use the means of violence at its disposal in order to bring the other state (or states) involved in the political process to behave more in agreement with i's wishes.

Assumption 5:
The environment of the states in the international system has experienced a disturbance, such that at least one of the states changes its behaviour to the extent that the weight of its demand behaviour towards one or more of the other states increases.

Theorem 13:
The probability that a political process between states de-escalates at a certain point in time (the probability that these states are able and willing to reduce the weight of their demand behaviour towards one another at a certain point in time), increases in proportion as, either their power diminishes more significantly, or the power differential between them becomes greater, or the costs of maintaining their demand behaviour at the level reached previously become higher (or any combination of the three).

Theorem 14:
The lower the legitimacy of an organization in the eyes of the human individuals participating in it (or some of them), the higher the probability that these human individuals will be prepared to reject or change the existing goals and rules of the organization in favour of other goals and rules.

Theorem 15:
The greater the legitimacy of an organization, the higher the probability that a human individual participating in that organization will value the marginal utility of an additional unit of credibility *vis-à-vis* other human individuals taking part in the organization, more highly than the marginal utility of an additional unit of economic resources or of resources that should strengthen its ability to weaken or even destroy the power of those other human individuals.

Assumption 5*:
The environment of the human individuals taking part in an organization has experienced a disturbance, such that at least one of those human

individuals changes his behaviour to the extent that the weight of his demand behaviour towards one or more of the other human individuals participating in the organization increases.

Theorem 16:
Working under the assumption that in an organization various human individuals advance more or less contradictory proposals for the resolution of a problem relevant to the organization but not covered by its rules, then the following applies: the less powerful the proponents of a particular proposal for the solution of this problem *vis-à-vis* the other human individuals participating in this political process, the more of their power, as compared to the latter, they will employ in inventing arguments in support of the solution advanced by them, and the less likely it becomes that this solution will be adopted.

Assumption 6:
The (physical and social) environment of the human individuals participating in the organization under consideration, experiences only minor disturbances.

Theorem 17:
The fewer disturbances the (physical and social) environment of the human individuals participating in the organization under consideration experiences, the higher the probability that these human individuals, in the context of the organization, will be able to adapt successfully to this environment.

Assumption 6*:
The initially stable (physical or social) environment of the human individuals participating in the organization under consideration, has experienced a fundamental change.

Theorem 18:
The higher an organization's legitimacy, the higher the probability that the human individuals taking part in it will react to a fundamental change in their environment by continuing to behave in the way they are used to.

Bibliography

Alchian, A.A. (1950), 'Uncertainty, evolution, and economic theory', *Journal of Political Economy*, 58.

Allison, G.T. (1971), *Essence of Decision*, Boston: Little, Brown & Company.

Apter, D.E. (ed.), (1964), *Ideology and Discontent*, New York: The Free Press.

Arrow, K.J. (1971), *Essays in the Theory of Risk-Bearing*, Amsterdam: North Holland Publishing Company.

Atkins, P.W. (1984), *The Second Law*, New York: W.H. Freeman & Company.

Axelrod, R. (1984), *The Evolution of Cooperation*, New York: Basic Books.

Barry, N. (1986), *On Classical Liberalism and Libertarianism*, Houndmills, Basingstoke: Macmillan.

Bates, R.H. (1983), *Essays on the Political Economy of Africa*, Cambridge: Cambridge University Press.

Bauer, P.T. (1981, 1982ed.), *Equality, the Third World and Economic Delusion*, London: Methuen.

Bauer, P.T. (1984), *Reality and Rhetoric. Studies in the Economics of Development*, London: Weidenfeld & Nicolson.

Bentham, J. (1982ed.), *An Introduction to the Principles of Morals and Legislation*, London and New York: Methuen.

Blümel, W., R. Pethig and O. von dem Hagen (1986), 'The theory of public goods: a survey of recent issues', *Journal of Institutional and Theoretical Economics*, 142.

Boulding, K.E. (1962, 1963ed.), *Conflict and Defense. A General Theory*, New York: Harper.

Boulding, K.E. (1966), 'The economics of knowledge and the knowledge of economics', *American Economic Review*, 58.

Braudel, F. (1949, 1975ed.), *The Mediterranean and the Mediterranean World in the Age of Philip II*, 2 vols, London: Fontana/Collins.

Buchanan, J.M., R.D. Tollison and G. Tullock (eds), (1980), *Toward a Theory of the Rent-Seeking Society*, College Station: Texas A & M University Press.

Buchanan, J.M. and G. Tullock (1962, 1965ed.), *The Calculus of Consent. Logical Foundations of Constitutional Democracy*, Ann Arbor: University of Michigan Press.

Bull, H. (1977), *The Anarchical Society. A Study of Order in World Politics*, London and Houndmills, Basingstoke: Macmillan.

Bunce, V. (1985), 'The empire strikes back: the evolution of the Eastern bloc from a Soviet asset to a Soviet liability', *International Organization*, 39.

Carr, E.H. (1939, 1964ed.), *The Twenty Years' Crisis: 1919–1939. An Introduction to the Study of International Relations*, London: Harper & Row.

Carr, E.H. (1953, 1966ed.), *The Bolshevik Revolution 1917–1923*, III, Harmondsworth: Pelican Books.

Carroll, L. (1871, 1954ed.), *Through the Looking Glass*, London: J.M. Dent & Sons.

Christensen, T.J. and J. Snyder (1990), 'Chain gangs and passed bucks: predicting alliance patterns in multipolarity', *International Organization*, 44.

Clausewitz, C. von (1989ed.), *On War*, Princeton, New Jersey: Princeton University Press.

Cohen, G.A. (1978, 1979ed.), *Karl Marx's Theory of History. A Defence*, Oxford: Clarendon Press.

Collingwood, R.G. (1946, 1957ed.), *The Idea of History*, New York: Oxford University Press.

Coser, L.A. (1956), *The Functions of Social Conflict*, London: Routledge & Kegan Paul.

Cyert, R.M. and J.G. March (1963), *A Behavioral Theory of the Firm*, Englewood Cliffs: Prentice-Hall.

Dawkins, R. (1986, 1988ed.), *The Blind Watchmaker*, London and Harmondsworth: Penguin.

De Jasay, A. (1989), *Social Contract, Free Ride. A Study of the Public Goods Problem*, Oxford: Clarendon Press.

Deutscher, I. (1954), *The Prophet Armed. Trotsky: 1879–1921*, New York: Vintage Books.

De Vree, J.K. (1982), *Foundations of Social and Political Processes*, Bilthoven: Prime Press.

De Vree, J.K. (1983), 'The behavioral function: an inquiry into the relation between behavior and utility', *Theory and Decision*, 15.

De Vree, J. K. (1986), 'Sapere aude! Over wetenschap and theorie van mens and samenleving', *Acta Politica*, XXI.

De Vree, J.K. (1990), *Order and Disorder in the Human Universe: the Foundations of Behavioral and Social Science*, 3 vols, Bilthoven: Prime Press.

Dougherty, J.E. and R.L. Pfaltzgraff, Jr. (1981ed. and 1990ed.), *Contending Theories of International Relations*, New York: Harper & Row.

Elster, J. (1979, 1984ed.), *Ulysses and the Sirens. Studies in Rationality and Irrationality*, Cambridge: Cambridge University Press.

Elster, J. (1983), *Sour Grapes. Studies in the Subversion of Rationality*, Cambridge: Cambridge University Press.

Evans, P.B., D. Rueschemeyer and T. Skocpol (eds), (1985), *Bringing the State back in*, Cambridge: Cambridge University Press.

Feigl, H. and W. Sellers (eds), (1949), *Readings in Philosophical Analysis*, New York: Appleton.

Ferguson, A. (1773ed.), *An Essay on the History of Civil Society*, London: Caddel.

Ferguson, A. (1792), *Principles of Moral and Political Science*, London and Edinburgh: Strahan, Cadell & Creech.

Freedman, L. (1981, 1989ed.), *The Evolution of Nuclear Strategy*, London: Macmillan.

Friedman, M. (1966), *Essays in Positive Economics*, Chicago: University of Chicago Press.

Gaddis, J.L. (1987), *The Long Peace. Inquiries into the History of the Cold War*, New York: Oxford University Press.

Galtung, J. (1971), 'A structural theory of imperialism', *Journal of Peace Research*, 8.

Gardiner, P. (1952), *The Nature of Historical Explanation*, London: Oxford University Press.

Gilpin, R. (1981), *War and Change in World Politics*, Cambridge: Cambridge University Press.

Gilpin, R. (1987), *The Political Economy of International Relations*, Princeton: Princeton University Press.

Gosses, F. (1948), *The Management of British Foreign Policy before the First World War. Especially during the Period 1880–1914*, Leiden: W. Sijthoff's Uitgeversmaatschappijen.

Gould, S.J. (1989), *Wonderful Life: the Burgess Shale and Nature of History*, New York: W.W. Norton.

Gourevitch, P. (1978), 'The second image reversed: the international sources of domestic politics', *International Organization*, 32.

Gowa, J. (1986), 'Anarchy, egoism, and third images: *The Evolution of Cooperation* and international relations', *International Organization*, 40.

Gray, C.R. (1972/73), 'The arms race is about politics', *Foreign Policy*, 9.

Grieco, J.M. (1988), 'Anarchy and the limits of cooperation: a realist critique of the newest liberal institutionalism', *International Organization*, 42.

Halperin, M.H. (1974), *Bureaucratic Politics and Foreign Policy*, Washington: The Brookings Institution.

Hampsher-Monk, I. (1992), *A History of Modern Political Thought. Major Thinkers from Hobbes to Marx*, Oxford: Blackwell.

Hardin, G.J. (1960), *Nature and Man's Fate*, London: Jonathan Cape.

Hardin, G.J. (1977), *The Limits of Altruism. An Ecologist's View of Survival*, Bloomington: Indiana University Press.

Hardin, R. (1982), *Collective Action*, Baltimore: The Johns Hopkins University Press.

Harmsen, G. (1968), *Marx contra de Marxistische Ideologen*, Den Haag: Kruseman.

Hayek, F.A. (1952, 1979ed.), *The Counter-Revolution of Science. Studies on the Abuse of Reason*, Indianapolis: Liberty Press.

Hayek, F.A. (1967), *Studies in Philosophy, Politics and Economics*, London: University of Chicago Press.

Hayek, F.A. (1982ed.), *Law, Legislation and Liberty. A New Statement of the Liberal Principles of Justice and Political Economy*, II, London: Routledge & Kegan Paul.

Head, J.G. (1962), 'Public goods and public policy', *Public Finance*, XVII.

Herz, J. (1950), 'Idealist internationalism and the security dilemma', *World Politics*, 2.

Hirschman, A.O. (1970), *Exit, Voice and Loyalty. Responses to Decline in Firms, Organizations and States*, Cambridge, Mass. and London: Harvard University Press.

Hobbes, T. (1947ed.), *Leviathan or the Matter, Forme and Power of a Commonwealth Ecclesiastical and Civil*, London: Basil Blackwell.

Hobson, J.A. (1975ed.), *Imperialism, a Study*, New York: Gordon Press.

Hogarth, R.M. and M.W. Reder (eds), (1987), *Rational Choice. The Contrast between Economics and Psychology*, Chicago: The University of Chicago Press.

Hume, D. (1981ed.), *A Treatise of Human Nature*, Oxford: Clarendon Press.

Hume, D. (1985ed.), *Essays, Moral, Political and Literary*, Indianapolis: Liberty Classics.

Hutchison, T.W. (1981ed.), *The Politics and Philosophy of Economics*, Oxford: Basil Blackwell.

Janis, I.L. (1982), *Groupthink*, Boston: Houghton Mifflin Company.

Janis, I.L. and L. Mann (1977), *Decision Making*, New York: The Free Press.

Jansen, M. and J.K. De Vree (1985, 1988ed.), *The Ordeal of Unity. The Politics of European Integration since 1945*, Bilthoven: Prime Press.

Jervis, R. (1978), 'Cooperation under the security dilemma', *World Politics* 31.

Kant, I. (1783, 1922ed.), *Prologomena zu einer jeden künftigen Metaphysik die als Wissenschaft wird auftreten können*, Berlin: Cassirer.

Kant, I. (1783, 1953ed.), *Prologomena to Any Future Metaphysics that Will Be Able to Present Itself as Science*, Manchester: Manchester University Press.

Kant, I. (1992ed.), *Perpetual Peace. A Philosophical Essay*, Bristol: Thoemmes Press.

Katzenstein, P.J. (1985), *Small States in World Markets. Industrial Policy in Europe*, Ithaca and London: Cornell University Press.

Keegan, J. (1993), *A History of Warfare*, London: Hutchinson.

Kennedy, P. (1987), *The Rise and Fall of the Great Powers. Economic Change and Military Conflict from 1500 to 2000*, New York: Random House.

Keohane, R.O. (ed.), (1986), *Neo-Realism and its Critics*, New York: Columbia University Press.

Keohane, R. (1989), *International Institutions and State Power: Essays in International Relations Theory*, Boulder: Greenwood Press.

Keynes, J.M. (1919, 1971ed.), *The Economic Consequences of the Peace*, Cambridge: Cambridge University Press.

Kissinger, H. (1994), *Diplomacy*, New York: Simon & Schuster.

Kolakowski, L. (1978, 1981ed.), *Main Currents of Marxism*, I & II, Oxford: Oxford University Press.

Kornai, J. (1986), 'The Hungarian reform process: visions, hope and reality', *Journal of Economic Literature*, XXIV.

Kossmann, E.H. (1987), *Politieke Theorie en Geschiedenis. Verspreide Opstellen en Voordrachten*, Amsterdam: Bert Bakker.

Krasner, S.D. (ed.), (1983), *International Regimes*, Ithaca: Cornell University Press.

Krasner, S.D. (1985), *Structural Conflict: the Third World against Global Liberalism*, Berkeley: University of California Press.

Kreps, D.M. (1990), *A Course in Microeconomic Theory*, New York: Harvester Wheatsheaf.

Krueger, A. (1974), 'The political economy of the rent-seeking society', *The American Economic Review*, 64.

Lakatos, I. and A. Musgrave (eds), (1970, 1974ed.), *Criticism and the Growth of Knowledge*, Cambridge: Cambridge University Press.

Liddell Hart, B. (1954, 1967ed.), *Strategy*, New York: Praeger.

Lieshout, R.H. (1984), *Without Making Elaborate Calculations for the Future*, Enschede.

Lieshout, R.H. (1992), 'Neo-institutional realism: anarchy and the possibilities of cooperation', *Acta Politica*, XXVII.

Longley, J. and D.G. Pruitt (1980), 'Groupthink: a critique of Janis's theory', *Review of Personality and Social Psychology*, 1.

Luce, R.D. and H. Raiffa (1957), *Games and Decisions. Introduction and Critical Survey*, New York: John Wiley & Sons.

Mackinder, H.J. (1904), 'The geographical pivot of history', *Geographical Journal*, XXIII.

Magdoff, H. (1969), *The Age of Imperialism*, New York and London: Modern Reader Paperbacks.

Mandeville, B. (1924ed.), *The Fable of the Bees: or, Private Vices, Publick Benefits*, Oxford: Oxford University Press.

Margolis, H. (1982), *Selfishness, Altruism and Rationality*, Cambridge: Cambridge University Press.

Marx, K. and F. Engels (1848, 1968ed.), *The Communist Manifesto*, New York and London: Modern Reader Paperbacks.

McKean, R.N. (1965), 'The unseen hand in government', *American Economic Review*, LV.

Mearsheimer, J.J. (1990), 'Back to the future. Instability in Europe after the Cold War', *International Security*, 15.

Medawar, P. (1984ed.), *Pluto's Republic*, Oxford: Oxford University Press.

Miliband, R. (1969, 1973ed.), *The State in Capitalist Society. The Analysis of the Western System of Power*, London: Quartet Books.

Mill, J.S. (1910ed.), *Utilitarianism, Liberty, Representative Government*, London: Everyman's Library.

Mill, J.S. (1843, 1981ed.), *A System of Logic, Ratiocinative and Inductive*, London: University of Toronto Press.

Morgenthau, H. (1946, 1965ed.), *Scientific Man* vs. *Power Politics*, Chicago: University of Chicago Press.

Morgenthau, H. (1978ed.), *Politics among Nations. The Struggle for Power and Peace*, New York: Alfred A. Knopf.

Mossner, E.C. and I.S. Ross (eds), (1977, 1987ed.), *The Correspondence of Adam Smith*, Indianapolis: Liberty Press.

Nagel, E. and J.R. Newman (1959, 1971ed.), *Gödel's Proof*, London: Routledge & Kegan Paul.

Nicholson, M. (1989, 1990ed.), *Formal Theories in International Relations*, Cambridge: Cambridge University Press.

Nozick, R. (1974), *Anarchy, State and Utopia*, New York: Basic Books.

Olson, M. (1965, 1971ed.), *The Logic of Collective Action. Public Goods and the Theory of Groups*, Cambridge, Mass.: Harvard University Press.

Ordeshook, P. (1986), *Game Theory and Political Theory: an Introduction*, Cambridge: Cambridge University Press.

Organski, A.F.K. (1958, 1968ed.), *World Politics*, New York: Alfred A. Knopf.

Osgood, R.E. (1962), *NATO. The Entangling Alliance*, Chicago: Chicago University Press.

Pellikaan, H. (1994), *Anarchie, Staat en het Prisoner's Dilemma*, Delft: Eburon.

Platt, R.M. (1964), 'Strong inference', *Science*, 146.

Popper, K.R. (1968ed.), *Conjectures and Refutations. The Growth of Scientific Knowledge*, New York: Harper & Row.

Popper, K.R. (1971ed.), *The Open Society and Its Enemies*, II, Princeton: Princeton University Press.

Popper, K.R. (1980ed.), *The Logic of Scientific Discovery*, London: Hutchinson.

Popper, K.R. (1982a), *The Open Universe. An Argument for Indeterminism*, London: Hutchinson.

Popper, K.R. (1982ed.b), *Unended Quest. An Intellectual Autobiography*, London: Fontana/Collins.

Popper, K.R. (1983), *Realism and the Aim of Science*, London: Hutchinson.

Popper, K.R. and J.C. Eccles (1981ed.), *The Self and Its Brain*, Berlin: Springer International.

Powell, L.F. (ed.), (1934), *Boswell's Life of Johnson*, II, Oxford: Clarendon Press.

Prigogine, I. and I. Stengers (1984), *Order out of Chaos. Man's New Dialogue with Nature*, Toronto: Bantam Books.

Quester, G.H. (1977), *Offense and Defense in the International System*, New York: John Wiley & Sons.

Rapoport, A. and M. Guyer (1966), 'A taxonomy of 2 x 2 games', *Peace Research Society (International), Papers*, VI.

Rawls, J. (1971), *A Theory of Justice*, Cambridge, Mass.: The Belknap Press of Harvard University Press.

Riker, W.H. and P.C. Ordeshook (1973), *An Introduction to Positive Political Theory*, Englewood Cliffs: Prentice-Hall.

Rosenau, J.N. (ed.), (1969), *International Politics and Foreign Policy. A Reader in Research and Theory*, New York: The Free Press.

Rosenberg, A. (1976), *Microeconomic Laws. A Philosophical Analysis*, Pittsburgh: University of Pittsburgh Press.

Rotberg, R.I. and T.K. Rabb (eds), (1989), *The Origin and Prevention of Major Wars*, Cambridge: Cambridge University Press.

Rousseau, J.-J. (1755, 1994ed.), *Discourse on the Origin of Inequality*, Oxford: Oxford University Press.

Rousseau, J.-J. (1761, 1917ed.), *A Lasting Peace through the Federation of Europe*, London: Constable.

Rousseau, J.-J. (1964ed.), *Oeuvres Complètes*, Paris: Gallimard.

Russell, B. (1918, 1957ed.), *Mysticism and Logic*, Garden City: Doubleday.

Russett, B. M. (1968), *Economic Theories of International Politics*, Chicago: Marham.

Savage, L.J. (1954), *The Foundations of Statistics*, New York and London: John Wiley & Sons.

Schelling, T. (1958), 'The strategy of conflict. Prospectus for a reorientation of game theory', *Journal of Conflict Resolution*, II.

Schelling, T.C. (1960, 1963ed.), *The Strategy of Conflict*, Cambridge, Mass.: Harvard University Press.

Schelling, T. (1966), *Arms and Influence*, New Haven and London: Yale University Press.

Schoeck, H., (1969, 1987ed.), *Envy. A History of Social Behaviour*, Indianapolis: Liberty Press.

Schumpeter, J.A. (1942, 1976ed.), *Capitalism, Socialism and Democracy*, New York: Harper & Row.

Schumpeter, J.A. (1954, 1982ed.), *History of Economic Analysis*, London: Allen & Unwin.

Schumpeter, J.A. (1955ed.), *Imperialism and Social Classes*, New York: Meridian Books.

Schumpeter, J.A. (1961ed.), *The Theory of Economic Development. An Inquiry into Profits, Capital, Credit, Interest, and the Business Cycle*, Cambridge, Mass.: Harvard University Press.

Simon, H. (1947, 1961ed.), *Administrative Behavior*, New York: Macmillan.

Simon, H. (1957), *Models of Man*, New York: John Wiley & Sons.

Skocpol, T. (1979), *States and Social Revolutions*, Cambridge: Cambridge University Press.

Smith, A. (1979ed.a), *The Theory of Moral Sentiments*, Oxford: Oxford University Press.

Smith, A. (1979ed.b), *An Inquiry into the Nature and Causes of the Wealth of Nations*, Oxford: Oxford University Press.

Smith, A. (1980ed.), *Essays on Philosophical Subjects*, Oxford: Oxford University Press.

Smith, T. (1979), 'The underdevelopment of development literature: the case of dependency theory', *World Politics*, 31.

Smoke, R. (1977), *War: Controlling Escalation*, Cambridge, Mass.: Harvard University Press.

Snidal, D. (1991), 'Relative gains and the pattern of international cooperation', *American Political Science Review*, 85.

Snyder, G.H. and P. Diesing (1977), *Conflict among Nations. Bargaining, Decision Making, and System Structure in International Crises*, Princeton: Princeton University Press.

Sowell, T. (1980), *Knowledge & Decisions*, New York: Basic Books.

Sprout, H. and M. Sprout (1965, 1979ed.), *The Ecological Perspective on Human Affairs. With Special Reference to International Politics*, Westport: Greenwood Press.

Steinbruner, J.D. (1974), *The Cybernetic Theory of Decision. New Dimensions of Political Analysis*, Princeton: Princeton University Press.

Stopford, J. and S. Strange (1991), *Rival States, Rival Firms. Competition for World Market Shares*, Cambridge: Cambridge University Press.

Strange, S. (1988), *States and Markets*, London: Pinter.

Strange, S. (1992), 'States, firms and diplomacy', *International Affairs*, 68.

Swanborn, P.G. (1981, 1987ed.), *Methoden van Sociaal-Wetenschappelijk Onderzoek*, Amsterdam: Boom.

Taylor, M. (1976), *Anarchy and Cooperation*, New York and London: John Wiley & Sons.

Taylor, M. (1987), *The Possibility of Cooperation*, Cambridge: Cambridge University Press.

Taylor, M. and H. Ward (1982), 'Chickens, whales and lumpy goods: alternative models of public goods provision', *Political Studies*, 30.

Thies, W.J. (1987), 'Alliances and collective goods. A reappraisal', *Journal of Conflict Resolution*, 31.

Thucydides (1954ed.), *The Peloponnesian War*, Harmondsworth: Penguin Books.

Tolstoy, L. (1898, 1938ed.), *What is Art? and Essays on Art*, London: Oxford University Press.

Van Doorn, J.A.A. (1988), *Rede en Macht. Een Inleiding tot Beleidswetenschappelijk Inzicht*, Den Haag: Vuga.

Von der Dunk, H.W. (1975), 'Het fascisme – een tussenbalans', *Internationale Spectator*, XXIX.

Wade, R. (1985), 'The market for public office: why the Indian state is not better at development', *World Development*, 13.

Wagner, R.H. (1983), 'The theory of games and the problem of international cooperation', *American Political Science Review*, 77.

Wallerstein, I. (1974), *The Modern World-System. Capitalist Agriculture and the Origins of the European World-Economy in the Sixteenth Century*, New York: Academic Press.

Walt, S.M. (1985), 'Alliance formation and the balance of world power', *International Security*, 9.

Waltz, K.N. (1954, 1959ed.), *Man, the State, and War. A Theoretical Analysis*, New York: Columbia University Press.

Waltz, K.N. (1979), *Theory of International Politics*, Reading, Mass.: Addison Wesley.

Waltz, K.N. (1981), 'The spread of nuclear weapons: more may be better', *Adelphi Papers*, 171.

Ward, H. (1987), 'The risks of a reputation for toughness: strategy in public goods provision problems modelled by chicken supergames', *British Journal of Political Science*, 17.

Webber, C. and A. Wildavsky (1986), *A History of Taxation and Expenditure in the Western World*, New York: Simon & Schuster.

Weiner, M. (1971), 'The Macedonian syndrome. An historical model of international relations and political development', *World Politics*, 23.

Williamson, O.E. (1975), *Markets and Hierarchies, Analysis and Antitrust Implications. A Study in the Economics of Internal Organization*, New York: The Free Press.

Williamson, O.E. (1985), *The Economic Institutions of Capitalism. Firms, Markets, Relational Contracting*, New York: The Free Press.

Wilson, F. (1985), *Explanation, Causation and Deduction*, Dordrecht: Kluwer Academic Publishers.

Yergin, D. (1977), *Shattered Peace. The Origins of the Cold War and the National Security State*, Boston: Hougton Mifflin Company.

Zinnes, D.A. (1976), *Contemporary Research in International Relations. A Perspective and a Critical Appraisal*, New York: The Free Press.

Index of Names and Subjects